Joyce and the Science of Rhythm

Joyce and the Science of Rhythm

William Martin

palgrave
macmillan

JOYCE AND THE SCIENCE OF RHYTHM

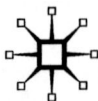

First published in 2012 by
PALGRAVE MACMILLAN®
in the United States—a division of St. Martin's Press LLC,
175 Fifth Avenue, New York, NY 10010.

Where this book is distributed in the UK, Europe and the rest of the world,
this is by Palgrave Macmillan, a division of Macmillan Publishers Limited,
registered in England, company number 785998, of Houndmills,
Basingstoke, Hampshire RG21 6XS.

Palgrave Macmillan is the global academic imprint of the above companies
and has companies and representatives throughout the world.

Palgrave® and Macmillan® are registered trademarks in the United States,
the United Kingdom, Europe and other countries.

ISBN: 978–1–137–27547–9

Library of Congress Cataloging-in-Publication Data

Martin, William, 1978–
    Joyce and the science of rhythm / by William Martin.
        p. cm.
    Includes bibliographical references.
    ISBN 978–1–137–27547–9 (alk. paper)
        1. Joyce, James, 1882–1941—Criticism and interpretation. I. Title.

PR6019.O9Z7269 2012
823'.912—dc23   2012014577

A catalogue record of the book is available from the British Library.

Design by Newgen Imaging Systems (P) Ltd., Chennai, India.

First edition: October 2012

10 9 8 7 6 5 4 3 2 1

Printed in the United States of America.

Dedicated to Peter Kuch

Contents

Illustrations

Abbreviations

CW	*The Critical Writings of James Joyce*, 1959.
D	*"Dubliners": Text, Criticism, and Notes*, 1969.
FW	*Finnegans Wake*, 1939.
JJ	*James Joyce: New and Revised Edition*, 1982.
Letters	*Letters of James Joyce, Vols I, II, and III*, 1957–1966.
P	*A Portrait of the Artist as a Young Man*, 1964.
PSW	*Poems and Shorter Writings: Including Epiphanies, Giacomo Joyce and "A Portrait of the Artist,"* 1991.
SH	*Stephen Hero*
U	*Ulysses*, 1984.

Acknowledgments

As the Inaugural Postdoctoral Fellow in Irish Studies at the University of Otago, I would like to thank Eamon Cleary for establishing the Chair of Irish Studies in 2006, a post that is still held by the Foundation Professor of Irish Studies, Peter Kuch. In gratitude for his mentorship over the past decade, I have dedicated this book to Professor Kuch, a great scholar and friend who was instrumental in establishing the fellowship of which I was the recipient. Professor Geoff Kearsley also deserves much thanks for supporting the project during my term as a lecturer in the Department of Media, Film and Communication. I would like to thank my parents, Geoff and Felicity Martin, for purchasing the computer that I used to write the final draft of this book. Last but not least, I would like to thank my loving wife Alex Bligh, whose ongoing love and support over the years has enabled the completion of this project.

Chapter 1

Introduction

The Science of Rhythm

At the turn of the twentieth century, scholars in the fields of physics, physiology, psychology, and prosody were engaged in the formation of a scientific discourse on rhythm that informed the critical and creative writings of modernist authors such as James Joyce. Contrary to the aesthetic conception of rhythm developed by the classical Greeks (Plato, Aristotle, and Aristoxenus), which is identified with the recurring temporal forms of music, poetry, and dance, scientists studying rhythm in the middle to late nineteenth century discovered periodic movements occurring in all spheres of nature. As "rhythm" was studied from a number of different perspectives, the term began to acquire a set of new connotations, including the vibrations of light and sound waves, the elliptical movement of planetary bodies, the cyclical growth of living organisms, as well as the perception of recurring, temporal patterns. In many ways, the development of the new "rhythmic" science was prefigured by Herbert Spencer's chapter on "The Rhythm of Motion" in *First Principles* (1880), for the English philosopher there develops a physical conception of rhythm as the periodic equalization of force that is applied to diverse fields such as evolutionary biology, physiology, psychology, and prosody. Significantly, Spencer traces the rhythms of music and poetry to the alternating phases of tension and relaxation that regulate the healthy functioning of the human body, thereby reducing the origin of art to periodic processes occurring in nature. In the domain of aesthetics, the discovery of rhythms in nature led to the reintegration of the "institution" of art into the sphere of everyday life (Bürger 1984), for the rhythmic forms of modernist poetry, prose, and drama became a *literary* expression of the periodic movements already occurring in the body. In the modernist writings of James Joyce, the interaction between the mechanical rhythms of the city and the organic movements of the body is recorded on the pages of *A Portrait of the Artist as a Young Man* and *Ulysses*, for the emergence of the interior monologue technique in these texts provides the perfect medium for describing how the periodic movements of the body structure the experience of space and time in a modern, industrial city.

Thanks to the recent publication of Michael Golston's *Rhythm and Race in Modernist Poetics and Science* (2008), many of the texts that contributed to the formation of this scientific discourse on rhythm have come to light, and it has now become possible to gauge the extent to which the work of modernists such as Pound, Yeats, and Joyce was informed by such ideas. In 1913, an experimental psychologist at Cornell University named Christian Ruckmich surveyed the field, his "Bibliography of Rhythm" containing more than 200 articles and books written in English, French, and German. Noting that the study of rhythm had been initially developed in "experimental psychology," a field first developed by Willhelm Wundt in his Leipzig laboratory, Ruckmich observed:

> The subject of rhythm has been carried into many fields both inside and outside the science of psychology: within, it has been related to attention, work, fatigue, temporal estimation, affection and melody; without, it has been frequently mentioned in connection with music, literature, biology, geology, gymnastics, physiology and pedagogy. (cited in Golston 2008, 2)

Although the scientific study of rhythm would never attain the status of an academic discipline, its rapid development in the first two decades of the twentieth century enabled it to be identified as an independent field of research, allowing Golston to coin the expression "rhythmics" to retrospectively describe the various investigations that contributed to the formation of this discourse. According to Golston, the period of modernism in English literature can be analyzed as an interaction between the stylistic practice of the modernist poets and the new science of "rhythmics," for as he puts it, "the innovations in form and prosody that characterize much Modernist poetry are based on a now forgotten set of ideas about rhythm" (2008, 4). For the purpose of studying the development of modernist poetry, free verse, and prose, the interaction between the fields of experimental psychology and prosody is of particular interest to the literary critic, as the theories of rhythm developed during this time not only worked to *motivate* the creation of new poetic forms, but also served to *legitimate* the stylistic experiments of modernists such as Pound, Yeats, and Joyce.

For the sake of outlining the relationship between "rhythmic" science and the legitimization of modernist poetry, it will be useful to make a brief comparison between Pound and Joyce, as we know that the American poet was directly familiar with the experimental techniques invented by the French phonologist, Abbé Rousselot. As a linguist and physiologist interested in studying the geographical and genealogical causes of dialectical variation, Rousselot invented a machine in the 1880s called the "phonoscope" that was able to graphically represent the duration and intensity of muscular contractions in the vocal apparatus. From a memoir describing his time in Paris in the 1910s, we know that Pound was familiar with the workings of this machine, for he writes: "The Abbé ... M. Rousselot ... had made a machine for measuring the duration of verbal components. A quill or tube held in the nostril, a less shaved quill or other tube in the mouth, and your consonants signed as you spoke them" (cited in Golston 2008, 65). For practitioners of *vers libre*, such as Pound, the invention of the phonoscope performed an important political function, for by measuring the duration and intensity of muscular contraction during the recitation of poetry, it provided a scientific explanation for the rhythmic principles of "free verse." Indeed, it is significant that Pound alludes to the composition of the "The Return" in the same memoir ("They return, One and by one, With fear, As half awakened each letter with a double registration of quavering"), for it suggests that the invention of the phonoscope inspired some of the free verse published in the first volume of *Des Imagistes* (1914). Coining the phrase "phonoscopic modernism," Golston argues that Pound sought to express imperceptible rhythms in his poetry that were either too rapid in frequency to be heard (the vibration of a tone) or too difficult to notate in the linear form of verse (intonation, volume, accent, gesture, pause, and so on). The invention of the phonoscope therefore served both to *motivate* and *legitimate* the free-verse experimentation of the modernist poets, for in the absence of metrical conventions, it provided an objective method for recording the inaudible and invisible rhythms of the voice.

As Pound included Joyce's "I hear an army" in the first anthology of Imagist poetry, we can establish a textual connection between the "free verse" of the two modernist authors, but it should be noted that Joyce had no direct knowledge of the experimental techniques developed by Rousselot. For the sake of reconstructing the impact of rhythmic science on the critical and creative writings of James Joyce, I will focus more on the discussion of rhythm in psychological textbooks of the late nineteenth century, as these texts give a coherent account of the physiological and psychological theories of movement and sensation that permeated the cultural milieu in Europe and North America. From his reading of Maher's *Psychology* (1895) at University College, Joyce would have possessed a general knowledge of eighteenth- and nineteenth-century psychology, ranging from the empirical accounts of Locke, Berkeley, Hume, and Kant, to the more materialistic theories of Bain, Spencer, Weber, Fechner, and Sully.[1] When attempting to gauge the influence of such ideas on the aesthetic theory of the young James Joyce, it is important to note that Maher presents many of these thinkers simply as straw men to be knocked down by the transcendental philosophy of Aristotle and Aquinas. Nevertheless, Joyce seems to have developed an independent interest in contemporary psychological science, for the aesthetic dialogues in *Stephen Hero* and *Portrait* contain allusions to Grant Allen's *Physiological Aesthetics* (1877), a work that explains the evolutionary origin of art in terms of "physiological psychology." In particular, Stephen's theory of the "epiphany" seems to have been inspired by the work of Allen, for the latter uses the example of a clock-face to illustrate the process by which the mind's attention is turned toward the intellectual dimension of the image.

According to his first biographer, Herbert Gorman, Joyce read the work of Herbert Spencer during his time at University College (*JJ*, 142), and it is likely that he read the chapter on "The Rhythm of Motion" from *First Principles* (1880) because the term "rhythm" becomes one of the central concepts of his aesthetic theory. Starting from the assumption that there can never be two physical forces that are perfectly in balance with one another, Spencer traces the origin of rhythm to the state of disequilibrium that results: "Rhythm results whenever there is a conflict of forces not in equilibrium" (1880, 254). By expanding the duration of the rhythmic phenomenon beyond the limits of human perception, Spencer is able to apply the term to describe any periodic motion in nature, ranging from the slow orbits of the planets to the rapid vibration of light waves to produce colors. In the context of nineteenth-century science, it is significant that Spencer alludes to the vibration of air particles to produce musical tones, for it shows that his account was informed by the acoustic theory of the German physicist Hermann von Helmholtz. Indeed, when Spencer discusses the acoustic phenomenon of beats—"recurring intervals of sound and silence which are perceived when two notes are struck together; and which are due to the alternate correspondence and antagonism of atmospheric waves" (1880, 253)—he alludes to the explanation given by Helmholtz in *On the Sensations of Tone as a*

Physiological Basis for the Theory of Music (1895), for the alternation between sound and silence is attributed to the interference between the differing forms of two vibrations. Building on the mathematical method of analyzing the interference of waves developed by Fourier and applied by Helmholtz to explain the different "timbre" (or "tone-color") of musical instruments, Spencer develops the concept of compound rhythms (secondary, tertiary, and quaternary) that accounts for the interference of one or more periodic phenomena. Significantly, he appeals to the visual image of the waves of the sea to illustrate his theory, an image that would have appealed to an aspiring poet such as the young Joyce: "We have again that which is furnished by the surface of the sea: every large wave bearing smaller ones on its sides, and these still smaller ones; with the result that each flake of foam, along with the portion of water bearing it, undergoes minor ascents and descents of several orders while being raised and lowered by the greater billows" (1880, 254). As the mathematical computation of compound rhythms provides a method for analyzing the interference of rhythms at different levels of complexity, we will see that this scientific theory also provides a model for explaining the manner in which the various elements or "parts" of poetry (rhythm, meter, accent, line, rhyme, and stanza) combine to form a structural impression of the poem as a whole.

We know that Joyce was familiar with the physical concept of rhythm as a periodic movement, for in the surviving draft of *Stephen Hero*, he contrasts the epochal rise and fall of the Roman Catholic Church to the rapid vibration of light waves: "The waves of the rise and fall of empires do not travel with the rapidity of waves of light and it will perhaps be a considerable time before Ireland will be able to understand that the Papacy is no longer going through a period of anabolism" (*SH*, 152). By using the term "anabolism," Joyce employs the terminology of biological science to suggest that the Roman Catholic Church is no longer evolving through the transformation of simple substances into more complex ones. More specifically, the term "wave" refers to the rise and fall of a rhythmic or periodic movement, and it is significant that Stephen differentiates his own *perception* of Rome's decline from the ignorance of Irish Catholics, for it demonstrates that the aesthete possesses a special capacity to perceive the rhythmic interaction of forces that govern the evolution of society. While Joyce probably read Spencer's chapter on "The Rhythm of Motion," the application of the physical concept of rhythm to the analysis of social change indicates that he may have already consulted Spencer's *The Study of Sociology* (1874).

Of course, Joyce possessed a 1918 edition of Spencer's work in his Trieste library; yet, it is possible that he read an earlier edition during his time at University College. Just as Joyce compares the rapid vibration of light waves to the rise and fall of Roman civilization, Spencer uses the concept of compound rhythms to describe the interaction of multiple social forces, writing in a memorable passage:

> In a society living, growing, changing, every new factor becomes a permanent force; modifying more or less the direction of movement determined by the aggregate of forces. Never simple and direct, but, by the cooperation of so many causes, made irregular, involved, *and always rhythmical*, the course of social change cannot be judged of in its general direction by inspecting any small portion of it. Each action will inevitably be followed, after a while, by some direct or indirect reaction, and this again by a reaction; and until the successive effects have shown themselves, no one can say how the total motion will be modified ... Surely, then, in such complex and slowly-evolving movements as those of a nation's life, all the smaller and greater *rhythms* of which fall within certain general directions, it is impossible that such general directions can be traced by looking at stages that are close together—it is impossible that the effect wrought on any general direction by some additional force, can be truly computed from observations extending over but a few years, or but a few generations. (1874, 105: my emphasis, WM)

Considering the aesthetic perspective adopted by Joyce (and his fictional alter ego, Stephen Dedalus), Spencer's account of social evolution as a rhythmic movement would have appealed to the young Irish writer, for it enables the aesthete to perceive the interaction of multiple social forces as a "wave," "curve," or "parabola" that is formed from the interference of different rhythms. Indeed, as the poet is an expert in constructing verse-rhythms, this innate capacity to perceive the periodic motions occurring in nature can be extended to the diagnosis of social tendencies.

From the perspective of literary modernism more generally, Spencer's chapter on the "Rhythm of Motion" should be seen as a revolutionary document, for not only does the *physical* concept of rhythm work to reintegrate the periodic movements of nature back into the sphere of everyday life, but the *physiological* concept of rhythm works to correlate the temporal forms of poetry and music with the muscular movements of the body. Drawing on the laws of thermodynamics developed by Helmholtz,[2] Spencer analyzes the bodily expenditure of energy as a rhythmic process, arguing that phases of work

must be balanced by phases of rest to prevent the onset of fatigue.
Indeed, most of the bodily processes that contribute to the sustenance
of life exhibit rhythmic cycles, such as the undulatory motions of the
stomach, the peristaltic movement of the intestines, or the pumping
of blood around the body. Significantly, Spencer relates the periodic
alternation between attention and relaxation to the embodied performance of dance, poetry, and music:

> The measure of a dance is produced by the alternation of strong mus-
> cular contractions with weaker ones ... Poetry is a form of speech in
> which the emphasis is regularly recurrent, that is—in which the muscu-
> lar effort of pronunciation has definite periods of great and less inten-
> sity: periods that are complicated with others answering to successive
> verses. Music more variously exemplifies the law. There are recurring
> bars, in each of which there is a primary and a secondary beat. There
> is the alternate increase and decrease of muscular strain implied by
> the ascents and descents to the higher and lower notes—ascents and
> descents composed of smaller waves, breaking the rise and fall of the
> larger ones, in a mode peculiar to each melody. (1880, 211)

As can be seen, Spencer relates the stresses of poetry to the muscular
contractions of the body and the tones of music to the tension of the
vocal chords, a theoretical gesture that works to reinscribe the embodied performance of music and poetry within the sphere of everyday
life. With regard to the development of poetic form, furthermore, the
physiological conception of rhythm challenges the generic distinction
between poetry and prose, for it can be seen that the temporal form of
everyday speech is now already shaped by the regular contractions of
the vocal apparatus: "Every sentence has its primary and secondary
emphases and its cadence containing a chief rise and fall complicated
with subordinate rise and falls" (212). Although Spencer's account
of physiological rhythms precedes the rise of rhythmic science by
two or three decades, he nevertheless outlines the direction of future
research, suggesting that the sensation of rhythm is motivated by the
corresponding movements of the body.

In the late nineteenth century, the German philosopher Wilhelm
Wundt founded the field of "physiological psychology," and con-
ducted a number of experiments with his students in his Leipzig laboratory that were designed to test the capacity of the mind to retain a
series of temporal stimuli. Published in the second volume of his
Grundzüge der Physiologischen Psychologie (1874), these experiments
exerted a decisive influence on the work of "experimental psychologists" working in North America, particularly Thaddeus Bolton (1894),

Robert MacDougal (1902), and Thomas Stetson (1905). Although never translated into English, an accessible account of these experiments appears in William James's *The Principles of Psychology* (1890), where it is argued that the mind can retain a longer sequence of impressions when temporal ideas are ordered into rhythmic groups. While these early experiments do not posit any connection between auditory sensation and tactile movement, a more popular summary of Wundt's rhythmic theory appeared in a text translated as *Outlines of Psychology* (1897), where the German psychologist correlates the feeling of tension and release with the contraction and relaxation of the muscles in the body. Observing that rhythmic movements such as walking and running are governed by the principle of *isochrony* (equivalent temporal periods), Wundt notes that the regular contraction and relaxation of the muscles in the limbs of the body give rise to a series of inner tactile sensations. As these "kinestheses" give birth to an exactly parallel series of *feelings* that are marked by similar changes in intensity, Wundt is able to correlate the psychological perception of rhythm to the contraction and release of the muscles in the body:

If we consider a single period in a series of rhythmical movements, there is always at its beginning and end a feeling of fulfilled expectation. Between the two limits of the period there is, beginning with the first movement, a gradually growing feeling of strained expectation, which suddenly sinks at the last moment from its maximum to zero, and gives place to the rapidly rising and sinking feeling of fulfillment. From this point on the same series is again repeated. Thus, the whole process of rhythmical touch movement consists, on its affective side, of a succession of two qualitatively antagonistic feelings. In their general character these feelings belong to the series of straining and relaxing feelings. One of these feelings is very rapid in its course, the other gradually reaches a minimum and then suddenly disappears. As a result, the most intense affective processes are crowded together at the extremes of the periods, and are made all the more intense through the contrast between the feeling of satisfaction and the preceding feeling of expectation. Just as this sharply marked limit between the different periods has its sensuous substratum in the strong outer and inner tactual impressions arising at this instant, as above pointed out, so there is a complete series of feelings of expectation corresponding to the continuous series of weaker inner tactual sensations accompanying the oscillatory movements of the limbs. (1897, 146–7)

Rather than describing the perception of rhythm in purely psychological terms, Wundt here traces the feelings of expectation and fulfillment to a series of inner tactile sensations that are associated with the periodic movements of the body. Nevertheless, by abstracting the feelings of expectation and release from the physical movements and kinestheses that underlie them, Wundt establishes the groundwork for a purely psychological theory of rhythmic sensation that *abstracts* the form of the rhythmic structure from the sensory material in which it is embodied.

From the perspective of prosodic science, the publication of Sidney Lanier's *The Science of English Verse* (1880) should be interpreted as the beginning of modern metrics, for the American author relates the psychological perception of rhythms to the conventional structures of English verse. Building on Spencer's concept of the "compound rhythm," Lanier constructs a hierarchical model of poetic structure that accounts for the different levels at which the human ear can perceive the phenomenon of rhythm. Beginning with the dimension of "quantity," Lanier defines the "primary rhythm" as "equally or simply proportional intervals of time ... marked off to our sense by any recurrent series of similar events" (62), suggesting that primary rhythms can be perceived by the eye and ear alike. To illustrate the perception of the primary rhythm, Lanier appeals to the example of a ticking clock, for not only is the duration between "ticks" exactly equal, but the mind makes a distinction between the higher pitch of the first "tick" and the lower pitch of the second "tack." By marking the recurrence of each temporal period with an "accent," the human mind automatically creates a "secondary rhythm" that corresponds to the foot in classical verse or the bar in music. For the method of scansion developed by Lanier, the perception of the secondary rhythm is highly significant, for he uses musical notation to represent the quantity of the syllables (quavers, crotchets, minims, and so on) and bar lines to differentiate between metrical groups. At the time of publication, Lanier's method was criticized for using musical notation to scan the rhythms of English verse—the most-cited example of his scansion of Hamlet's famous soliloquy (172) (Figure 1.1).

As can be seen from the transcription, the time signature 3/8 indicates that the primary rhythm is determined by a monotonous series

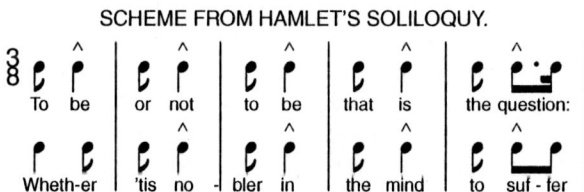

SCHEME FROM HAMLET'S SOLILOQUY.

Figure 1.1 Lanier's scansion of Hamlet's soliloquy.

of quavers (eight notes) that are ordered into groups of three by the secondary rhythm. By using accents, Lanier is able to distinguish the element of stress from the element of quantity; yet, his scansions are compromised by his tendency to subordinate the rhetorical rhythm to the primary and secondary rhythms. In his *History of English Prosody from the Twelfth Century to the Present Day* (1910), for example, George Saintsbury criticized the use of musical notation to scan lines of English verse, writing "however keen his musical ear may have been, his prosodic one must have been very dull" (vol. 3, 494–5). Despite the occasional misapplication of the theory, Lanier's treatise ought to be recognized for distinguishing the perception of rhythm from the conventions of meter, and relating the hierarchical structure of the poem to the interaction between rhythms of differing levels of complexity.

There is textual evidence to suggest that Lanier's hierarchical model of rhythmic structure was directly influenced by the rise of rhythmic science. Indeed, Lanier's concept of the "primary" or "secondary" rhythm can be traced to the compound rhythms of Spencer, for in a chapter titled "Of Rhythm throughout all those Motions which we call 'Nature,'" Lanier states that "Mr. Herbert Spencer claims to have observed such a prevalence of this rhythmic periodicity throughout nature as to convince him that it is universal" (1880, 248). Although Lanier was not primarily concerned with physical rhythms, Spencer's mathematical method of analyzing the interference of different wave forms seems to have inspired the hierarchical model of poetic rhythm presented in *The Science of English Verse*, for Lanier uses the terms "tertiary" and "quaternary" to describe higher-order structures such as the "phrases" or "lines" of verse. Indeed, once the regularity of the primary and secondary rhythm has been established, the monotony of the temporal series is disrupted by the perception of tertiary rhythms that are determined by the length of the phrase, the position of the logical accent, or the perception of alliteration. Rather than defining the poetic line as a regular number of rhythmic units or feet, a method that would remain bound to the orthographic conventions of the literary text, Lanier focuses on the phenomenon of sound that is actually heard by the ear, defining the line in terms of the recurrence of silences or rhyming words at the end of phrases. In addition to this fourth-order rhythm, revealed to the ear through the metrical equality between the lines, there is the fifth-order rhythm determined by the recurrent form of the stanza, and the sixth-order rhythm that arises from the repetition of stanzas to form a complete poem. As we have seen, the analysis of poetry as the interference of multiple rhythms creates a new conception of poetry as the structural relation between the parts and the whole of the work of art.

With the invention of an experimental technique for measuring the tendency of listeners to impose metrical forms of auditory stimuli, Thaddeus Bolton developed the concept of the "wave of attention" to describe how the subjective experience of time is structured by the perception of rhythmic forms. In a classic article titled "Rhythm" (1894), Bolton integrates the distinction between primary and secondary rhythms into a psychological theory of rhythmic sensation, for he states that "The regular recurrence of sounds and silences constitutes primary rhythm, and a grouping of these sounds by means of intensity, pitch or tone-color, constitutes the secondary rhythm—the bar in music and the foot in poetry" (Bolton 1894, 174). In order to prove the existence of these secondary rhythms in the minds of his experimental subjects, Bolton designed an electrical instrument called a "chronograph" that used a rotating drum to open and close an electrical current, thereby generating a primary rhythm composed of a series of ticks. As the tempo and intensity of the ticks could be varied by altering the speed of the drum's rotation, Bolton used the apparatus to test the tendency of experimental subjects to order the recurring ticks into groups of two, three, or four. Significantly, Bolton observed that many respondents would tap their fingers to actualize the rhythm, confirming the kinesthetic relationship between the physiological and psychological dimensions of rhythm posited by Wundt. In order to describe how the mind synthesizes a series of discrete events into a single, undivided act of consciousness, however, Bolton develops the concept of the "wave of attention":

> The conscious state accompanying each wave of attention "grasps together or unifies all the impressions that fall within the temporal period of a wave. As the result of a series of attentive efforts, a series of auditory impressions takes the form of a sequence of groups. This rhythmical grouping is due to the unifying activity of the mind; it is an attempt to conceive a series of sounds in a simpler form. When the mind acts upon a continuous series of auditory impressions, it groups all the impressions that fall within the period of a wave of attention, and conceives them as a single impression or a unity. Each succeeding wave groups a like number, so that the series is conceived in the form of groups. If the single impressions are separated by a greater time interval than the normal period of a wave of attention, each impression stands alone as the sole object of consciousness. (1894, 220)

In his conclusion, Bolton makes it clear that each "wave of attention" is an organic unity, for the discrete elements of the temporal series are conceived as parts that are synthesized into the form of a whole.

He states that the temporal events "form an organic unit which is the essential condition of a number of impressions entering into a state of consciousness" (1894, 213). As Bolton's results tend to confirm the hypothesis that the mind tends to impose an order upon a temporal series of undifferentiated stimuli, the structural concept of rhythm as an organic totality is naturalized as the temporal form of psychological experience.

Although the scientific discourse on rhythm remained largely confined to the academic sphere, Lanier's treatise on *The Science of English Verse* brought about a revolution in English prosody that would have far-reaching consequences. The most notable successor to Lanier was an American "metrist" named T. S. Omond, who developed a concept of the "period" that reconciled the concept of the primary or secondary rhythm with the classical system of feet. After positioning his own work within the context of the musical school (Joshua Steele, John Ruskin, Sidney Lanier, and J. P. Dabney), Omond gives a more general account of the rhythmic phenomenon, beginning with the statement that "Meter is the body of verse, as emotional thought is the source" (1903, 1). While this Cartesian distinction between the body and soul seems to relegate the "meter" of verse to the material dimension of the text (the written words or spoken syllables), the subsequent identification of "meter" with the performance of rhythmical actions reveals an experience of temporality that underlies the physical movements: "The sailor pulling at his ropes, the blacksmith beating on his anvil, the tramp of a marching regiment—all the old familiar illustrations— regularity of recurrence is the principle these show at work" (1903, 2). By focusing on the phenomenon of regular recurrence, Omond demonstrates that there is a *temporal correspondence* between external actions and inner feelings, reducing the essence of verse to the pure experience of time that underlies the composition of verse: "All metre is essentially rhythmical ... it consists of equal units, uniform as regards duration" (1903, 2). Viewed in this context, it becomes clear that Omond's central contribution to modern prosody is the abstraction of *time* from the syllables of verse, for as he puts it: "If syllables do not recur with regularity, we must fall back on that which underlies these—on the time-spaces or periods of duration in which syllables are, as it were, embedded" (1903, 3). Omond therefore develops a new concept of the "period" that *conditions* the arrangement of the syllables, formulating the basic principle that "*Isochronous* periods form the units of metre" (1903, 4). By constructing a metaphysical opposition between the body and soul of verse, Omond abstracts the *psychological experience of the underlying rhythm* from the metrical organization of verse, and therefore anticipates the development of modern prosody as recently codified by Derek Attridge (1982).

While it is difficult to determine whether Joyce ever read Omond's *Study of Metre*, he was nevertheless exposed to Lanier's notion of the "primary rhythm" through the literature of the period, for the decadent poet and critic Arthur Symons describes the pure sensation of rhythm as "the executive soul" of Stéphane Mallarmé's poetry. According to Richard Ellmann, Joyce read *The Symbolist Movement in Literature* (1899) during his time at University College, and there is textual evidence to suggest that he appropriated Symons's account of the method of poetic composition from the chapter on "Mallarmé."[3] In his attempt to reconstruct Mallarmé's method of composition, Symons holds that the poetic symbol begins with the simple intuition of a rhythmic form, for as he puts it: "he [Mallarmé] has received, then, a mental sensation: let it be the horror of the forest. This sensation begins to form in his brain, at first probably no more than a rhythm, absolutely without words" (1899, 132). Alluding here to the concept of the "primary rhythm" first developed by Lanier, Symons abstracts the psychological experience of rhythm from the poetic diction in which the images of the poem are expressed. As the bare sensation of the rhythm precedes the selection of the words and phrases, it is conceptualized as both a *temporal form* that conditions the revelation of the poetic symbol as well as a *spatial structure* that leads to the concealment of the creative process. Significantly, Symons attributes a guiding role to the intuition of rhythm in the mind of poet, because "guided always by the rhythm, which is the executive soul (as in Aristotle's definition, the soul is the form of the body), words come slowly, one by one, shaping the message" (1899, 133). From the perspective of the development of Joyce's aesthetic theory, this must be interpreted as a highly significant statement, for Symons equates the perception of the primary rhythm with the *soul* of an Aristotelian substance.

From his general familiarity with the laws of classical prosody, the psychology of the nineteenth century, and Symons's critical study of the French symbolists, it appears that Joyce developed a dualistic account of the rhythmic phenomenon that includes both *a practical understanding of (1) the metrical rhythm* and *(2) a theoretical understanding of the structural rhythm*. In the context of Stephen's aesthetic philosophy, the "soul" or "substance" of the image is associated with the structural rhythm, an idealizing tendency that tends to conceal his practical understanding of rhythm as meter (see Ch. 3). Despite the stress on the spatial form of the image in Joyce's aesthetic theory, the surviving manuscript of *Stephen Hero* indicates that the perception of the structural rhythm is conditioned by the intuition of the primary or secondary rhythm; for a fragment from chapter XXV posits that "[the feet?] of verse are the first conditions which the words must submit to, the rhythm is the esthetic result of the senses, values and relations of the words thus conditioned" (*SH*, 25). Due to the fragmentary state of the manuscript, it is impossible to know the exact terminology employed by Joyce to describe the primary and secondary rhythms (meters, feet, stresses?) that condition the composition of verse; yet, it is evident from this passage that the Irish author had already developed the structural conception of rhythm that first appears in the Paris notebook of 1903 (see Ch. 3).

The discussion of Stephen's prosody in *Stephen Hero* reveals that Joyce identifies the rhythm of poetry with both the temporal form that *conditions* the selection of the words, as well as the spatial structure that comes into being from the higher-order interference of the secondary, tertiary, and quaternary rhythms (meter, accent, and line). Alluding to Carlyle's definition of the symbol as quoted in the introduction to *The Symbolist Movement in Literature*—"In a symbol ... there is yet concealment and revelation" (Symons 1899, 4)—Stephen links the revelatory structure of the symbol to the tension between the *process* and *product* of creation, for he asserts: "the beauty of verse consisted as much in the concealment as in the revelation of the construction but it certainly could not proceed from only one of these" (*SH*, 25). As the metrical rhythm is associated with the "executive soul" of the poem, the primary rhythm that conditions the selection of the words, it is associated with the creative *process*. By contrast, the structural rhythm only emerges from the completion of the poem as an artistic *product*, as the formal relations between the parts can only be perceived in terms of their position within the whole. By maintaining the tension between the process (metrical rhythm) and the product (structural rhythm), Stephen implicitly rejects Symons's claim that "in the final result there must be no sign of the making, there must be only the thing made" (1899, 133), maintaining that the final product must not conceal the experience of temporality that originally inspired the composition of the poem. From the preceding discussion, it is clear that Symons's notion of rhythm as a "mental sensation" is derived from the psychological theory of rhythmic sensation, a theory that received its most forceful expression in Lanier's conception of the primary rhythm. From the appropriation of such ideas in the draft of *Stephen Hero*, it has emerged that there is a constant tension in Joyce's work between the practical intuition of rhythm as a temporal pattern and the aesthetic apprehension of rhythm as a spatial structure.

The Influence of Quackenbos's
Practical Rhetoric on the Prose of
Stephen Hero

As it is well known, Joyce develops a structural conception of rhythm in the Paris notebook (1903) that is reproduced in the aesthetic dialogue of *Portrait*, and the term acquires some of the connotations ascribed to it by psychologists and prosodists such as Spencer and Lanier; yet, it is more likely that Joyce's definition was informed by the classical conception of beauty as harmony developed by Aristotle and Aquinas. For the sake of reconstructing the intellectual development of the young James Joyce, I will undertake an investigation into the sources of his aesthetic theory, but it should be recognized that the rise of the rhythmic science had a more profound impact on his *rhythmic practice*. While Joyce's knowledge of rhythmics was limited to his general awareness of psychological science in the late nineteenth century, he nevertheless studied from rhetorical manuals such as John Duncan Quackenbos's *Practical Rhetoric* (1896), a textbook that he possessed in his Trieste library. Significantly, this rhetorical manual includes a lesson on "Versification" that would have shaped the style of his early poetry. While other commentators have asserted that Joyce mainly drew on *Practical Rhetoric* during the composition of the "Aeolus" episode of *Ulysses* (Gillespie 1983), the allusions to Quackenbos's textbook in *Stephen Hero* indicate that he probably studied it during his time at University College (or at least during his early years in Trieste). As Quackenbos seeks to legitimate the principles of rhetoric in terms of the leading scientific authorities of the day—in particular Herbert Spencer's "Essay on the Philosophy of Style" (1892) and Grant Allen's *Physiological Aesthetics* (1877)—this textbook can be used to measure the extent to which rhythmic science informed Joyce's stylistic practice. Even if Joyce did not read any of the scientific authorities cited in *Practical Rhetoric*, he nevertheless studied many of its lessons, demonstrating that his early literary style as a poet and essayist was *indirectly* shaped by the emergence of rhythmics in the late nineteenth century.

The surviving manuscript of *Stephen Hero* gives a realistic description of Joyce's time at University College Dublin, and chapter XV gives us an indication of the extent to which his prose style was shaped by his attendance at classes in English composition taught by W. P. Coyne. In the second chapter of this book, I will contend that Joyce drew on Quackenbos's *Practical Rhetoric* when formulating the basic principles of his prosody; yet, the authenticity of this source can be verified by out-lining the allusions to the lesson on "Literary Style" in Joyce's unpub-lished manuscript. In chapter XX, Joyce gives an account of Stephen reading an essay titled "Art and Life," a fictional document that fuses the content of the two essays that Joyce originally presented to the Literary and Historical Society at University College: "Drama and Life" (January 20, 1900) and "James Clarence Mangan" (February 15, 1902). In "Art and Life," Stephen places particular emphasis on the selection of words or images, for he imagines the artist "standing in the position of media-tor between the word of his experience and the world of his dreams—a mediator, consequently gifted with the twin faculties, a selective faculty and a reproductive faculty" (*SH*, 82). As indicated by this passage, the faculty of selection is directly related to the world of experience, for it is the vocation of the literary artist to select memorable words and images from the scenes of everyday life.

While the reference to the term "faculty" brings to mind the language of neo-Kantian psychology, it is most likely that Joyce developed his theory of the literary imagination from Quackenbos's lesson on "The Imagination" in chapter XV of *Practical Rhetoric* (1896), for both authors use the metaphor of the "treasure-house" to describe the space in which images are retained in the memory. In the section titled "The Image-Making Faculty," Quackenbos describes the manner in which remem-bered images are transformed into the material of artistic creation:

> The simplest action of this faculty is the reproduction of a remem-bered image. Whatever *impresses* the mind through the senses leaves behind it a representative in the memory. Every object that we have seen is represented by a memory image. It is with memory images that imagination deals. They remain stored in the mind's *treasure-house*, to be reproduced, when occasion arises, in the mental field. It is easy, when at a distance from home, to construct in your mind a picture of the street on which you live, or of the library in which you study; the fact that you can do so proves to you that you have an image-making faculty. (1896, 27: my italics, WM)

It is significant that Quackenbos uses the metaphor of the "treasure-house"todescribethespaceofthememory,forthesameexpressionoccurs in a passage of *Stephen Hero* that depicts the young artist memorizing the images and words that appear during his walk through the city:

> As he walked thus through the ways of the city he had his ears and eyes ever prompt to receive *impressions*. It was not only in Skeat that he

found words for his *treasure-house*, he found them also in the mouths
of the plodding public. (*SH*, 36: my italics, WM)

Considering that the related words "impresses" and "impressions" are
also used to describe the way in which Stephen constructs a picture of
the street, there seems to be a strong correspondence between the two
passages. In addition to the reproduction of past images, Quackenbos
also describes the process by which the artist selects images to be
used in the composition of new aesthetic wholes. In a section of
the same lesson titled "Taste in the Workshop of the Imagination,"
the Professor of Rhetoric writes that "From among the many forms of
Beauty assembled by the creative faculty, a selection must be made"
(28). As the terms "reproduction" and "selection" are used in successive sections of *Practical Rhetoric* to describe the dual operations of
the creative "faculty," it can hardly be doubted that Joyce drew on
this source when composing *Stephen Hero*.[4]

It seems that Joyce consulted the lessons in *Practical Rhetoric* as a
means of developing his original style as an essayist, for the literary
program outlined in *Stephen Hero* is oriented toward the selection
of poetic words and phrases that reflect the individual temperament
of the artist. In the section on "Literary Style," Qackenbos writes
that "style is the manner of expressing thoughts by the selection and
combination of words" (1896, 135), specifying that the quality of the
author's style will depend on the particular choice of words, their
number, and arrangement into sentences or paragraphs. Significantly,
Quackenbos outlines a program of education that involves investigating the etymological origin of words, for in a paragraph on the
"Sources of Diction," he advises the young writer "to accept no
expression without a reason—to add no word to his working list from
example or hearsay alone, until he has thoroughly informed himself
as to its history, derivation, spelling, pronunciation, exact meaning
and standing" (1896, 137). It is only when we take into account this
imperative to understand the history and value of words that we can
understand the following passage from *Stephen Hero*:

> He was at once captivated by the seeming eccentricities of the prose
> of Freeman and William Morris. He read them as one would read a
> thesaurus and made a garner of words. He read Skeat's etymological
> dictionary by the hour and his mind, which had from the first been
> only submissive to the infant sense of wonder, was often hypnotised by
> the most commonplace conversation. People seemed to him strangely
> ignorant of the value of the words they used so glibly. (*SH*, 32)

It is clear from this passage that Stephen has prescribed for himself an educational program designed to improve his knowledge of the origin and history of words. The allusion to "Skeat's etymological dictionary" only reinforces the impression that the development of Joyce's literary style was shaped by *Practical Rhetoric*, for in a note at the end of chapter XIII, Quackenbos states that "for a purely etymological dictionary, none other is equal to Professor Skeat's" (141). In an exercise appended to the same lesson, furthermore, the author advises the student to compile a "list of twenty words, gathered from the writings of Defoe, Carlyle, Coleridge, Dickens," an exercise that parallels Stephen's task. In a subsequent conversation with Father Butt, Stephen differentiates between the value of words in the "literary tradition" and the "market place," suggesting that words become "debased" when used in everyday conversation. As *Practical Rhetoric* also contains sections on the various origins of words, including "Words Entering Language through Commercial or other Intercourse" and "Hybrid or Mongrel Words," it is also possible that Joyce developed his theory of nominal value from reading the same work.

It is clear that Joyce undertook research into the history of words to improve the style of his English composition, as he provides a justification for the method in his essay on "The Study of Languages." Probably written during his matriculation year (1899), Joyce argues that the study of the grammar of language can be considered a science, for "the orthography and etymology are admitted as known," and "they are studied in the same manner as tables in Arithmetic, surely and accurate" (*CW*, 27). By emphasizing the scientific nature of linguistic research and the mathematical basis of etymology, Joyce presumably alludes to Max Müller's newly founded "Science of Language," for the German scholar had recently delivered a number of lectures at Oxford to publicize his method. Significantly, Quackenbos points students toward Müller's *Three Lectures on the Science of Language and Its Place in General Education* (1889) in the same lesson. If Joyce had consulted this text, and it is highly likely that he did, he would have come across a passage in which the origin of language is related to the rhythmic coordination of social actions:

> With regard to the sounds accompanying our notions, we know from physiology that under any strong muscular effort it is a relief to the system to let our breath come out strongly and repeatedly, and by that process to let the vocal cords vibrate in different ways. That is the case with savages, and it is the case even with us. These natural sounds accompanying our acts, are called *clamor concomitans*. Navvies when

they have to lift a heavy weight together, shout *Yo heo*. Sailors when they pull together, have their own monotonous song. Even children when they march or dance, break out naturally in some kind of rhythmic sing song. Here we have at all events a hint—for I will say no more—how this natural music which accompanied the acts of early people, this *clamor concomitans*, could have supplied the outward signs of the inward concepts of these acts. (1889, 34)

Viewed in its historical context, Müller's allusion to "physiology" is highly significant, for it suggests that his account of the origin of words was influenced by the "physiological psychology" that underlies the scientific discourse on rhythm. As Müller seeks to refute the thesis that words arise through the imitation of animal calls, he posits an intellectual relationship between the rhythm of the verb and the continuous activity of the physical action, founding the conventional meaning of words through the rhythmic coordination of social action. There are strong grounds to assert that Joyce consulted this passage, or at least was indirectly influenced by Müller's theory, for he writes in *Stephen Hero* that "he seemed to hear the simple cries of fear and joy and wonder that are antecedent to all song, *the savage rhythm of men pulling at the oar*" (*SH*, 37: my emphasis, WM). Not only does Joyce allude to the communal sounds made by sailors when "pulling" on their oars, but he also ascribes an evolutionary origin to the phenomenon of rhythm, claiming in the same passage that he "caught glimpses of emergent art as one might have a vision of plesiosauros [sic] emerging from his ocean of slime" (*SH*, 37).

As the concept of the *clamor concomitans* posits a temporal correspondence between the sound of words and the rhythm of bodily actions, it also provides a model of artistic creation, for it suggests that the literary author can communicate the social meaning of actions through the choice of specific words and phrases whose rhythm contains a temporal reference to an unfolding action. In *Stephen Hero*, Stephen develops a theory of the rhythmic gesture that relates the metrical form of poetry to the primitive cries and movements of animals. Due to Joyce's own preference for the Elizabethan ballad, Stephen cites one of Ariel's songs from *The Tempest*; yet, this text is also chosen because the second verse features the primitive cries of a dog:

> Come unto these yellow sands,
>   And then take hands:
> Curt'sied when you have, and kist,—
>   The wild waves whist,—
> Foot it featly here and there;

And, sweet sprites, the burden bear.
   Hark, hark!
   [*Burden dispersedly, within.*
   Bow-wow.]
The watch-dogs bark.
   [*Burden dispersedly, within.*
   Bow-wow.]
Hark, hark! I hear
The strain of strutting chanticleer.
                    [*Cry*: Cock-a-diddle-dow] (Bullen 1907, 1)

Distinguishing his own conception of the rhythmic gesture from the doctrine of the elocution Professor, who simply defines rhythm as "emphasis," Stephen performs the song in a dramatic manner, "making a graceful anapaestic gesture with each arm" (*SH*, 189). As the opening line begins with a trochaic inversion that disrupts the iambic meter of the song, the repetition of two short (or unstressed) syllables creates a triple rhythm that Stephen performs with his anapestic gesture. Significantly, the animal cries of the watch-dogs ("Bow wow!") are dramatized as a burden sung by all the performers, linking the performance of the rhythm to the coordination of social action.[5] While the rhythmic gesture of Ariel's song represents the descent of art into life, in the sense that a musical form is used to encode the performance of the dramatic gesture, Stephen's theory of the rhythmic gesture is supposed to explain the emergence of rhythmic forms in the context of everyday life. After performing Ariel's Song, Stephen says to Cranly: "I would like to go out into Grafton St some day and make gestures in the middle of the street" (*SH*, 189).

The allusion to "Ariel's Song" can be interpreted as a transitional moment in the development of Joyce's theory of rhythm, for although Stephen's interpretation of the poem depends on the metrical concept of rhythm, he becomes increasingly concerned with the visual gesture that accompanies the embodied performance of the song. In one of his youthful epiphanies, Joyce alludes to the watch-dog from Shakespeare's song, observing:

Dull clouds have covered the sky. Where three roads meet before a swampy beach a big dog is recumbent. From time to time he lifts his muzzle to the air and utters a prolonged sorrowful howl. People stop to look at him and pass on; some remain, arrested, it may be, by that lamentation in which they seem to hear the utterance of their own sorrow that had once its voice but is now voiceless, a servant of laborious days. Rain begins to fall. (*PSW*, 168)

Although this epiphany is written as a short prose poem, and does not display any discernible metrical properties, the allusion to the "prolonged sorrowful howl" can be interpreted as a "rhythmic gesture," for the sound of the dog's howl, recurring "from time to time," arrests the attention of the people. When Joyce posits a sympathetic relationship between the voice of the dog and the voiceless onlookers, he is alluding to Herder's theory that language evolves from the primitive cries of animals (Herder 1966). Indeed, it is precisely the *sympathetic vibration* between the voice of the dog and the ear of the human that reveals the meaning of the epiphanic moment. As it is well known, Stephen Dedalus placed specific emphasis upon the use of the word "arrest" in the aesthetic dialogue of a *Portrait*, a term that marks the transition of consciousness from the kinetic involvement with physical objects to the static contemplation of aesthetic images. According to Sandra Tropp, Joyce appropriated this term from Alexander Bain's *Mental and Moral Science* (1872), for with regard to the apprehension of games, the physiological psychologist writes that "we are in a peculiar state of arrested attention, which, as an agreeable effect, is often desired for itself" (Bain 268, cited in Tropp 2008, 229). As we will see, Bain's notion of "arrested" attention provides a good model for the Joycean epiphany, and informs Stephen's later account of the mind focusing its attention on the face of Ballast clock in chapter XXV.

Practical Rhetoric and the Scientific Discourse on Rhythm

Assuming that the development of Joyce's youthful prose style was shaped by the lessons in *Practical Rhetoric,* we can now begin to measure the extent to which his practical understanding of rhythm was shaped by rhythmic science. In particular, the allusions to Herbert Spencer's "Essay on the Philosophy of Style" (1892) in Quackenbos's manual reveal that the study of rhetoric and versification was being shaped by a new appreciation of the role which rhythm plays in regulating the movements of the body and maintaining the balance between the work and rest. Indeed, Quackenbos's manual contains no fewer than 16 direct references to Spencer's work, including two lengthy quotations on the use of concrete terms and figurative language from the essay on style. In the opening sentence of the preface, Quackenbos writes: "Herbert Spencer, in his 'Essay on the Philosophy of Style', observes that maxims contained in works on composition and rhetoric are presented in an unorganized form, and proceeds to systematize the scattered precepts under one leading principle, economy" (3). While this principle is modified to accommodate the classical conception of beauty as "harmony," a term that becomes synonymous with "rhythm" in Stephen's aesthetic theory, the principle of economy can nevertheless be interpreted as the basis of modern rhetoric as codified in Quackenbos's manual.

In his essay on style, Spencer derives the principle of economy from a review of the existing literature on the subject, concluding that the received maxims of rhetoric all emphasize "the importance of economizing the reader's hearing or attention"; in other words, "to present ideas that they may be apprehended with the least possible mental effort" (Spencer 1892, 3). In this revolutionary document, Spencer uses the physiological concepts of effort and fatigue as metaphors to describe the waxing and waning of the mind's attention. The basis of this metaphor is the notion that words of rhetoric are "symbols of thought" (3) that can be organized in such a manner as to maximize the effect upon the reader. As the reader only has a "limited amount of mental power available," the symbols must present ideas in the most direct manner possible. According to Spencer, "the more time and attention it takes to receive and understand each sentence, the less time and attention can be given to the contained idea; and the less vividly will the idea be conveyed" (3). The principle of economy therefore dictates that the selection and arrangement of the symbols exactly mirror the thought processes they are supposed to represent. When constructing sentences, for example, adjectives must precede nouns, for the mind perceives an image of the predicate before it grasps the meaning of the subject. Spencer also expresses a preference for the use of metaphors rather than similes, as they present the images directly to the mind. In summary, the principle of economy dictates that the orator constructs sentences that maximize the force of the utterance, using Anglo-Saxon words (rather than Latin terms), inversions, metaphors, and concrete terms to minimize the mental energy devoted to the interpretation of the symbols.

When applied to the temporal form of poetry, the principle of economy proscribes that the poet must adopt a regular meter, for any disruption to the metrical pattern will capture the mind of the reader, diverting his or her attention from the images and ideas contained in the poem. According to Spencer, the diction of poetry exemplifies the economic use of diction, for the exaggerated use of inversions, metaphors, epithets, and concrete terms all tend to increase the force of the expression. Yet, poets do not simply wish to express thoughts and ideas, they also wish to express "idealized emotions," and therefore require an "idealized language of emotion" (1892, 32). For Spencer, the cadences of music provide such an idealized language as there seems to be direct correspondence between the rise and fall of the melody and the rise and fall of human emotion: "As the musical composer catches the cadences in which our feelings of joy and sympathy, grief and despair, vent themselves, and out of these germs evolves melodies suggesting higher phases of feeling; so the poet develops from the typical expressions in which men utter passion and sentiment" (1892, 32–3). From this analogy between music and poetry, we can see that the poet relies on the musical dimensions of language to express strong emotions, and this function is performed by the adoption of a regular rhythm. It is at this point of his discourse that Spencer relates the perception of rhythm to the attention of the mind, for the alternating phases of stress and relaxation provide the most economical method of communicating human emotions to the reader:

> For if, as we have seen, there is an expenditure of mental energy in the mere act of listening to verbal articulations, or in that silent repetition of them which goes on in reading—if the perceptive faculties must be in active exercise to identify every syllable—then, any mode of so combining words as to present a regular recurrence of certain traits which the mind can anticipate, will diminish that strain upon the attention required by the total irregularity of prose. Just as the body, in receiving a series of varying concussions, must keep the muscles ready to meet the most violent of them, as not knowing when such may come; so, the mind in receiving unarranged articulations, must keep its perceptives active enough to recognize the least easily caught sounds. And as, if the concussions recur in a definite order, the body may husband its forces by adjusting the resistance needful for each concussion; so, if the syllables be rhythmically arranged, the mind may economize its energies by anticipating the attention required for each syllable. (1892, 34–5)

As we noted earlier, the concept of "mental fatigue" relies on an analogy between physical and mental effort; yet, the perception of a rhythmic pattern provides the perfect illustration of this analogy, for the body learns to coordinate its movement through the performance of rhythmic actions. Anticipating the development of experimental psychology, Herbert Spencer therefore develops a metaphorical concept of "mental fatigue" that can explain the pleasurable feelings associated with the perception of a rhythmic pattern, for the tension associated with the anticipation of the beat is relieved by its arrival at the expected moment.

Considering that Quackenbos's entire treatise is informed by Spencer's essay, we can assume that he understood the relationship between the physiological rhythms of the body and the metrical conventions of poetry. In a section of *Practical Rhetoric* (1896) on "The Elements of Audible Beauty," Quackenbos writes that "Rhythm, or uniform movement in time, involving the regular succession of stress and relaxation, of long and short tones, is aesthetic" (48). While this definition still remains tied to the classical conception of rhythm as a sequence of short and long syllables (or musical *tones* in the case of lyrical song), the reference to a "uniform movement in time" is an acknowledgment that the body produces rhythmic movements that can be separated from the material of either music or poetry. In the "Further Reading" section, Quackenbos cites Grant Allen's *Physiological Aesthetics* (1877), a study that applies the theories of Spencer, Bain, Helmholtz, and Herman to the field of aesthetics. In the introduction, Allen outlines the basic principle of "physiological psychology," stating that: "all mental phenomena are the subjective sides of what are objectively cognised as nervous functions; and that they are in consequence as rigorously limited by natural laws as the physical processes whose correlatives they are" (1877, 2). In the chapter on "Hearing," Allen bases his definition of rhythm on the supposed correspondence between physiology and psychology, for the "muscular energies" of the body are compared to the "attention" of the mind:

> Now, what the rhythm of music and dance is to our muscular energies, the rhythm of music and poetry is to the ear. Its main constituent as pleasure is the regularity of its recurrence, and the consequent possibility of relaxing our attention to the accentuation or arrangement of chords. While syllables irregularly thrown together require a certain amount of jumping from point to point, syllables placed in a regular order of short and long allow us to withdraw our attention from their accent, and to expect a continuance of the same harmonious and easily followed succession. (1877, 115)

As can be seen, the equivalence between "stress" and "relaxation," "long" and "short," in Quackenbos's treatise can be traced to this passage in *Physiological Aesthetics*, for the analogy between physiological movement and psychological attention is made explicit. According to Allen, an "organic rhythm" is set up whenever the organs of the body "perform their function at the exact moment of expectation" (117), producing a feeling of pleasure from the ease of continuing the movement. Similarly, whenever the syllables of verse conform to the underlying rhythm, the mind derives pleasure from the fulfillment of the expectation, allowing listeners to divert their attention from the performance of the rhythm to the meaning of the words. The pleasure and pain associated with poetry can therefore be traced to either the fulfillment or disruption of the regular rhythm, for as Allen puts it, "the aesthetic pleasure of meter depends upon the existence of an expectant state, realized in the auditory apparatus as a recurrent organic rhythm of nascent stimulation: while the aesthetic discomfort of bad versification depends upon the breach of this expectation, and consequent upsetting of the organic rhythm" (1877, 116).

As a disciple of Herbert Spencer, Grant Allen interprets all mental processes as correlatives of physiological processes, and draws on the thermodynamics of Helmholtz to describe the human body as a machine that constantly requires energy to maintain its healthy functioning. While the feeling of pain is associated with physical processes that deplete the amount of energy in the body (work, movement, fatigue), the feeling of pleasure is associated with the repletion of that lost energy (repose, repair, nutrition). As the senses of sight and hearing are not involved in the fulfillment of the basic life functions, however, and are not usually susceptible to physical pleasure and pain, they become capable of discriminating between beauty and ugliness in a purely intellectual manner. According to Allen, it is only through an act of *attention* that the aesthetic quality of the object comes into view, an act which is not involved in the fulfillment of any life function, for as he puts it, "The aesthetically beautiful is that which affords the Maximum of Stimulation with the Minimum of fatigue or waste, in processes not directly connected with the vital functions" (39). In a later passage, Allen evokes the specific example of a clock to illustrate the manner in which the mind focuses on the aesthetic qualities of visual or auditory sensations:

> When the higher coordinating structures are occupied in transforming or correlating such transmitted energies, we are in a state of Attention to our sense-impressions; as in the case of observing the dial, or listening to the tick of the clock. (199)

As we will see, Stephen also chooses the example of the clock to demonstrate his theory of the epiphany in *Stephen Hero*, but the image also possesses a deeper significance in the scientific literature of the era.

According to Sandra Tropp (2008), Joyce was already familiar with Grant Allen's work during his first trip to Paris, an interest that may have been spurred by the citations in *Practical Rhetoric*. In a letter written to his mother on January 25, 1903, Joyce writes "Tell stannie to send me *at once* (so that I may have it by Thursday night) my copy of Wagner's operas and if he can enclose with it a copy of Grant Allen's 'Paris' " (*Letters II*, 25). This request for Allen's travel guide indicates a prior familiarity with his nonscientific works, and allusions in *Ulysses* indicate that Joyce was familiar with Allen's scandalous novel, *The Woman Who Did* (1895). More specifically, the surviving manuscript of *Stephen Hero* contains a direct allusion to the work of Allen, for Stephen draws on the image of a clock-face to illustrate the act whereby the mind turns its attention from the sensible material of the image to its intellectual form. Turning his friend's attention to "the clock of the Ballast office," Stephen reports: "I will pass it time after time, allude to it, refer to it, catch a glimpse of it. It is only an item in the catalogue of Dublin's street furniture. Then all at once I see it and I know at once what it is: epiphany" (*SH*, 216). By selecting the "clock" as an example of an epiphany, Joyce is ironically suggesting that the rhythmic ticking of the clock underlies the spatial perception of the image. According to Stephen's description, the mind passes from the sensible to the intellectual dimension of the image by focusing its attention: "Imagine my glimpses at that clock as the gropings of a spiritual eye which seeks to adjust its vision to an exact focus. The moment the focus is reached the object is epiphanised" (*SH*, 216–17). It is no coincidence that Stephen selects the clock as an example, for it is precisely the object used by experimental psychologists of the era to test the speed of consciousness and the capacity of the mind to retain series of impressions.

When placed in the context of nineteenth-century psychology, Allen's reference to the ticking of a clock ought to be interpreted as allusion to an experiment performed by Wilhelm Wundt that was designed to measure the reaction-time of consciousness toward the occurrence of physical sensation. As early as 1862, Wundt had performed a thought experiment on what he called a "thought-meter," a machine consisting of a swinging clock that sounded two bells whenever the pendulum reached the extreme of either arc (Rieber 1980). In order to test the "reaction-time" of consciousness, Wundt focused his attention on the timescale whenever the bell sounded, but found that he always perceived the position of the pendulum to be slightly displaced from the extreme of the timescale. Due to the delay of approximately one-tenth of a second between the aural sensation (the sounding bell) and the visual sensation (the position of the pendulum), Wundt concluded that the mind only attends to one sensation at a time. As the voluntary act of focusing the mind's attention on the position of the pendulum is caused by a reaction to the involuntary act of hearing the bell, Wundt further concluded that the act of thought itself takes some time. From a philosophical standpoint, Wundt took this thought experiment as evidence for the ideal existence of voluntary acts, using the term "apperception" to distinguish the focused attention of the mind from the background "perception" of the physical sensations. Considering that Allen uses the example of the clock to illustrate the act of focusing the mind's attention, and transforming the energy of the sensation into an ideal experience, it is highly likely that he is alluding to the concept of "apperception" developed by Wundt in his *Grundzüge der Physiologischen Psychologie* (1874). Although Allen does not directly cite Wundt in his work, he nevertheless claims to have been working in the field of "Physiological Psychology," and therefore must have possessed some knowledge of the German scholar whose *magnum opus* served to define the field.

A Note on Method and a Summary of the Work

As indicated above, our analysis of the impact of rhythmic science on Joyce's critical and creative writings is not limited to an investigation of the *sources* of his aesthetic theory, for as the "physiological psychology" of the late nineteenth century reveals for the first time, the rhythmic *competence* of the literary author is determined by a set of habitual practices that may or may not be the product of self-conscious knowledge. In order to clarify the method of this book, therefore, it will be useful to distinguish between three levels of analysis, including the study of (1) discourse, (2) influence, and (3) stylistics. Over the course of the next four chapters, I will be pursuing these three levels of analysis simultaneously; yet, as one or the other becomes more or less prominent at different stages of the argument, I will take this opportunity to outline the content of the various chapters.

In the second chapter of this book, subtitled "Rhythm as Meter," I will gauge the extent to which Joyce's *rhythmic practice* as a critic and poet was shaped by both the psychology of rhythm and the principles of nineteenth-century prosody. As Joyce was both a student and a teacher of English literature, I argue that his dramatic approach to prosody was informed by the scientific *discourse* on rhythm, for the style of his own poetry and criticism was shaped by the *disciplinary practices* of the educational institutions in both Dublin and Trieste.

Beginning with Joyce's classical education at Clongowes Wood College in County Kildare and Belvedere College in Dublin, I will suggest that Joyce possessed a practical understanding of classical meters through his study of Latin poetry. Upon his admission to University College in Dublin, however, Joyce would have become familiar with some of the debates concerning English prosody at the turn of the twentieth century, for the manuscript of *Stephen Hero* demonstrates an awareness of the conflict between the "quantity" (feet) and "quality" (stress) that remained largely unresolved prior to the 1903 publication of Omond's *A Study of Metre*. Through his attendance at lessons in English Composition and his own experimentation with verse composition, it is probable that Joyce became exposed to more modern systems of prosody. In this regard, it is significant that he owned a copy of Quackenbos's *Practical Rhetoric* (1896), for the rhetorical manual contains a lesson on "Versification" that attempts to reconcile the rhythmic feet of classical prosody with the physiological psychology of the late nineteenth century. As we shall see, Joyce takes for granted an understanding of rhythm *qua* meter, and develops a new dramatic approach to prosody that focuses on the position of the rhetorical accents.

As it is well known, Joyce modeled the lyrics of *Chamber Music* on the style of the Elizabethan ballad, a traditional form that remains at odds with the stylistic experimentation of his later novels. Despite the apparent conservatism of these early poems, Joyce's penchant for British folk songs can be interpreted as symptomatic of late-Victorian attempts to reunite the arts of poetry and music, an aesthetic ideal famously invoked by Wagner in *Opera and Drama* (1895). Inspired by the musical experiments of Yeats and Florence Farr, who had perfected the art of chanting poetry to the tones of a psaltery designed by Arnold Dolmetsch, Joyce also attempted to translate his own poetry into music through the composition of "airs" on the piano. Striving to attain the "condition of music" idealized by Pater in his famous study of *The Renaissance* (1899, 140), Joyce reduces the content of his poems to a subtle play of sound and color, the images of musical instruments providing a visual parallel to the regularity of the underlying rhythms. Despite the idealizing tendency of these early verses, Joyce composed them with the aim of having them set to music, and his unrealized plans of performing British folk songs with Oliver St. John Gogarty reveal a countervailing tendency of translating art into life. Indeed, to the extent that the musical arrangement and performance of lyric poetry *incorporates* the motor patterns of the body into the form of English verse, and reintroduces the dimension of time into its reception,

Joyce's preference for the ballad reveals an affinity with the physiological approach to the study of rhythm. Considering that Sidney Lanier's *The Science of English Verse* used the symbols of musical notation to transcribe the primary and secondary rhythms of poetry, Joyce's own attempts to reunite the arts of poetry and music should be interpreted as reflecting the *zeitgeist* of the late-Victorian era.

In the third chapter of this book, subtitled "Rhythm as Gesture," I will measure the *influence* of rhythmic science on the aesthetic theory developed by Joyce in the Paris notebook and articulated by Stephen Dedalus in the aesthetic dialogue of *Portrait*. Following a thoroughly traditional method of literary exegesis, I will identify the sources that Joyce drew upon when composing the entries of the Paris notebook (1903), for it is in this context that he *self-consciously* formulates the definition of rhythm as the set of formal relations between the parts and the whole of an aesthetic image. As we will see, Joyce drew heavily on Samuel Butcher's translation and commentary on *Aristotle's Theory of Poetry and Fine Art* (1895), a text that includes a long section on the understanding of rhythm in ancient Athens and classical Greece. In the first instance, Joyce draws on the organic conception of drama as the "wholeness" and "perfection" of the tragic plot (*mythos*), for it is precisely the *causal* relationship between beginning, middle, and end of the play that determines the fate of the hero (and the life of the organism). While this text reveals the classical authorities behind Joyce's structural conception of rhythm, Butcher's treatise can be interpreted as an attempt to legitimate the classical conception of rhythm in terms of the leading scientific theories of the day, for he posits a rhythmic correspondence between the gestures of the body and the spiritual movements of the soul reminiscent of Spencer and Wundt. In *Stephen Hero*, Joyce develops a theory of the rhythmic gesture that orients the mind of the esthete toward the perception of conversations and poetic images that reveal the emergence of rhythmic forms in the context of everyday life. From the "epiphanies" that Joyce collected during his time at University College, it is clear that he attempted to transcribe the rhythmic form of everyday conversations, particularly moments when the "beat" or the "pulse" of the interaction is disrupted. To show how Joyce translated his theory into practice, I will analyze the dialogues in two stories from *Dubliners* ("Grace" and "Ivy Day"), suggesting that the beats of dialogue perform the important function of socializing speakers and revealing the sources of dysfunction paralyzing Irish society around the turn of the twentieth century.

As it will become clear from our analysis of *Dubliners*, there is a certain gap between Joyce's rhythmic theory and practice, for as one of the most experimental of all modernist writers, Joyce's creativity as a literary author almost always exceeded his capacity to describe the principles of his own *stylistic* practice. In the context of his dramatic dialogues, for example, Joyce focuses on pivotal exchanges in which the logic of narrative is revealed, isolating moments that highlight the normalizing force of conversation as the primary form of social interaction. To *supplement* Joyce's theory of the rhythmic gesture, therefore, I will draw on some concepts developed in discourse analysis and sociolinguistics, particularly the notions of *kairos* and *chronos* developed by Erickson and Schultz (1982) in their study of college interviews. Similarly, when it comes to studying the narrative form of Joyce's *Portrait* in Chapter 4 (subtitled "Rhythm as Ex-tension"), it should be recognized that the first draft of "A Portrait of the Artist" only outlines the basic form of the *künstlerroman* to be developed in the published version of the novel. While Joyce himself refers to the experience of the hero as a "fluid succession of presents" that must be represented in the past, and therefore demonstrates some theoretical understanding of narrative form; the concepts of "narratology" can nevertheless help us to understand the full dimension of Joyce's stylistic practice in *Portrait*. Indeed, with the dramatic presentation of lyrical fragments at critical moments of the novel, Joyce fuses the "narrative-time" of the literary performance with the "story-time" of the plot, achieving the condition of "zero-degree narrative" described by Genette in *Narrative Discourse* (1980). Drawing on Bakhtin's concept of the "chronotope," I will suggest that the direct perception of rhythmic forms reveals a new form of temporal experience in the modernist novel, a "rhythmic chronotope" (my term) that fuses the sensation of the hero with the physical movements of the natural environment and the industrial city. When Joyce directly presents the rhythmic experience of Stephen Dedalus, I will suggest that the author reveals the "tension" that motivates the biographical development of the hero, for it will be argued that Stephen's personality is "stretched" between music of the maternal sphere (the metrical rhythm) and the intellectual image of the paternal sphere (the structural rhythm).

If there is a stylistic trait that distinguishes Joyce as a modernist writer, then it is the tendency toward the direct presentation of temporal experience, a tendency that is revealed in the diary entries at the end of *Portrait* and fully developed in the "interior monologues" of *Ulysses*. Although the sensations, thoughts, and feelings passing through Bloom's and Stephen's stream of consciousness seem to be purely "psychological" in character, I will argue in Chapter 5 (subtitled "Rhythm as Movement") that the temporal *form* of each thought process is motivated by the reception of physical rhythms, the performances of physiological rhythms, and the memory of psychological rhythms. In the "Sirens" episode, Joyce demonstrates an awareness of acoustic science, for Bloom meditates on the mathematical ratios governing the harmony of musical tones. Following Plock (2009), I will suggest that Joyce was familiar with the work of the Irish physicist John William Tyndall, whose lectures on *Sound* summarize many of the experiments performed by Helmholtz in his groundbreaking *On the Sensations of Tone as a Physiological Basis for the Theory of Music* (1895). In "Proteus," furthermore, we will see that the changing orientation of the visual field is motivated by the movement of the body in space. As Stephen compares the meters of his poetic verses to the rhythm of walking, he reveals that the "ineluctable modality of the visible" is ordered by the sensation of rhythm, for each "step" of the body can be correlated with an alteration to the visual field. In "Lestrygonians," finally, we will see the emergence of the "stream of life" as a metaphor for the circulation of machines, commodities, and money in the modern metropolis. Inspired by the metaphysics of Heraclitus and the philosophy of Bergson, Joyce uses the image of the river Liffey to dramatize the "flux" of the modern city, linking the experience of time to the recurrence of musical refrains in Bloom's stream of consciousness.

To summarize, therefore, this book will interpret the many aspects of "rhythm" that are manifested in Joyce's creative and critical writings, an approach that is not limited to the discovery of historical sources or the identification of metrical conventions, but rather seeks to reconstruct the basic principles of the scientific discourse on rhythm that emerged in the late nineteenth century and the impact it had on Joyce's stylistic practice. Indeed, at various stages of Joyce's literary career, different aspects of rhythm become more prominent, whether it be the metrical rhythms of *Chamber Music*; the dialogical rhythms of *Dubliners*; the narrative tension of *Portrait*; or the physical, physiological, and psychological rhythms of *Ulysses*. As already stated, there is a tendency throughout the Joycean *corpus* for the author to fuse the "narrative-time" with the "story-time," a stylistic principle that leads to the breakdown of narrative categories in *Ulysses*. With the disappearance of genre, however, the fragmentary form of the interior monologue allows various types of speech-act and rhythm to float on the stage of the imagination, and this hybrid style is explored to its fullest potential in *Finnegans Wake*. With the composition of the "Anna Livia Plurabelle" episode, Joyce synchronizes all these aspects of rhythm into a "polyrhythmic" text that incorporates elements of action, dialogue, poetry, and dream-thoughts into layered, multidimensional narrative. By analyzing the recording that Joyce made of this episode for the Orthological Institute in 1929, we should be able to describe the unique "rhythmic competence" of the author, revealing an alliterative meter of four accents that returns us to the tetrameters of the *Chamber Music* cycle.

Chapter 2

"If Thou but Scan it Well"

Rhythm as Meter in Chamber Music

Introduction

In the "Nestor" episode of *Ulysses*, Stephen Dedalus meditates on the definition of movement from Aristotle's *Physics* (III.i.200.10–11),[1] a phrase that Joyce himself encountered during his first trip to Paris in 1903: "It must be a movement then, an actuality of the possible as possible. Aristotle's phrase formed itself within the gabbled verses and floated out into the studious silence of the library Saint Genevieve where he had read, sheltered from the sin of Paris, night by night" (*U*, 2:67–70). Considering that the theme of the episode is history, however, it is probable that this definition of movement also refers to the experience of time-passing, for Aristotle also defines time as a "measure of motion" in the *Physics* (IV.xii), a measure that might be used to count the periods (or beats) that structure the "meters" of verse. Indeed, when Aristotle's phrase *forms itself* in the silent space of Stephen's imagination, his meditation on the meaning of history is mediated by the sensation of a regular rhythm, for the acoustic images of the words are superimposed on a schoolboy's performance of Milton's *Lycidas*:

> *Weep no more, woeful shepherd, weep no more*
> *For Lycidas, your sorrow is not dead,*
> *Sunk though he be beneath the watery floor* (*U*, 2:64–6)

Here, the rhythm of verse plays an important role in facilitating the remembrance of historical events, for Milton's poem recalls the drowning of his friend, Edward King. The supernatural image of King walking the waves provides a rhythmic schema for describing the *eternal return* of the deceased in the haunting imagery of the poem. As Talbot cannot read, he relies on the regular rhythm to remember the words. When he mechanically repeats the line, "*Through the dear might of him that walked the waves,*" Stephen gently reminds him to "turn the page." Viewed in the context of Joyce's own career as an English teacher, the scene in "Nestor" serves to highlight the central importance of poetic recitation to his teaching style, a preoccupation that would have required some theoretical understanding of prosody at the turn of the twentieth century.

As James Joyce was both a teacher and student of English literature, we can assume that his style as a poet was shaped by a discourse on rhythm that was embodied in the institutions of the education system around the turn of the twentieth century. When I use the term "discourse" to describe the emergence of rhythmic science in the late nineteenth century, however, it should be noted that I am using it in the Foucauldian sense to indicate both the discursive rules that govern the inclusion and exclusion of statements (Foucault 1972), as well as the disciplinary practices that accompany the embodiment of discourses within scientific and educational institutions (Foucault 1977). In order to understand the impact of this discourse on the rhythmic practice of the young Joyce, we must take into account his education in classical meters at Belvedere College, his study of English composition at University College, as well as his time as a language teacher at the Berlitz School in Trieste. As alluded to in the "Nestor" episode, Joyce also worked for a short time as a primary school teacher at Clifton School in Dalkey (Spring 1904), and the large number of poetic quotations indicate that Joyce regularly called on his students to recite verses. The specific allusion to "Lycidas" in "Nestor" supports the contention that Joyce drew on Quackenbos's *Practical Rhetoric* (1896) when developing his own approach to prosody in *Stephen Hero*, for the specific lesson on "The Definition and Theory of Poetry" asks students to explain why "Lycidas" (among other examples) is an instance of poetry (417). Indeed, Milton's *corpus* seems to have furnished Quackenbos with considerable literary material to illustrate his prosodic theory, for the lesson on "Versification" asks students to scan lines from "L'Allegro" and "Il Penseroso" (438). As each lesson contains a "Further Reading" section that guides more inquisitive students toward the theoretical justification for the rhetorical precepts contained in the textbook, such reference lists provide the contemporary critic with a useful means of demonstrating how the scientific discourse on rhythm impacted on the literary style of modernist authors such as Joyce.

In the late nineteenth century, most teachers and students employed the terminology of classical prosody to scan the stress-based meters of English verse, using the terms "iambic" and "trochaic" to describe the shape of feet either ending or beginning with stresses. Despite this adherence to tradition, the leading prosodists of the day were beginning to integrate the insights of experimental psychology into their systems, particularly the notion that *the perception and production of motor rhythms* precede the self-conscious arrangement of syllables to form lines of verse.

As we have seen, the leading proponent of the new approach was Sidney Lanier (1880), for not only did he integrate the insights of Helmholtz's acoustic theory into his discussion (differentiating the duration, pitch, volume, and timbre of each syllable), but he also employed the conventions of musical notation to quantify the duration of the syllables in English verse. While it is unclear whether Joyce read Lanier's work, Quackenbos's "Lesson on Versification" contains references to Parsons's *English Versification* (1891), a text that distinguishes between the "duple" and "triple" movements that constitute the underlying rhythms of English verse. As Joyce composed many of his early lyrics with the intention of having them set to music, most of his poems possess a strong underlying rhythm that is either duple or triple in form. Rather than positing a simple causal link between the prosody of the late nineteenth century and the development of Joyce's poetic style, it would be more accurate to say that both poets and critics of the era were searching for a rhythmical means of uniting the arts of poetry and music, seeking to realize Pater's claim that "all art constantly aspires to the condition of music" (1899, 140). Indeed, what emerges from an interpretation of the lyrics contained in *Chamber Music* is an experience of time that cannot be reduced to the quantification of the syllables on the page, but rather points to the embodied performance of rhythm in the context of a recurring musical ritual.

Quantity and Quality

As a young student at Clongowes College, Joyce was required to study Latin, and his early lessons would have been devoted to learning its grammar and syntax. Although the study of "prosody" or "meter" would not have been the subject of these lessons, Joyce would have been intuitively aware of the role which rhythm performs in facilitating the memorization of grammatical tables. In the second section of *Portrait*, Joyce describes a typical Latin lesson in which Father Arnall asks a student named Jack Lawton to decline the noun *mare* (sea, ocean). Unable to complete the exercise, the student apparently "stopped at the ablative singular and could not go on with the plural" (*P*, 47). Here we can see that each step of the rhythm corresponds to a grammatical category, and it is therefore due to the established order of the categories that Stephen Dedalus is able to determine which element is missing. If Joyce had reported the sound of the drill, it would have contained three beats with an unrealized fourth beat, because Lawton would have said: "*mare, maris, mari*" omitting the final "*mari*" from the series. When another student named Fleming makes the false assertion that the noun *mare* has no plural (*maria, marium, maribus*), this makes him the prime candidate for a beating, which is duly delivered when the Prefect of Studies enters the room. It is significant that Joyce here reproduces the immediate experience of the pandybat striking the hand, for the rhythm of this ritual parallels the exercise of reciting Latin declensions: "Fleming held out his hand. The pandybat came down on it with a loud smacking sound: one, two, three, four, five, six" (*P*, 49). By counting out the number of each blow, Joyce emphasizes the rhythmic correspondence between the related activities of parsing grammatical tables and administering corporal punishment, a correspondence that reveals the association between the rules of classical prosody and the discipline of the classroom.

Although *Finnegans Wake* was written in Joyce's mature years, Joseph Schork has shown that many of the expressions refer to exercises that Joyce would have memorized as a schoolboy (1997, 21–2). One example is the comic transliteration of the declension of demonstratives (*hic, haec, hoc; huius, huius, huius; huic, huic, huic*), which is parsed as, "hicky hecky hock, huges huges, hughy hughy hughy" (*FW*, 454:15–16). This list is remarkable not only for its completeness, but also for the repetition of the same element in the nominative, genitive, and dative singular, because it is the position of the word in the rhythmic series (three groups of three) that discloses its grammatical function. In the second book of the *Wake*, Joyce describes the contents of a grammar lesson in which Shaun, Shem, and Issy are exposed to distinctions of gender, mood, and tense. At the beginning of the lesson, we are told that "Soon jemmijohns will cudgel about some rhythmatick or other over Browne and Nolan's divisional tables" (*FW*, 268:7–9). Here the term "rhythmatick" alludes to the quantitative meters of classical verse, for the word is a hybrid of "rhythm" and "mathematics." This tale of Shem and Shaun quarrelling over the rules of prosody brings to mind the lines from the autobiographical chapter of the book, where Joyce describes his two *personae* as "like a thoroughpaste prosodite, masculine monosyllables of the same numerical mus" (*FW*, 190:34–6). While Schork focuses on the allusion to Horace's *mus*, the "mouse" born from the labor of the mountain (which perhaps contains a pun on the Greek *musē*), Joyce is perhaps pointing out that both *Shem* and *Shaun* have names composed of a monosyllable.

In Kennedy's *The Public School Latin Primer* (1866), a manual that formed the basis of Latin grammar in Victorian schools, "the general rules of quantity" are summarized in five points, rules that provide a means of determining whether a vowel is long by nature or position:

GENERAL RULES OF QUANTITY:
1. Every diphthong and contracted syllable is long.
2. Primitives give their own quantity to their derivatives.
3. A vowel coming before a vowel will be short.
4. Any vowel becomes long by Position, which two consonants follow; as *trīstis* : or which in the same word *j* follows or *x* or *z* : so *ājax*, *āxis*, *Amāzon*.
5. A vowel, though short by its own power, is doubtful if a mute consonant with a liquid after it follows; thus you will say rightly (*lugŭbre* melos) a mournful melody, or *lugŭbre*.
   a. *Gn* always makes a long syllable, as *āgnus* and *īgnis*: and likewise *gm*; which *tēgmen* and *āg-men* shew. (1866, 117)

As it can be seen from these rules, the duration of long and short syllables is entirely dependent on the conventions of classical orthography, which simply assume that the addition of a consonant increases the amount of time taken to pronounce the syllable. From a "Note on Prosody" included as an appendix to Kennedy's textbook, Joyce would have become familiar with the various types of rhythmic feet employed in Latin poetry (iambs, dacytls, spondees, anaepests, tribrachs, and so on), as metrical schemes are given for the Dactylic Hexameter, the Dactylic Pentameter, the Iambic Trimeter, the Sapphic Stanza, and the Alcaic Stanza (1866, 150–2). Unfortunately, the use of the Roman alphabet to transcribe the sound of English words does not produce an accurate representation of the duration of syllables, for the addition of a consonant does not necessarily lengthen the vowel that it terminates. Despite the fact that the prosody of English verse is determined either by the number of syllables or the position of the stresses, it is highly likely that Joyce would have learnt to apply the classical rules to the analysis of English verse. Joyce alludes to this practice when he writes: "quantity counts though accents falter" (*FW*, 270:2). Indeed, it was a common practice for many prosodists to treat a stressed syllable as "long" and an unstressed syllable as "weak," despite the fact that many stressed syllables in English are short. Perhaps, Joyce was pointing out this contradiction between quality and quantity when he stated that "the O of woman is long" (*FW*, 270:25–6), for although the duration of the syllable is short, the stress is placed on the first syllable of "woman," which causes the ear to hear it *as if* it were long.

During his time at Belvedere College, Joyce would have been exposed to the poetic aspects of Latin, and it is during his study of Ovid and Horace that he would have become familiar with the rules of classical prosody.[2] In his biography, Herbert Gorman reproduces *O Fons Bandusiae*, a youthful translation of a Horation Ode that Joyce completed at Belvedere. According to Sullivan in *Joyce among the Jesuits* (1958), the foundation of the Intermediate Education of Board of Ireland in 1871 altered the curriculum at Catholic schools. Whereas the study of classical and modern literature had formerly been focused on the structure and style of the literary work, and the ideas contained within it, the new approach meant that "translation was considered an end in itself, and the approach to language, by way of syntax and etymology, and even historical grammar, was linguistic rather than purely or properly literary" (Sullivan 1958, 71). This new philological approach would have been complemented by the method of literary explication called "Prelection," a method enshrined in the *Ratio Studiorum*, a statute regulating the form of instruction and administration at Catholic schools. The method of "Prelection" consists of five steps: reading; translation; explication; analysis of poetical or rhetorical structure; and *eruditio*. During the first and third steps of the "Prelection," Joyce would have been exposed to the rules of Latin prosody, which would have required some knowledge of the different types of "feet" formed from the combination of short and long syllables. Following these guidelines, Sullivan attempts to reconstruct the plan of the lesson:

> In the classroom on the day the ode was assigned, Joyce's instructor first read the poem aloud, distinctly, accurately, according to meter, in a tone adjusted to convey the mood and feel of Horace. He then interpreted it, giving either a paraphrase or, more probably, a translation of the Latin. Following the translation, he identified the meter and, writing one or two lines on the blackboard, scanned them, marking off short and long quantities and locating the caesura. (1958, 76)

While this reconstruction is based on the teaching of a Latin text, the purpose of the lesson was to compose an English translation, and this would have required both the rules of Latin and English prosody to be examined. As a consequence, Joyce would have been faced with the dilemma of translating the quantitative meters of Latin into the qualitative (or stress-based) meters of English. For the sake of determining the manner in which Joyce negotiated this contradiction between quantity and quality, let us compare the Latin text of Horace's *O Fons Bandusiae* with the English translation of the young Joyce. The Latin ode is composed in the basic meter known as an "Asclepiad," which varies in length according to the form used, but is always formed around the nucleus of a choriamb (¯˘˘¯). When studying Horace's Ode (3.13), Joyce's Latin teacher would have scanned the syllables on the blackboard, thereby demonstrating the conventions of the "The Fourth Asclepiad." The first two lines of this meter are composed of two choriambs that are surrounded by a *basis* (a bisyllabic foot) at the beginning and the end of the line. The third and fourth lines are shorter, containing only a single choriamb at the center of the line, and completed by a monosyllable and basis, respectively (West 2002, "Metrical Introduction," xviii–xix). Thus, the first two stanzas of Horace's would feature choriambs in the following positions:

O fons Bāndŭsĭae, splēndĭdĭōr vitro,
dulci dīgnĕ mĕrō nōn sĭnĭ flōribus,
cras donābărĭs hāedo,
cui frons tūrgĭdă cōrnibus
    primis ēt vĕnĕrēm et prōelĭă dēstinat.
frustra: nām gĕlĭdōs ĭnfĭcĭēt tibi
rubro sānguĭnĕ rīvos
lascivī sŭbŏlēs gregis. (West 2002, 118)

In translating Horace's Ode, Joyce does not attempt to reproduce the quantitative scheme of the original, but uses a four-beat line that begins with a trochaic foot. Significantly, Joyce fuses the first two strophes of the Ode into a single stanza of seven lines, imposing a new rhyme scheme (ABBACCC).

Bríghter than gláss Band<u>úsian Spr</u>íng
    For méllow wíne and flówers méet,
The mórrow thée a kíd shall bríng
    Bóding of rívalry and swéet
<u>Lóve in his sw</u>élling hórns. In váin
Hé, wánton óffspring, déep shall stáin
Thy cléar cold stréams with crímson ráin. (*PSW*, 71: my underline, WM)

As Latin and English possess different metrical systems, it is difficult to compare the two; yet, the use of trochaic inversions at the beginning of lines 1, 3, and 5, demonstrates that Joyce did attempt to capture the movement of Horace's choriambs, which acts as the metrical signature of the Asclepiad. Indeed, Joyce reverses the order of the first two Latin phrases, such that the first choriamb (*Brighter than glass*) becomes the rhythmic signature of the poem as a whole. As the effect of acceleration created by the use of trochaic opening must be compensated by a pause before the second phrase (*Bandusian spring*), Joyce creates a caesura that reflects the division between the first two phrases of the Latin text. Further choriambs are constructed in the phrases "Boding of ri-valry" and "Love in his swel-ling," marking the persistence of the classical source. Toward the end of the stanza, the correspondence between the lines of the original and its translation begins to break down; and although Joyce employs a consistent rhyme scheme, the rhythm of the last three lines is almost wholly determined by the position of the rhetorical accents. Thus, the accent on "cold" can either be demoted to maintain the underlying pulse of the four-beat rhythm, or the reader can dwell on the meaning of each word, pronouncing the phrase "cléar cóld stréams" as three distinct, monosyllabic feet.

In the surviving draft of *Stephen Hero*, Joyce gives us a partial description of a lecture in which Stephen Dedalus is taught the laws of classical and modern prosody. Although the chronology of this episode seems to indicate that it occurred at University College, in which case the character of Father Butt would seem to have been modeled on the Professor of English, Father Darlington (Noon 1957, Ch. 1); the description of the English teacher corresponds closely to the appearance of Joyce's English teacher at Belvedere, George Dempsey. According to Sullivan, Dempsey was "a tall thin man with gray hair and a moustache the color of old hay" (1958, 85). This closely resembles the description of Joyce's teacher in *Stephen Hero*, for he writes that "Father Butt had always his hands full of papers and his soutane very soiled with chalk. He was an elderly greyhound of a man and his vocal ligaments, like his garments, seemed to be coated with chalk" (*SH*, 31). As this scene is supposed to reflect the development of Stephen's own esthetic philosophy, it is significant that he begins to elaborate a theory of rhythm that contradicts Father Butt's approach to the question of meter. Although there are two pages of the manuscript missing at this point of the text, it can be inferred that Joyce's teacher gave his pupils some instruction as to how a line of verse should be scanned and read. It seems that Dempsey (or Darlington) took a strictly quantitative approach to the measurement of feet, for Stephen apparently finds "Father Butt's reading of verse and a schoolgirl's accurate reading of verse intolerable" (*SH*, 31). In order to remedy this defect, Stephen proposes a hybrid theory that would take into account the dramatic role of the rhetorical accent in determining the meaning and weight of each phrase. When he proscribes that "Verse to be read according to its rhythm should be read according to its stresses; that is, neither in according to the feet nor yet with complete disregard to them" (*SH*, 31), Stephen equivocates between a classical approach to meter that analyzes the quantitative "feet" of the line, and a modern English approach that focuses on the qualitative "stresses" of the line. Without resolving the difference between these two methods, Joyce adopts a compromise position that can be interpreted as symptomatic of the conflict between the classical and psychological approaches to the subject of rhythm.

The Lesson on "Versification"

As Stephen purports to develop his own theory of prosody, and explicitly contradicts the approach adopted by the Professor of English, Father Butt, it is possible that he consulted an *alternative* source that enabled him to develop a looser, more flexible approach to the scansion of English verses. According to a fellow student at University College, C. P. Curran, Joyce's reputation as an essayist was enhanced by his regular attendance at classes in English composition, for "in this class, open to students of any year, Joyce, a newcomer, heard his essays read as models" (1968, 6). If we assume that the surviving manuscript of *Stephen Hero* gives us a partial description of Joyce's own education at University College, it would appear that he distinguished himself first and foremost as an essayist, for "There was a special class for English composition and it was in this class that Stephen made his name. The English essay was for him the one serious work of the week. His essay was usually very long and the professor, who was a lead writer on the *Freeman's Journal*, always kept it for last" (*SH*, 32). If the class had been taught by a scholastic such as Father Darlington, the Prefect of Studies, then one might have expected the lessons to have been based upon Aristotle's *Rhetoric* or Cicero's *De Oratore*; yet, the classes were in fact taught by W. P Coyne, an economist who published articles on economics and literature in the *Freeman's Journal* and the *Lyceum* (Curran 1968: 12). Considering the humanistic and scientific perspective adopted by Joyce's teacher, it is probable that the content of these lessons was based on the modern principles of style laid out in Herbert Spencer's *The Philosophy of Style* (1892) or Alexander Bain's *English Composition and Rhetoric* (1867). Although there is no explicit mention of a rhetorical manual in Curran's memoir, Joyce possessed a copy of John Duncan Quackenbos's *Practical Rhetoric* (1896) in his Trieste library, and it is probable that he studied from this textbook during his time at University College. As Quackenbos's manual contains an independent lesson on "Versification," it is likely that Joyce developed his own approach to the prosody of English verse through the completion of the exercises contained in this textbook.

As we have seen, Stephen equivocates between a quantitative and qualitative approach to English prosody, and this ambiguity is reflected by the nomenclature of *Practical Rhetoric*, for Quackenbos uses the quantitative ratios of the classical feet to categorize the stress-based meters of English verse. In the first instance, Quackenbos highlights the primary role of "accent" or "stress" in determining the rhythm of English, but it can be seen that his definition of rhythm is already informed by the emergence of rhythmic science, for the recurrence of the stresses is linked to the "alternation of tension and relaxation" in the muscles of the body: "English verse is characterized by rhythm, *the alternation of tension and relaxation*, involving the regular recurrence of accent, or stress of voice. A rhythmic succession of words is thus divisible into distinct pulses or movements, appreciable by the ear; these are known as Measures or feet" (1896, 418: my italics, WM). By relating the auditory perception of rhythm to the distinct pulses or movements of the voice, Quackenbos implicitly rejects the quantitative approach to English prosody, for it is no longer the inherent duration of the syllables that determines the rhythm, but rather the temporal coordination of the physical movement through the recurrence of stresses or accents. Despite this accentual approach, Quackenbos adopts the names of the classical feet to categorize the various combinations of stressed and unstressed syllables that constitute the "rhythmic units" of English verse, for he writes in a footnote that "length or quantity depends almost entirely on accent, it is customary to denote unaccented syllables with a breve (˘), the mark used to indicate a short syllable in Latin; and accented syllables with a macron (ˉ) which marks long syllables in Latin" (419). From this note, it can be seen that Quackenbos equates stressed syllables with long syllables, a theoretical fiction that enables him to use the feet of classical prosody to categorize the accentual rhythms of English verse. Thus, he can define disyllabic and trisyllabic feet in terms of the combination of accented and unaccented syllables (Figure 2.1).

The Principal Feet occurring in English Verse are: —

DISYLLABIC.
(Adapted to double movement.)

{
THE IAMBUS, consisting of an unaccented followed by an accented syllable; as, *to-day.*

THE TROCHEE (in Greek, *running, tripping*), consisting of an accented followed by an unaccented syllable; as, *twinkle.*

THE SPONDEE (from the Greek *spondai, a solemn treaty*), consisting of two accented syllable; as, *downright.*
}

TRISYLLABIC.
(Triple movement.)

{
THE DACTYL (from the Greek *daktulos, a finger* which has one long joint and two short ones), consisting of an accented syllable followed by two unaccented syllables; as, *tenderly.*

THE ANAPEST (*struck back*), the dactyl *reversed*, consisting of two unaccented syllables followed by one that is accented; as, *Isabelle.*
}

Figure 2.1   The table of feet from *Practical Rhetoric*, p. 419.

As can be seen from this table, the categories of classical prosody are grafted on to the rhythms of English verse, because the quantitative proportion between short and long syllables is reconfigured in terms of the presence or absence of accents (or stresses). Furthermore, the structure of Quackenbos's table implies that stressed syllables *realize* the beats of the underlying rhythm, because he further specifies that disyllabic feet are "adapted to double movement" and trisyllabic feet are "adapted to triple movement." By making this further distinction between the double or triple form of the underlying rhythm and the disyllabic or trisyllabic shape of the feet, Quackenbos implies that the psychological intuition of the rhythm precedes the adaption of the rhythm to the metrical structures of verse. Significantly, the translation of "trochaic" as *running* or *tripping* echoes the self-description of Malachi Mulligan at the beginning of *Ulysses*, for Stephen's nemesis designates himself as "sunning and tripping like the buck himself" (*U*, 1:42). In the same episode, Stephen notes that Malachi Mulligan's name is composed of "two dactyls," confirming the association in Joyce's mind between Gogarty's comic poetry and the system of classical feet.

Of course, when analyzing the "table of feet" reproduced in *Practical Rhetoric*, it should be noted that Quackenbos is not formulating a new theory of English prosody, but rather incorporating elements from other systems to construct a matrix of rhythmic and metrical correspondences. As Quackenbos lists a number of prosodic manuals in the "Further Reading" section appended to the lesson on "Versification," it should be a fairly simple matter to reconstruct the sources of his hybrid system. With regard to the classification of the rhythmic feet, it is likely that he drew upon Brewer's *Orthometry* (1893), for the latter makes a distinction between "disyllabic" and "trisyllabic" feet, and uses macrons and breves to denote the stressed and unstressed syllables of English verse. Significantly, Brewer cites the definition of rhythm contained in Guest's *History of English Rhythms* (1882), which is remarkable for the author's stress upon the spatial arrangement of the rhythmic structure: "Rhythm in its widest sense may be defined as a law of succession. It is the regulating principle of every *whole* that is made up of proportionate parts, and is as necessary to the regulation of motion, or to the arrangement of matter, as to the orderly succession of sounds" (2). Significantly, there is an equivocation in this definition, for not only is rhythm defined as a temporal "law of succession," but it also refers to the proportionate arrangements of the parts to form a whole, a structural conception of rhythm that antici-pates Joyce's own definition in the Paris notebook (see Ch. 3).

With regard to the *adaption* of the syllables to the underlying rhythm, however, it is clear that Quackenbos draws on Parsons's *English Versification* (1891), for the latter holds that "the unit of rhythm is commonly called a foot," clarifying that "there are four principal kinds of feet—two of double movement, and two of triple movement" (8). By referring to rhythm as a *movement* that underlies the meters of verse, Parsons constructs a model of poetic sensation and creation that is grounded in the periodic movements of nature. When it comes to listing examples of rhythm in nature, Parsons highlights the correspondence between the motion of the waves and the pulsation of the blood around the body, for the rhythmic phe-nomenon is present both *within* and *without*: "in the rise and fall of leafy branches in the springtime ... in the rolling in of the billows toward the shore; and, as if in response to these, the beating of our hearts, felt with regular pulsations in all parts of our bodies" (1891, 3). According to Parsons, English verse is constituted by a succession of accented syllables, with each accent either preceded or followed by one or two unaccented syllables. As the movement (or pitch) of the voice rises and falls according to the presence or absence of an accent, Parsons compares the rhythm of speech to the motion of the waves, for "to compare it with the waves of the sea, it will be a series of crests subsiding into hollows, or a series of hollows rising into crests" (1891, 8). Thus, the disyllabic shape of a trochaic or iambic foot corresponds to a series of sound waves, which Parsons represents in Figure 2.2.

Thus: | ∩◡ | ∩◡ | ∩◡ | ∩◡ | ∩◡ |

Or: | ◡∩ | ◡∩ | ◡∩ | ◡∩ | ◡∩ |

Figure 2.2   Parsons's sound waves (1891, 8).

Tick - y | tack - y - tick - y | tack - y - tick - y | slam bam | Bam !

Figure 2.3   Lanier's scansion of a minstrel dance.

By comparing the rise and fall of the voice to the waves of the sea, Parsons is able to locate the phenomenom of rhythm in a physical movement, such that the disyllabic and trisyllabic feet can be understood as the embodiment of a "double movement" or a "triple movement." As we will see, the periodic motion of the sea functions as a source of poetic inspiration for Stephen Dedalus in both *Portrait* and the "Proteus" episode of *Ulysses*, and it is possible that Parsons's text provides the model for this type of poetic creation.

Submerged within the "Further Reading" section of *Practical Rhetoric*, the elements of Parsons's textbook illustrates the extent to which the principles of rhythmic science were being incorporated into the study of prosody, and embodied in the disciplinary practices of the educational system in both North America and Britain. From the chapter on "Rhythm," it is clear that Parsons was familiar with the concept of the primary rhythm from *The Science of English Verse* (1880), for he includes the perception of visual rhythms in his definition: "Rhythm, in its most comprehensive sense, is the recurrence of similar phenomena at regular intervals of space or time, thus showing itself to the eye or the ear" (Parsons 1891, 5). In a chapter titled "Comic Forms," Parsons also reproduces the musical scansion of a minstrel dance by Sidney Lanier, a transcription that uses the "tick" and the "tock" of a clock to illustrate the primary rhythm of the beating foot (135) (Figure 2.3).

Significantly, Parsons also draws a distinction between "accent" and "emphasis" in his more general account of "stress," a distinction that incorporates the psychological concept of "attention" into the interpretation of poetic rhythms, for as Parsons puts it, "to give attention to the strong syllables and the weak ones at the same time, requires effort, and this effort has its limits" (1891, 6). While the concept of "accent" is limited to the *metrical* stresses of verse, the concept of "emphasis" links the position of the stresses to the *meaning* of the words, a rhetorical rhythm that may act in counterpoint to the metrical rhythm. In a chapter "On Reading Verse," Parsons makes it clear that the proper interpretation of the rhythm requires that the reader pay attention to the difference in force between the metrical accents and the points of rhetorical emphasis, a dual intention that leads to the following proscription: "We are not to find out, first of all, how to scan it, and then, dividing it up into feet, to put the accent in the proper places, regardless of the meaning, but we are to read it to express as completely as possible the thought and feeling in the mind of the writer, letting accent and emphasis fall naturally where they will" (1891, 68). By linking the position of the rhetorical stresses to the meaningful syllables of prominent words, Parsons reveals a source of *tension* between the metrical and rhetorical rhythm that may have influenced Joyce's own approach to the composition and interpretation of English verse.

As we have already seen, Joyce begins to develop the principles of his own prosody in the draft of *Stephen Hero*, for he objects to the strictly quantitative approach of his teacher, Father Butt, who mechanically adheres to the succession of *metrical* accents. To recapitulate, Stephen holds that "Verse to be read according to its rhythm should be read according to its stresses; that is, neither in according to the feet nor yet with complete disregard to them" (*SH*, 31). While the exact meaning of Joyce's terminology remains unclear, this passage identifies the conflict between the *metrical* and *rhetorical* stresses of English verse that corresponds to Parsons's distinction between "accent" and "emphasis." In *Stephen Hero*, Joyce adopts an accentual system of notation to indicate the stresses in some lines from the second stanza of Byron's "On this day I complete my thirty sixth year," a method that seems to correspond closely to Parsons's approach:

> My dáys are *in* the yéllow léaf
> The *flow*ers and frúits of lóve are góne
> The wórm, the cánker *and* the gríef
> Are míne al*one*. (*SH*, 31: my italics, WM)

Although Stephen claims that "there was only one possible way of rendering the first quatrain of Byron's poem" (*SH*, 31), the use of only three accents to scan a line that clearly contains four beats demonstrates that Joyce has chosen to mark only the syllables that carry some specific rhetorical emphasis. By failing to mark the stresses on

"in," "flow-," and "-lone," Joyce makes it clear that he has subordinated the metrical rhythm (the "feet") to the rhetorical accents (or
"stresses") that express the meaning and intention behind the phrase.
Such an approach seems to concord with the method adopted by
Parsons, for he modifies the scansion of a line from Shakespeare in
such a manner that the metrical accent on "the" is demoted: "that
héals the wóund, and cúres not the disgráce" (1891, 70).

From the scansion of Byron's verse in *Stephen Hero*, it is clear that
Stephen adopts the same approach as Parsons; yet, it remains unclear
how Joyce arrived at the same method. While it is possible that Joyce's
teacher (W. P. Coyne) consulted Parsons's textbook during his classes
in English composition at University College, it is more likely that the
spirit of Parsons's system entered into the lesson on "Versification" in
Practical Rhetoric (1896). In fact, Quackenbos suggests that lines of
blank verse can be scanned according to the position of the accents,
for as he puts it:

> Blank verse is the most elevated of all measures, and as such it is the
> appropriate vehicle for our epic and dramatic poetry. In the regular
> line, the accents are five in number; but these may be diminished to
> quicken the movement. Hence, in dramatic poetry, we should expect
> to find lines of five accents the exception; and such is the case in
> Shakespeare. Thus the first line below, from "Paradise Lost," has the
> five regular accents; the second, four; the third, from Shakespeare's
> "Julius Caesar," only three:
>
> > "In ádamántine cháins and pénal fíre."
> > "Agáinst the thróne and mónar*chy* of Gód."
> > "These cóuchings *and* these lówly cóurtes*ies*."
>
> In order to secure the desired rhythmic effects, the trochee, the spondee,
> two short syllables, and even occasionally the anapest, may by poetic
> license be substituted for the iambus; and a syllable without accent
> may be added to the line. A correct ear and a delicate taste are essential
> to success in blank verse. (1896, 431: my italics, WM)

Although Byron's poem is not composed in blank verse, containing
lines of eight or nine syllables, Joyce's method of scansion indicates
that he was attempting to *dramatize* this lyrical poem. Considering
that Joyce does not accent the stressed syllables that lack rhetorical emphasis ("in," "flowers," "alone"), it would seem that he has
directly adopted Quackenbos's accentual approach to the scansion of
blank verse, for the latter does not accent the final syllable of "mon-
archy" (in the second example) or the ultimate syllable of "courtesies"

(in the third example). It can therefore be inferred that Stephen Dedalus is seeking to develop a more *dramatic* approach to the scansion of English verse that both *takes for granted* a theoretical understanding of the relationship between the underlying rhythm and the shape of the feet (iambs, trochees, dactyls, and anapests) and searches for a phrasal rhythm that expresses the dramatic intention suggested by the meaning of the phrase.

The contention that Stephen adopts a *dramatic* approach to the scansion of tetrameters is supported by a passage from "Lestrygonians" where Bloom composes a rhyming couplet to describe the motion of a gull flying above the river Liffey:

> *The hungry famished gull*
> *Flaps over the water's dull.*
>
> That is how poets write, the similar sounds. But then Shakespeare has no rhymes: blank verse. The flow of the language it is. The thoughts. Solemn.
>
> *Hamlet, I am thy father's spirit*
> *Doomed for a certain time to walk the earth.* (U, 8:62–8)

In this passage, Bloom compares his own tetrameters to the blank verse of Shakespeare, suggesting that in the absence of rhyme, the natural rhythm or "flow of the language" provides an ordering principle. Despite the fact that Bloom misquotes the lines of blank verse from *Hamlet*, they might nevertheless be scanned as two tetrameters, for the rhetorical emphasis falls on the following syllables: "Hámlet, Í am thy fáther's spírit | Dóomed for a certain tíme to wálk the earth." While the outcome of the scansion depends on the actor's interpretation of the phrase, it is nevertheless "the thoughts" that guide the placement of the accents, for the emphasis must be placed on the words that communicate the intention of the speaker to his or her listeners. By eliding the difference between lyrical tetrameters and dramatic pentameters, Joyce therefore demonstrates that the speaker can emphasize the rhetorical rhythm over and above the metrical rhythm that is *automatically enacted* by the motor movements of the body.

Rhythmic Science and the Ideal of Music

In the late nineteenth century, the physical concept of rhythm was identified with the vibration of musical tones, a conflation of metrical and harmonic rhythms that led to the idealization of music as the poet's source of inspiration. In a lesson on the "Definition and Theory of Poetry," Quackenbos argues that rhythm differentiates poetry from prose, for "while prose implies intellectual and emotional life, poetry requires in addition rhythmic life" (1896, 411). Although rhythm is the temporal form of poetry, an alternation between tension and relaxation that is realized through the motor patterns of the body (and the vocal apparatus), this conception of "rhythmic life" leads to the *idealization* of the rhythmic phenomenon as the spiritual substance of poetry. Citing Edmund Clarence Stedman's papers on *The Nature and Elements of Poetry* (1892), Quackenbos argues that the spiritual content of poetry is expressed in "poetic vibrations," for he correlates the physical vibrations of colors and sounds with the psychical operation of the mind:

> In the operation of each of our senses, what is actually communicated to the brain is some kind of vibration, the function of such vibration being to convey through bodily organs to the mind a knowledge of the external world. This principle has been extended into the realm of emotional thought by Mr. Stedman, who conceives of poetic vibrations as in like manner thrilling the soul. (1896, 412)

Viewed in the context of late-nineteenth-century aestheticism, this notion of "poetic vibrations" can be interpreted as a symptom of both the emergence of rhythmic science—in particular, the physiological explanation for the sensation of colors and musical tones—and the influence of Pater's study of *The Renaissance*, for the Oxonian had famously asserted that "all art constantly aspires to the condition of music" (1899, 140). As we will see, the ideal of uniting poetry and music leads to a contradiction in the poetry of the era, for while the embodied performance of rhythm causes the institution of art to pass into life—the process of "desublimation" described by Peter Bürger in his *Theory of the Avant-garde* (1984)—the idealization of rhythm transforms life into art, for the temporal experience of poetry becomes a mere reflection of spiritual thought. Indeed, the poems collected in *Chamber Music* tend to epitomize this contradiction, for while Joyce's preference for the Elizabethan ballad emphasizes the embodied performance of rhythm, the Paterian ideal of music reduces the sensuous form of poetry to a mere "symbol" of thought.

For the sake of appreciating the impact of the new rhythmic science on Joyce's understanding of meter—a practical form of knowledge that may have been habitual rather than self-conscious—it will be useful to consult the "Further Reading" sections contained at the end of the lessons in Quackenbos's *Practical Rhetoric*, for these bibliographic entries reveal the extent to which rhetorical manuals of the late nineteenth century were beginning to incorporate the insights of physiological psychology. In this regard, Stedmen's lecture titled "What is Poetry?" registers the influence of rhythmic science on the aestheticist movement of the late nineteenth century. Delivered at John Hopkins University in 1892, Stedman's comments reveal the extent to which Helmholtz's acoustics and Spencer's *First Principles* had permeated the institution of literature in both North America and Britain at the close of the nineteenth century. Assuming his audience to be familiar with rhythmic science, Stedman states "there is small need to descant upon the universality of rhythm in all relations of force and matter, nor upon its inherent consonance with the lightest, the profoundest, sensations of the living soul," asking his listener to acknowledge that there is "a psychological impulse behind every physical function" (1892, 51). Alluding to the "physiological psychology" of Helmholtz, Spencer, and Wundt as the "new empiricism" of the day, Stedman claims that this new science is guided by intuition that nevertheless understands the meaning of these natural vibrations:

> But our new empiricism, following where intuition leads the way, comprehends the function of vibrations: it perceives that every movement of matter, seized upon by universal force, is vibratory; that vibrations, and nothing else, convey through the body the look and voice of nature to the soul; that thus alone can one incarnate individuality address its fellow; that, to use old Bunyan's imagery, these vibrations knock at the ear-gate, and are visible to the eye-gate, and are sentient at the gates of touch of the living temple. The word describing their action is in evidence: they "thrill" the body, they thrill the soul, both of which respond with subjective, interblending vibrations, according to the keys, the wave-lengths, of their excitants. (1892, 51–2)

As we will see (Ch. 5), Helmholtz compares the nerve fibrils in the ear to the keys of a piano, revealing the physiological basis of Stedman's metaphor, for the poet is said to respond with "subjective, interblending vibrations" that transform the movements of nature into the spiritual substance of poetry. While it is unlikely that Joyce ever read Stedman's lecture on poetry, the condensation of this theory in Quackenbos's *Practical Rhetoric* assured that he had limited exposure to such ideas, particularly the notion that the sensation of musical tones and colors could be immediately translated into poetic thoughts.

As revealed by Stedman's speculative account, the physiological psychology of the late nineteenth century provided a *scientific legitimation* for the Romantic conception of the poet as genius, for the sensation of musical tones provides an immediate way of translating the periodic (or *rhythmic*) motions of nature into the ideas of poetry. Considering that the vibration of musical tones provides the perfect illustration of this theory, furthermore, it seems to lend scientific authority to Pater's claim that "all art constantly aspires to the condition of music" (1899, 140). Of course, when Pater made this claim in his famous study of *The Renaissance*, he was not actually asserting that all the arts should *become* music, but rather that each art form should strive to attain the ideal unity of form and content that is exemplified by the vibration of musical tones. Indeed, Pater maintains that each art form should strive to express itself in a way that remains true to the nature of its sensuous material, for as he puts it, "Each art ... having its own peculiar and incommunicable sensuous charm, has its own special mode of reaching the imagination, its own special responsibilities to its material" (1899, 136). According to such a view, the function of criticism is to determine the limits within which an artwork remains faithful to the particular material in which its form is embodied. While the aim of Pater's philosophy may have been to maintain the irreducibly sensuous element of every aesthetic experience, the effect of this doctrine on modernist poetics was ultimately to reduce the content of all artistic expression to a mere reflection of form. Ironically, when the sensuous experience of painting or poetry becomes the perfect expression of its subject matter, the form and content of art become indistinguishable from one another, and the work of art attains the condition of music (at least metaphorically).

In his chapter on "On the School of Gorgione," Pater criticizes the German critic and dramatist Gotthold Lessing for attempting to measure poetry by its capacity to be translated into painting (and vice versa), maintaining that each art form should be judged by the extent to which it perfectly expresses the nature of its own material: "of colour, in painting; of sound, in music; of rhythmical words, in poetry" (1899, 135). Nevertheless, he maintains that some works of art can attain the condition of another art form through a process of *alienation* which enables the various art forms to "lend each other new forces" (1899, 139). Thus, Pater discusses the notion that sculpture approaches the condition of color embodied in painting, or poetry the spatial structure of sculpture, citing "the analogy between a Greek tragedy and a work of Greek sculpture" (1899, 140) as one of his chief examples. In general terms, Pater maintains that the "mode of handling" should become an end in itself, causing the colors of the painting to stand for the landscape, or the rhythm of the poem to capture the expressed emotions. When it comes to illustrating his theory,

however, it is contradictory that Pater appeals to the embodied performance of lyrical poetry, for not only does the poem seem to attain
the condition of music, but it actually *becomes* music:

> The very perfection of such poetry often seems to depend, in part, on a
> certain suppression or vagueness of mere subject, so that the meaning
> reaches us through ways not distinctly traceable by the understanding,
> as in some of the most imaginative compositions of William Blake,
> and often in Shakespeare's songs, as pre-eminently in that song of
> Mariana's page in *Measure for Measure*, in which the kindling force
> and poetry of the whole play seems to pass for a moment into an actual
> strain of music. (1899, 143)

In my view, this passage should not be interpreted as a mere *aberra-
tion*, but rather as an essential contradiction at the heart of Pater's
theory, for it expresses the tendency of late-Victorian poets to translate their poetry into music, real or ideal. Considering that Pater
alludes to the dramatic performance of the Elizabethan ballad in the
context of a Shakespearian play, it is highly likely that this passage
influenced the motivations of the young James Joyce.

   In one of Joyce's youthful poems preserved on the verso page of
Stanislaus commonplace book, the Irish writer completes his thought
with the lines: "I hear the viol and the flute, | The sackbut and the
psaltery" (*PSW*, 94). While the "viol," "flute," and "sackbut" are
clearly allusions to the music of the baroque period—the type of
instruments that were being revived by Arnold Dolmetsch at the turn
of the twentieth century—the allusion to the "psaltery" refers more
specifically to the attempts made by Florence Farr and W. B. Yeats to
reunite the arts of speech and music (see Farr 1909). In "Speaking to
Musical Notes," an essay that Joyce would have read when first published in *The Monthly Review* (May 1902), Yeats does not prescribe
how the melody of a poem should be intoned, but merely stresses the
prohibition that the natural rhythm and melody of the verse should
not be subordinated to an artificial, musical arrangement: "Whenever
I spoke of my desire to anybody they said I should write for music,
but when I heard anything sung I did not hear the words, or if I
did their natural pronunciation was altered and their natural music
was altered, or it was drowned in another music which I did not
understand" (Yeats 1961, 14). Indeed, the positive account of the
new art only emerges from the performances of the actress Florence
Farr, who began to emphasize the natural pitch of her voice by pluck-
ing a single stringed instrument at private recitals at Yeats's London

apartment. Initially, Yeats and Farr had experimented with the quarter tones of Tibetan music; yet, Arnold Dolmetsch persuaded them to adopt the tonal system of Western music, designing and building a Psaltery for Farr in 1902. Although the "New Art" remained an oddity to most listeners, the collaboration between Yeats and Farr persisted for the better part of a decade (including an American tour in 1907), and inspired the composition of many poems, including the prelude to *The King's Threshold*. By alluding to the "psaltery" in one his youthful poems, Joyce was clearly signaling that he intended to unite the arts of poetry and music through the performance of his own poetry.

Although Joyce was not wholly responsible for inventing the title of *Chamber Music*, the name is an accurate reflection of his early poetry, as the lyrics are densely packed with allusions to "strings" and "harps," and seemed to be more concerned with rhythm and sound of the words than any extrinsic source of reference. In *My Brother's Keeper* (2003), Stanislaus Joyce claims the credit for naming the collection, stating that Jim "had not yet found a title for his collection of poems, and as usual, he asked me for suggestions. One of these *Chamber Music*, he adopted. It had seemed to me suitable to the passionless love themes and studious grace of the songs" (175). Considering Stanislaus's tendency to overestimate his influence on his brother, we must infer that Joyce himself played some role in choosing the title, a selection justified by the analogy between poetry and instrumental music in the imagery of the cycle. At first glance, the title suggests that Joyce originally composed his verses as songs. Indeed, by analyzing the typical stanzas used in *Chamber Music*, which must possess a consistent rhythm and rhyme scheme in order for the melody to be repeated, Myra Russel (1981) has argued that Joyce modeled his lyrics on the Elizabethan songs of Byrd, Campion, Dowland, or Morland. Such a view is *partially* confirmed by a letter which Joyce wrote to G. Molyneux Palmer in 1909, an Irish musician who set a number of the verses to music: "I hope you may set all of *Chamber Music* in time. This was indeed partly my idea in writing it. The book is in fact a suite of songs and if I were a musician I suppose I should have set them to music myself" (*Letters I*, 67). In citing this letter, I would like to stress that setting the words to music was only "partly" Joyce's intention when writing the verses, a qualification that is highly significant because it introduces an element of ambiguity into the generic status of the poems: either the lyrics were composed for musical setting, in which case the emotions contained in the words need to be *translated* into an appropriate melody (performance, passing into life); or the lyrics were composed for their own sake, in which case the ideal of music is simply a *metaphor* for the organic unity of the work—that is, the extent to which the verses achieve that fusion of form and content espoused by Pater in his study of *The Renaissance* (1899).

If we consider the opening lyric of the *Chamber Music* cycle, which Joyce describes as a "prelude" in his letter to Molyneux Palmer, we can see that he seeks to resolve the contradiction between art and life by taking the performance of music as the subject matter of the poem. The desired fusion of form and content is therefore achieved through a self-reflexive strategy that dramatizes the poet as the "love" or *Amor* of the poem, and his Muse as the musical instrument that he is playing:

> Strings in the earth and air
>   Make music sweet;
> Strings by the river where
>   The willows meet.
>
> There's music along the river
>   For love wanders there,
> Pale flowers on his mantle,
>   Dark leaves on his hair.
>
> All softly playing,
>   With head to the music bent.
> And fingers straying
>   Upon an instrument. (*PSW*, 13)

In contrast to many of the other poems in the cycle, where the persona takes the first person, and either addresses his beloved in the second person or describes her in the third, the objectification of the poet as "love" has the effect of creating a self-reflexive relation between the poet and his creation. The source for this character may be the figure of *Eros* from Plato's *Symposium*, who is personified as a semidivine messenger, occupying the limit between the mortal and immortal worlds. Such an interpretation is supported by the generative relationship between the earth and the sky, *Gaia* and *Ouranos*, who in Greek mythology are responsible for the creation of the world. An alternative source for Joyce's "love" might be the *Amor* of Dante's *Vita Nuova* (1992), the god who mediates between the troubadour and the idealized figure of Beatrice. Joyce has fused these two sources, but the inverse consequence of this strategy is to objectify the subject of the poem as the very medium in which the song is embodied, for the poet's Muse is present only as the "instrument" upon which the poet's fingers are "straying." As a framing device, this "prelude" therefore alludes to the "strings" in which the poems are to be composed, and if the song never actually *becomes* music in the act of adaptation, it will at least attain the ideal condition of music as the *metaphorical content* of the poem as such. As we have seen, Pater's aesthetic system contains a fundamental ambiguity, for although the condition of music seems to function as the unattainable ideal of all the arts (the absolute fusion of form and content), the actual *performance* of poetry and its adaptation as the words of a song constitute both the realization of this ideal and the reintegration of art into the praxis of life. While he was working as a poet and journalist in Paris, Joyce became interested in the revival of British and Irish folk music that began to gather momentum in the finale decade of the nineteenth century. On the same day (December 15, 1902) that he sent the finished version of "All day I hear the noise of waters" to his friend J. F. Byrne, he wrote to his mother requesting *A Book of British Song* (1904), a text recently published by John Murray in London (*Letters II*, 21). It seems that he did in fact receive this volume, edited by Cecil Sharp, because it contains the words and music to the ballad "Turpin Hero," which provided Joyce with the title for *Stephen Hero*, and is later discussed in the aesthetic dialogue of *Portrait*.[3] While Joyce's main interest in this ballad seems to have been the mixture of dialogue and narration, moving from the first person to the third person as the ballad progresses, it also provides a good example of how the rhythm of a verse is adapted for use in a musical setting. As the duration of each syllable can be notated using quavers, crotchets, or minims (including dotted rhythms), the use of musical notation provides a convenient way for restoring the quantitative duration to English verse, and in this sense, can be seen as a rapprochement with the classical system of rhythmic feet. In contrast to the established rules of classical prosody, however, which categorize the movement from unstress to stress as "iambic," the rhythm of "Turpin Hero" begins with an anacrusis, such that the first syllable of each line precedes the strong beat of the bar. While a prosodist would scan the opening line as "Says Í | to the láwyer, | for tó | be cúte," the musical arrangement places the first syllable before the strong beat of the bar, effectively transforming it into a trochaic meter: "Says | Í to the | láwyer | fór to be | cúte" (Bauerle 1982, 127–9). As the number of syllables varies from line to line, furthermore, Joyce would have been familiar with the technique of substituting bisyllabic and trisyllablic feet, which in this context would have been similar to the alternation between spondees and dactyls characteristic of the Homeric meter.

Joyce's interest in the revival of British folk music can perhaps be traced to the influence of Wagner, for in "The Artwork of the Future" (1895), the German composer and poet develops a concept of the folk that is linked to the organic conception of the community. According to Timothy Martin, Joyce had begun collecting Wagnerian material as early as 1899, for his early critical essays are littered with allusions to his operas and prose writings (Martin 1991, Ch. 1). Assuming that Joyce was familiar with the Wagnerian conception of the "folk," it is not surprising that he returned to the folk ballads of the Elizabethans in his search for an authentic form of lyrical expression. On March 9, 1903, Joyce wrote to his brother Stanislaus, requesting that he purchase and send him an anthology of *Twelve Elizabethan Songs* (1902) edited by Janet Dodge (*Letters II*, 35). From a Wagnerian point of view, Joyce may have been interested in this anthology because it contained three songs by Thomas Campion, one of the few Elizabethans to have written both the words and music to his own songs. As a schoolboy, Joyce had regularly performed Dowland's "Weep no more ye sad fountains" (Joyce 2003, 161), and therefore would have been pleased to discover the piano score for "Time stands still with gazing on her face" in the same anthology. It is most likely that Joyce was collecting the musical scores of Elizabethan songs because he wished to pursue a career as a tenor, an ambition that was only partly tempered by his failure to win first prize in a singing contest. On returning to Dublin in 1904, Joyce wrote to his friend Oliver St. John Gogarty at Oxford:

> Dear Gogarty: I sent you back the budget. I am still alive. Here is a more reasonable request. I am singing at a garden fete on Friday and if you have a decent suit to spare or a cricket shirt send it to them. I am trying to get an engagement in the Kingstown Pavilion. Do you know anyone out there? My idea for July and August is this—to get Dolmetsch to make me a lute and to coast the south of England from Falmouth to Margate singing old English songs. When are you leaving Oxford? (*Letters I*, 54)

As the letter is signed "Stephen Daedalus," it is clear that he associates his fictional *persona* with the musical side of his personality, which in this instance is to be brought to life through the performance of "old English songs." Unfortunately, Dolmetsch refused to make a Lute for Joyce, and the proposed tour was never forthcoming.

Despite the failure of Joyce's musical career, his planned tour of English watering places demonstrates that he was composing lyrics for the purpose of performing them to music. For Joyce, *alias* Stephen Dedalus, the performance of music was not only a means of developing the aesthetic side of his personality, but an authentic way of expressing his emotions. Joyce's personal identification with the poetry and music of the Elizabethans is confirmed by another letter sent to Nora in July of 1904, where he transcribes the words to a song written by Henry VIII, expressing "very delicately and musically the vague and tired loneliness which I feel" (*Letters II*, 44). In his transcription, Joyce notes that they have been written for music:

Song
(for music)
Ah, the sighs that come from my heart
They grieve me passing sore!
Sith I must from my love depart.
Farewell, my joy, for evermore. (*Letters II*, 45)

While this song can be interpreted simply as the subjective expression of the lyrical artist, Joyce's act of sending it to his beloved Nora shows that it can perform a *dramatic function*, insofar as it embodies the emotions of the sender and communicates it to the addressee. Indeed, the songs of Elizabethans were often performed on the dramatic stage, either in the plays of Shakespeare or the Comedies of Jonson (Fuller 1977), and it is to the latter that Joyce alludes in *Portrait*, quoting a line from *The Vision of Delight* (Jonson 1890, 221). As the song "I was not wearier where I lay" is taken from this masque, a courtly drama which evolved from the medieval festival, it can be seen as an instance of art intruding into the sphere of life, an impression only reinforced by the fact that the members of court would often perform the roles of classical Gods and Heroes. Comparing the decadence of such rituals with the erotic intentions of the troubadours, Joyce writes in *Portrait* that: "His mind, in the vesture of a doubting monk, stood often in shadow under the windows of that age [the Elizabethan age], to hear the grave and mocking music of the lutenists or the frank laughter of waist coateers until a laugh too low, a phrase, tarnished by time, of chambering and false honour stung his monkish pride and drove him on from his lurking-place" (*P*, 176). By alluding to the dramatic context in which the Elizabethan ballad was performed, Joyce attempts to reintegrate the tradition of English poetry into the practice of life, a project that he attempted to realize through his proposed tour of the British Isles singing the songs of the folk tradition.

Chamber Music

The poems collected in *Chamber Music*, published by Elkin Matthews in 1907 (see Nelson 1985), represent the culmination of Joyce's early activity as a poet, and can be seen to aspire the ideal condition of music as well as attempting to translate art into life through the *performance* of poetry. As we have already seen, there is a tension in Joyce's larger literary project between the structural rhythm of the poem as a whole and the movement of the underlying rhythm, for while the former is oriented toward the ideal space of the literary imagination, the latter is grounded in the actual performance of poetry and music. In order to reconcile the metrical and structural concepts of rhythm, we need to focus on those rhythmic elements that allude to *the dramatic situation of the poem as a whole*. Indeed, if we are to follow the method devised by Joyce himself in *Stephen Hero*, we need to focus upon the position of the rhetorical accents, for Stephen Dedalus only places "emphasis" on those accents that draw the reader's attention to the meaning of the words.

The most predominant rhythmic feature of Joyce's early poetry is the persistence of a four-beat line, which usually resolves itself into stanzas of four or six lines (heptets or sextets). According to Derek Attridge (1982), the four-by-four structure is the most basic form of all English verse, for most nursery rhymes and folk songs tend to be composed in this simple meter. As folk songs are the product of a communal tradition which does not distinguish rigorously between poetry and music, the quantity of the syllables must naturally conform to the regularity of the underlying beat, and can vary in duration and stress according to the metrical context in which they are used (Attridge 1982). As the form of these songs is based on an intuition of the underlying rhythm, and not governed by the rules of classical prosody, the rhythmic form of the foot remains variable (trochees and anapests are often substituted for iambs), and the number of syllables realizing a beat can range from one to three. The presence of triple rhythms (three syllables per beat) makes explicit the connection between Joyce's poetry and the folk tradition, because the alternation between bisyllabic and trisyllabic feet reveals the dominance of the underlying rhythm over the quantity and position of the syllables. Thus in the ninth poem of the cycle ("Winds of May," IX), a ballad that resembles Swinburne's "Love at Sea,"[4] Joyce alternates freely between trochees and dactyls to create an effect of acceleration that embodies the circular dance of the wind on the sea:

Wínds of Máy, that <u>dánce on the</u> séa,
<u>Dáncing a</u> ríng aróund in glée

From fúrrow to fúrrow, while óverhéad
The fóam flies úp to be gárlandéd,
In sílvery árches spánning the aír,
Sáw you my trúe love ánywhére?
Wélladáy! Wélladáy!
Fór the wínds of Máy!
Lóve is unháppy when lóve is awáy!   (*PSW*, 21: my underline, WM)

In contrast to the opening couplet, which begins with a falling rhythm (trochaic), the subsequent lines revert to an rising pattern (iambic), demonstrating that the line can begin either with the realization of a beat or an offbeat. As a consequence, a higher-order rhythm is created by the alternation between falling and rising rhythms, and this is reflected in the actual meaning of the poem, for while the waves are crashing down at the beginning of the poem, they are rising in the second half to form the circular symbol of a garland. The beats of the underlying rhythm are then made explicit by the refrain "Welladay! Well-aday!," for a single syllable is used to articulate the first beat of the line. Despite this emphasis on the metrical rhythm, which attempts to recreate the movement of the waves, Joyce is also attempting to construct a structural rhythm, for the image of his beloved is embodied in the dance of the wind and the waves. By removing the fourth beat from the second line of the refrain "For the winds of May __," Joyce shows that his beloved is absent, and although the final line restores the original rhythm, the memory of the missing fourth beat remains in the final image: "Love is unhappy when love is away." Here we can see that the poet's beloved *is* the missing fourth beat of the refrain, for it is the rhythm that creates both expectation of her appearance, as well as the awareness of her absence. At this point, we might say that the underlying rhythm is momentarily coordinated with the rhetorical intention behind the poem, such that the *rhythmic gesture* of the whole begins to show itself.

Through the technique of rhyme, Joyce creates a series of harmonic correspondences that reinforce the structural rhythm of the poem as a whole. As Myra Russel has pointed out, the *ababcc/dedeff* is the most commonly used scheme in the Elizabethan ballad, and the same form is used by Joyce in nine of his poems. Another common form is the *abcb/defe* scheme, which appears in another nine of Joyce's poems. Indeed, Joyce's strict adherence to such rhyme schemes demonstrates his fidelity to the genre of the Elizabethan ballad; yet, his innovation consists in the use of assonance and alliteration to create a series of harmonic echoes *within* the line. In the opening stanza of XV, for example, the movement from the "o" sound at the beginning of the

line to the long "e" at the center, creates a melodic contour that is
more forceful than the end rhyme:

> *From* dewy *dreams,* my soul arise,
>   *From love's deep* slumber and from death,
> For *lo,* the *trees* are full of sighs
>   *Whose leaves* the morn admonisheth (*PSW*, 27: my italics, WM)

As the rhetorical emphasis is placed on each "ee" sound, the effect of
this assonance is to increase the intensity of the slumber, musically
evoking the depth of the poet's dreams. A similar technique is used
in XXVIII, where the assonance between "deep" and "sleep" reinforces the soporific effect: "Sing about the long deep sleep." In other
poems, Joyce uses alliteration to capture the movement of nature, such
as "rivers rushing," "foam flies," and "silvery arches spanning the air"
(IX). Joyce also uses onomatopoeia to emphasize the musical aspects
of language and the capacity of words to imitate natural sounds. In
the opening line of XXIII, the verb "to flutter" captures the light and
airy manner beating of the poet's heart ("This heart that flutters near
my heart"), an effect reinforced by the airy vowel sound of "heart."
In most poems, however, assonance and alliteration are used in combination with one another, and can be used to make the tone light or
heavy, according to the dramatic situation. The effectiveness of this
technique is best illustrated in XXV, where the light dance of the Muse
("Lightly come or lightly go") becomes burdened by the heaviness of
the poet's heart: "Love and laughter song confessed | When the heart
is heaviest." Here we can see that the length of the final vowel sounds
decreases the tempo of the poem and burdens the tone, creating a clear
contrast between the light opening and heavy conclusion. In this way,
Joyce creates a *dramatic reversal* between the first and second stanzas,
for the light is no longer the embodiment of the Oread dancing on
mount Helicon, but rather the manner in which the clouds "lightly"
enwrap the valley, veiling the muses from the gaze of the poet.

  In direct opposition to the natural tendency of the ballad form,
which tends to subordinate rhetorical stress to the regularity of
the underlying rhythm, Joyce composes a number of lines that are
intended to disrupt the recurring pattern. This is most clear in VIII
("Who goes amid the green wood"), for the third line of each stanza
includes an additional word that alters the position of the rhetorical
accent. In the first stanza, for instance, Joyce writes:

> Who goes amid the green wood
>   With springtide all adorning her?

Who goes amid the *merry* green wood
To make it merrier (*PSW*, 20: my italics, WM)

As the first line is composed of four beats, the third beat must be realized by a monosyllable ("green"), and this forces the reader to place rhetorical stress on the adjective. In the third line, however, the insertion of "merry" alters the quantity of "green," for it is now simply the second short syllable of a dactyl (*"merry* green"), a rhythmic modification that causes it to lose its rhetorical emphasis. Directly alluding to the rhetorical effects of this technique, Joyce notes that the insertion of the new adjective makes the wood *merrier* ("To make it merrier"). Similar rhetorical points are made by the addition of "sweet" before "sunlight," "sunny" before "woodland," and "own" before "true love." In each case, the rhetorical emphasis is shifted to the first of the two adjectives, and the poet thereby increases the sincerity with which he praises his lover. The same technique is used in XVI, where the opening line ("O cool is the valley now") is altered by the addition of a new adjective ("O cool and *pleasant* is the valley"), shifting the emphasis to the aesthetic satisfaction of the image. Through the harmonic manipulation of the metrical elements, Joyce's technique is to add adjectives, bringing about an increase in rhetorical intensity and sincerity. Too delicate to be registered at the level of semantics, these melodic variations create subtle changes in tone color and intensity that are registered only at an emotional level.

The rhetorical accent also performs a pivotal role in III ("At that hour when all things have repose") because it is almost impossible to render the rhythm of this poem without emphatically pronouncing those syllables that actualize the five beats of the line. Although the reader might wish to elide the opening syllables in an attempt to establish an iambic rhythm, we are forced to dwell on the monosyllables, for both "At" and "O" must carry an accent to establish the rhythm: "*At* that hour when all things have repose | *O* lonely watcher of the skies" (my italics, WM). The effect of these monosyllables is to slow the tempo, allowing the performance to achieve the "repose" alluded to in the opening line. Indeed, the rhetorical intent behind this technique is to create a feeling of stasis in which the different parts of the poem resonate with each other, creating a sense of the structural rhythm. Thus, it is only on the condition of repose or *stasis* that the music is heard in the ideal space of the literary imagination: "When all things repose do you alone | Awake to hear the sweet harps play." By repeating the same imagery in various parts of the poem, Joyce makes explicit the "equality" of the rhythmic patterns, as in the line "Play on, invisible harps, unto love," which

echoes the earlier mention "Of harps, playing unto love to unclose."
We can therefore say that the repetition of melodic motifs increases
the sense of the structural rhythm, an effect that is created through
subtle shifts in syntactical order and rhetorical emphasis. When this
technique is pursued to its limit, the underlying rhythm is entirely
disrupted, for the reader can no longer intuit a metrical pulse, but
must search for corresponding points of rhetorical emphasis. In IV
("When the shy star goes forth in heaven"), the four-beat line is continually contradicted by the proliferation of rhetorical accents, and
the rhythm is entirely disrupted in the second stanza, when Joyce
breaks the line with a colon: "Nor muse: who may this singer be |
Whose song about my heart is falling?" Although these lines can be
scanned as iambic tetrameters, the position of the rhetorical accents
contradicts the position of the stresses, and the rhythmic structure of
the poem begins to break down, approaching the condition of *vers
libre*.

Joyce uses the technique of inversion to emphasize the correspondence between the various parts of the poem, and to alter the rhetorical status of the lexical elements. In II ("The Twilight Turns from
Amethyst"), a ballad written in the style of a "fourteener," Joyce
inverts the position of the adjectives, highlighting the growing intensity of the blue tone color:

> The twilight turns from amethyst | To deep and deeper blue (1/2)
> The twilight turns to darker blue | With lights of amethyst (11/12)

Here the stresses on "deep" and "deeper" create the effect of heightened rhetorical emphasis, corresponding to the intensification of the
color. In the final line, "darker" carries the emphasis, such that the
blue dominates the lingering "lights" of the amethyst. Alluding to the
German concept of *klangfarbe* ("clang-tint" or "tone-color") Joyce
establishes a correspondence between emotions and colours, because
the "the lamp fills with a pale green glow" and the muse "bends upon
the yellow keys" of an old piano. In this instance, the inversion is
used as a framing device for the poem as a whole, suggesting that
it embodies the structural rhythm. A similar technique is used in V,
where the order of the opening refrain ("Lean out of the window,
Goldenhair, | I heard you singing a merry Air") is inverted at the end
of the poem. Indeed, most of the poems in *Chamber Music* contain
repeated motifs, which are altered either by changing the order of the
lines (*strophic inversion*) or changing the order of the words (*syntactical inversion*). An example of the latter is to be found in XXIV, where

the position of the verb "to come" is syntactically inverted, depending on the rhetorical emphasis of the line and its role in the structure of the poem as a whole:

Silently she's *combing* (1)
Combing her long hair (2)
And still she's *combing* her long hair (7)
I pray you cease to *comb*, (9)
Comb out your long hair (10)

Here we can see that the repetition of the "ohm" sound creates a series of harmonic associations between the different lines, but each "comb" contains a different degree of emotional intensity, causing the activity of combing to be perceived from several different angles.

The refrain performs an important function in the Elizabethan ballad, for it marks the recurrence of the melody and expresses the central idea of the poem. As Joyce's poems rarely exceed the 16 lines of the four-by-four structure, refrains are usually limited to the recurrence of a single line, which may or may not be positioned at the end of the stanza. The opening line of VI ("I would in that sweet bosom be") is repeated at the close of the first stanza, creating a refrain-like effect; yet, the line is modified in the second stanza to prevent the onset of monotony ("I would *be ever in that heart*"). Indeed, Joyce chooses to vary the refrains to slightly alter the rhetorical meaning. The most persistent refrain is perhaps "My dove, my beautiful one, | Arise, arise!" (X), but even this line is subjected to strophic inversion in the second stanza, and truncation at the end of the poem. A more productive approach would be to analyze the recurrence of individual words and phrases as refrains in their own right, as is indicated by Joyce's own quotation marks in XXXIV. Here we can see that the original motif is divided into a number of refrains that allude back to the unity of the opening line:

Sleep now, O sleep now,
O you unquiet heart!
A voice crying "*Sleep now*"
Is heard in my heart.

The voice of the winter
Is heard at the door.
O *sleep*, for the winter
Is crying, "*Sleep* no more."

My kiss will give you *peace now*
And quiet to your heart

Sleep on in *peace* now
O you unquiet heart. (*PSW*, 46: my emphasis, WM)

By citing the refrain "sleep now" in the body of the poem, Joyce relates
the recurrence of motifs to the identity of the speaking subject, for the
harmonic effect creates a division in the poet's personality. Indeed, the
refrain is identified with the voice of the heart, an emotional faculty
that is distanced from the intellect of the poet, who reflects on his emotions and translates them into rhythmic form. By separating the *emotional content* of the poem from the *intellectual technique*, a dimension
of irony begins to intrude into Joyce's lyrics, and this reinforces the
pervading sense of erotic perversity that underlies most of the lyrics.
For Joyce, the rhythmic and harmonic aspects of the poem are a mathematical code for transcribing the emotions of the troubadour, as is
indicated by the lines, "That mood of thine, O timorous, I Is his, if thou
but scan it well" (XXVI). It is here suggested that the lady will discover
the troubadour's true intentions if she pays attention to the rhyme and
rhythm of the poem; yet, this implies the separation between the intellectual and emotional sides of poetry, which introduces an element of
irony that is recognized by author and reader alike.

The final two poems of the *Chamber Music* cycle announce the eruption of a distinctly modernist style in Joyce's poetry, for the regularity
of the underlying rhythm is disrupted by a series of musical effects that
emphasize the structural rhythm. According to Myra Russel, "there is
no way to fit the last poem, XXXVI, into a structure even remotely like
the Elizabethan," for "[w]ith an alternating meter of five and six stresses
to a line, the rhythm is irregular and difficult" (1981, 140). While the
first line can indeed be scanned as an iambic pentameter (with an anapest in the fourth foot), the remainder of the stanza disrupts the flow
of the rhythm, particularly the fourth and sixth lines, where the agent
("charioteers") and action ("stand") are placed at the end of the line,
and adjectival phrases present an array of juxtaposed images:

I hear an army charging upon the land,
    And the thunder of horses plunging, foam about
        their knees:
Arrogant, in black armor, behind them stand,
    Disdaining the reins, with fluttering whips, the
        Charioteers. (*PSW*, 48)

In the first two lines, Joyce employs trisyllabic substitution ("*charging
upon*") to imitate the rhythm of the galloping horses. This technique

creates a sense of acceleration as the riders come into view. The assonance between "thunder" and "plunging" creates a sense of descending movement that communicates the power of the riders and their dominance of the land. Yet, as soon as the rhythm is established, the word "arrogant" stands in stark contrast to the preceding material, as though the word itself were striking a pose. The "black armor" of these knights appeals to the eye, not simply for the firmness and strength of the diction, but also for its metrical isolation. Each phrase of the antithesis possesses an accent that cannot be reduced to any metrical scheme. Through his use of parataxis, which is clearly marked by his use of punctuation, Joyce creates a static image of the riders, simultaneously presenting them from multiple points of view. Through his use of assonance ("disdaining the reins") and alliteration ("with fluttering whips"), furthermore, Joyce creates a sense of motion in rest, the riders appearing before the eyes as a blur of motion. The cumulative effect of all these techniques is to create a poem whose organic unity no longer derives from the mechanical regularity of a metrical rhythm, but rather from the tension between the individual elements of the poem as a whole.

Conclusion

Moving from an account of Joyce's rhythmic education at Belvedere and University College toward an appreciation of this rhythmic praxis as preserved in the poems of *Chamber Music*, we have seen that there is a tension between the rhetorical accents and the underlying rhythms that structure the musical performance of ballads and songs. Although Joyce may not have read the work of prosodists such as Sidney Lanier or T. S. Omond, his basic understanding of modern meter was informed by the work of John Duncan Quackenbos, whose lesson on "Versification" unites the different strands of prosodic theory in circulation at the turn of the twentieth century. Significantly, the physiological psychology of Wundt and Spencer intrudes into Quackenbos's manual, particularly the concept of rhythm as the alternation between tension and relaxation in the periodic movements of the body. To the extent, furthermore, that the *musical performance of poetry* reintegrates the movements of the body into the sensation of rhythm, we have seen that Joyce was able to successfully reintroduce the dimension of quantity and duration into the experience of reading and performing English verse. According to the theory of prosody developed in *Stephen Hero*, Joyce wished to stress the meaning of the rhetorical accents above the mechanical regularity of the underlying rhythm, and it is this tendency to disrupt the reader's sensation of rhythm that distinguishes *Chamber Music* as an early example of "modernist" poetry. Although Joyce conforms closely to the genre of the Elizabethan ballad, he uses assonance and alliteration to create musical effects, a new method of composing poetry that contributes to the construction of what he calls the "structural rhythm."

Chapter 3

"The Most Commonplace Conversation"

Rhythm as Gesture in Dubliners

Joyce wrote most of *Dubliners* between 1904 and 1907, and the stories collected in this volume provide the critic with ample material to test the theory of the "rhythmic gesture" developed in *Stephen Hero* (see Introduction), as the Irish author was also working on this manuscript during his early years in Trieste. As we have already seen, the scientific discourse on rhythm had an impact on the metrical style of the young James Joyce, as his dramatic approach to the scansion of verse was informed by the lesson on "Versification" in Quackenbos's *Practical Rhetoric* (1896). While Joyce may not have been fully aware of the influence of rhythmic science on his own metrical style, the surviving manuscript of *Stephen Hero* demonstrates an increasing awareness of psychological science, particularly the theory of "attention" developed in Alexander Bain's *Mental and Moral Science* (1872) and Grant Allen's *Physiological Aesthetics* (1877). Although Stephen Dedalus relies on the classical authorities of Aristotle and Aquinas to develop the basic principles of his aesthetic theory—sources that would have been authoritative for his Jesuit teachers at University College—his theory of the "rhythmic gesture" is informed by a much wider variety of sources than hitherto recognized. As we shall see, Joyce develops a structural conception of rhythm as the relationship between the parts and the whole of an aesthetic image in the Paris notebook of 1903, a definition that seems to have been inspired by the organic theory of drama developed in Aristotle's *Poetics*. Although Joyce drew on such classical sources when developing his aesthetic theory, he also consulted more modern texts such as Butcher's *Aristotle's Theory of Poetry and Fine Art* (1895), a translation and commentary that contribute a classical perspective to the scientific discourse on rhythm.

The Structural Conception of Rhythm in the Paris Notebook

While Joyce's critics have spilled much ink investigating the sources of his aesthetic theory, scant attention has been paid to the theory of rhythm developed in the Paris notebook, perhaps for the reason that the "rhythmic science" of the late nineteenth and early twentieth centuries has hitherto remained obscure. In *Portrait*, Stephen Dedalus tells Father Darlington that he is working on an aesthetic theory that has been guided "by the light of one or two ideas of Aristotle and Aquinas" (*P*, 187), and it must be admitted that these classical thinkers remain the primary authorities for investigating the sources of Joyce's own aesthetic theory. In *The Aesthetics of James Joyce* (1992), the French critic Jacques Aubert has suggested that Joyce read parts of Aristotle's *Oeuvres* in the classic translation of J. Barthélémy-Saint-Hilaire, basing his argument on a number of quotations that Joyce recorded in Paris (see Aubert 1992, appendix B, 131–7). Taking for granted the authority of these classical sources, I would like to contend that Joyce also consulted a number of commentaries that were beginning to incorporate the insights of rhythmic science. While Aubert suggests that Joyce consulted a contemporary French translation and commentary of *La Poetique d'Aristote* by Hatzfeld and Dufour (1899), the entries in the Paris notebook indicate that Joyce was relying more heavily on Samuel Butcher's *Aristotle's Theory of Poetry and Fine Art* (1895), a text that includes the original Greek, an English translation, and an extended commentary on Aristotle's aesthetic system. In this important work, Butcher interprets the *Poetics* in a manner that incorporates the principles of Aristotle's metaphysics and psychology; yet, his commentary also seeks to legitimate the Aristotelian theory in light of the leading scientific and aesthetic theories of the late nineteenth century. More specifically, Butcher's commentary includes an extended discussion of Greek music that reflects the emergence of rhythmic science in the late nineteenth century, particularly the attempts of late-Victorian prosodists to reunite the arts of poetry and music.

Joyce recorded the entries on aesthetics during his second trip to Paris, a sojourn which dates from January 1903 until the death of his mother in August of the same year. From the content of the first entry in the Paris notebook—dated by the author to February 13, 1903—it is clear that Joyce was interpreting the *Poetics* through the lens of Aristotle's psychology, for he differentiates the dramatic emotions (terror and pity) from the kinetic impulses that motivate the body to either move toward a pleasant object or flee from a painful object:

> Desire is the feeling which urges us to go to something and loathing is the feeling which urges us to go from something; and that art is improper which aims at exciting these feelings in us whether by comedy or tragedy. (CW, 143)

Viewed from the perspective of nineteenth-century psychology, Joyce's negations of these kinetic emotions should be interpreted as a strategy designed to *purge* the physiological dimension of the dramatic spectacle, a transformative response to the spectacle that was associated with the Aristotelian theory of *catharsis* or "purgation." In 1857, the German scholar Joseph Bernays published a pamphlet titled *Zwei Abhandlungen über Die Aristotelische Theorie Des Drama*, which suggested that the tragic spectacle had the same effect on the soul as that of medicine on the body. Significantly, Butcher summarizes the "purgation" theory in his commentary, writing:

> Pity and fear, artificially stirred, expel the latent pity and fear, which we bring with us from real life, or at least, such elements in them as are disquieting. In the pleasurable calm, which follows when the passion is spent, an emotional cure has been wrought. (Butcher 1895, 229)

According to Butcher, the proper experience of tragedy does not cause the spectator to "fear" his own destruction, rather the "terror" of drama is mediated by the "pity" the spectator feels for the tragic hero, transforming the hero's *pain* into a form of aesthetic *pleasure*. As the spectator perceives the character of the hero to be "like" his own, the situation of the tragic hero comes to represent the universal nature of humanity. Similarly, Joyce traces the origin of the dramatic spectator to the feeling of empathy that unites the spectator with the suffering of the hero, for "terror is the feeling which arrests us before whatever is grave in human fortunes and unites us with the human sufferer" (CW, 143). Considering that both Butcher and Joyce appeal to a universal notion of humanity to distinguish the ideal feelings of terror and pity from their pathological counterparts, it would seem that Joyce was drawing on *Aristotle's Theory of Poetry and Fine Art* when composing even the earliest entries in the Paris notebook.

The opening entry of the Paris notebook suggests that the subsequent entries should be interpreted within the context of the *Poetics*, including the structural definition of rhythm as the formal relations between the parts and the whole of an aesthetic image. In his chapter titled "The Function of Tragedy," Butcher claims that poetry is a "representation of the universal," basing his claim on the notion that "the characters it depicts, the actions and fortunes of the persons with whom it acquaints us, possess a typical and universal value" (1895, 240). Significantly, Butcher traces the universality of the tragic situation to the organic unity of the plot, for "The artistic unity of plot, *binding together the several parts of the play in close inward coherence*, reveals the law of human destiny, the causes and effects of human suffering" (240: my italics, WM). Significantly, the feelings of terror and pity associated with the perception of the dramatic situation are caused by the sequence of events that determine the suffering of the tragic hero. Indeed, it is this notion of *dramatic causality* that links Joyce's theory of the dramatic emotions to the structural conception of rhythm, for it is precisely the *relation* between the individual character of the hero and the organic unity of the dramatic plot that constitutes the tragic situation. In Book XIII of the *Poetics*, Aristotle makes it clear that the organic unity of the "plot" is constituted by the ordered relation between the parts and the whole, for as he puts it:

> The plot must, as in a tragedy, be dramatically constructed; it must have for its subject a single action, whole and complete, with a beginning, a middle, and an end. It will *thus resemble a single and coherent picture of a living organism*, and produce the pleasure proper to it. (cited in Butcher 1895, 176)

Although the word "structure" does not appear anywhere in Aristotle's text, the term appears in Butcher's commentary on "The Dramatic Unities," for he writes "The whole (*holon*) in which it is manifested is complete (*teleion*) in its parts, the parts themselves being arranged in a fixed order (*taxis*) and structurally related so that none can be removed, none transposed, without disturbing the organism" (254–5). Once again, Butcher stresses the relationship between the organic unity of the work and the dramatic causality that determines the fate of the hero, for: "Within the single and complete action which constitutes the unity of a tragedy, the successive incidents are connected together by an inward and causal bond,—by the law of necessary and probable sequence, on which Aristotle is never tired of insisting" (255).

Having reconstructed the context in which Joyce formulated the entries in the Paris notebook, we are now in a position to interpret the meaning of the structural definition of rhythm. In an entry dated to March 25, 1903, the young Joyce writes: "Rhythm seems to be the first or formal relation of part to part in any whole or of a whole to its part or parts, or of any part to the whole of which it is a part ... Parts constitute a whole as far as they have a common end" (*CW*, 145). Despite the abstract manner in which the definition is formulated, the context surrounding the other entries in the Paris notebook indicates that Joyce was paraphrasing the organic theory of tragedy developed by Aristotle and elaborated by Butcher. Indeed, throughout the chapter titled "The Dramatic Unities," Butcher refers to the events of the plot as *parts* (beginning, middle, and end), and places particular emphasis on the condition of "wholeness" that binds these parts together. Significantly, the "end" of the plot is not simply the last event of the play, but also the "final cause" that reveals the necessary fate of the tragic hero. According to Butcher, "the end is linked to the beginning with inevitable certainty, and in the end we discern the meaning of the whole: *to telos megiston apantōn*" (1895, 263). Significantly, this conception of the tragic plot as a perfect whole enables the critic to reduce the temporal order of events to a spatial configuration. Consequently, the musical significance of rhythm as a metrical pattern is increasingly displaced by its architectural significance as harmony, symmetry, and proportion. Furthermore, the analogy between works of art and living organisms allows the dramatic conception of the "end" to be transferred to the sphere of artistic or natural production, for the term might refer to either the "form" of a technical product or the "soul" of a living animal. In the context of Joyce's developing esthetic theory, this metaphysical notion of an end is extended to the perfection or completion of any natural process, an understanding he would have gleaned from Butcher's explanation: "Each individual thing has an ideal form towards which it tends, and in the realization of this form, which is one with the essence (*ousia*) of the object, its end is attained" (155).[1] Considering that the ultimate aim of Stephen's esthetic theory is to perceive the *quidditas* or "whatness" of the aesthetic object, it would seem that this notion of the "end" as the wholeness of the rhythmic structure is also that which guides the process of aesthetic apprehension.

In the next entry of the Paris notebook, written only two days later (March 27), Joyce meditates on the meaning of an Aristotelian phrase that is quoted directly in Butcher's commentary: *ē technē mimeitai tēn phusin*. Translating the phrase in the traditional manner, "Art imitates nature," Butcher rejects the Platonic interpretation of art as a mere "copy" of nature, for "the original saying was never meant to differentiate between fine and useful art, nor indeed could it possibly bear the sense that fine art is a copy or reproduction of natural objects" (1895, 110). Indeed, Butcher maintains that art is a technical activity like any other, and collapses the distinction between artistic and natural processes, for the reason that nature itself is "the productive principle of the universe" (110). As all substances are created from the synthesis of form and matter, whether produced by a craftsman or nature itself, Butcher posits an *analogy* between natural and artistic processes: "In the *Physics*, the point of comparison is that alike in art and in nature there is a union of matter (*hylē*) with constitutive form (*morphē*), and that the knowledge of both elements is requisite for the natural philosopher as for the physician and architect" (110–11). For the purposes of the current study, the key part of this argument is the use of the term "alike," for Joyce also constructs an analogy between artistic and natural processes, writing in the Paris notebook: "Aristotle does not here define art; he says only, 'Art imitates Nature' and means that the artistic process is like the natural process" (*CW*, 145). Considering the similarity between these two explanations, there can hardly be any doubt that Butcher's commentary is the authoritative source for the entries contained in the Paris notebook. Viewed in this context, the "end" of dramatic work becomes synonymous with the "form" of a substance, for the process of artistic production is guided by the "idea" of the product in the soul of the maker (just as the perfection of a natural substance is guided by its form as final cause). Indeed, when nature itself is conceived as the product of a divine creator, the artist becomes a God-like figure. As Butcher puts it, "art in its widest acceptation has, like nature, certain ends in view, and in the adaption of means to ends catches hints from nature who is already in some sort an unconscious artist" (111). Consequently, the structural rhythm of the aesthetic whole should be interpreted as the *form* of a technical object, a reorientation that allows Joyce to analyze the aesthetic phenomenon from the perspective of production (as opposed to the mere reception of the dramatic spectacle).

In the *Poetics*, Aristotle uses the term "rhythm" in the traditional sense to refer to the meters of classical poetry. It may therefore come as a surprise to discover that Joyce uses the same term to refer to the organic structure of the dramatic artwork. How are we to explain this contradiction between the metrical and structural conceptions of rhythm, or in other words, the temporal and spatial aspects of poetry? In Book I of the *Poetics*, Aristotle defines rhythm as one of the three "means" of imitation that constitute the essence of Greek music: rhythm (*rhythmos*), language (*logos*), and harmony (*harmonia*). In Butcher's translation, the concept of the "means" or "medium" is explained in the following terms: "For as there are persons who, by conscious art or mere habit, imitate and represent various objects through the medium of colour and form, or again by the voice; so in the arts mentioned above, taken as a whole, the imitation is produced by rhythm, language and 'harmony', either singly or combined" (7). Within this context, the term "rhythm" becomes synonymous with the classical conception of "meter," for it refers to the particular combination of short and long syllables used to compose lyric (dithyramb), epic (dactylic), tragedy (trochaic), or comedy (iambic). Despite this strict association between rhythm and meter, Aristotle goes on to clarify that dancers imitate emotions and actions by means of "rhythmical movements" (*dia tōn schematizomenōn rhythmōn*; 1447a, 27–8), revealing that the metrical rhythm has a visual aspect that transforms the temporal form into a dramatic gesture. In his commentary on this passage, Butcher concedes that these gestures "are indeed less perfect manifestations of these qualities than music, whose rhythmical and ordered movements have a special affinity with the nature of the soul"; but nevertheless maintains some form of temporal correspondence between the passions of the soul and the gestures of the body, for the reason that "they are not conventional symbols, but living signs through which the outward frame follows and reflects the movements of the spirit; they are a visible token of the inner unity of body and soul" (128). Considering that Stephen Dedalus develops a theory of the "rhythmic gesture" in *Stephen Hero*, it is evident that Joyce was aware of the correspondence between inner feelings and external gestures. To the extent, furthermore, that the performance of classical tragedy was inseparable from the rhythms and harmonies of Greek music, there are grounds to assert that the "rhythmic gesture" translates the metrical rhythms of poetry into the structural rhythms of painting and sculpture.

While Butcher purports to be interpreting the Aristotelian theory of music from a purely historical point of view, his account of the temporal correspondence between rhythmic movements and inner feelings appears to have been informed by the rhythmic science of the late nineteenth century. In the first instance, the priority given to the concept "rhythm" in Butcher's treatise reflects the growing interest in the topic in Europe and North America, an interest invigorated in the field of classics by the rediscovery of Aristoxenus's treatise on *The Elements of Rhythm* (1989) by the German scholar, Rudolf Westphal (1883). For example, in an article titled "On the Equivalence of Rhythmical Bars and Metrical Feet" (1892), the American scholar Milton Humphrey cites Westphal to argue that the Greek performance of music was based on an intuition of equivalent temporal periods. Purporting to "omit all theorizing about nerve-waves from the ear to the brain," Humphrey ironically demonstrates an awareness of physiological psychology, using the terms "rhythmic sense" and "rhythmic effect" to describe the production and perception of rhythms. Abstracting the meters of classical verse from the material of language, furthermore, Humphrey appeals to a psychological conception of rhythm developed by Lanier, for "the rhythm of music and poetry, both ancient and modern, not only depends on quantity, that is, time, but requires the recurrence of approximately equal units" (159). By positing a temporal correspondence between metrical bars and rhythmic feet, Humphrey recapitulates the musical notation used by Sidney Lanier in *The Science of English Verse* (1880), where the "recurrence of approximately equal units" is defined as the psychological sensation of the primary rhythm.

Reflecting trends in modern psychology and acoustics, classicists of mid-to-late nineteenth century sought to ground the essence of poetry in the unity of Greek music (rhythm, words, and melody), a project that was brought to completion via the publication of Monro's *The Modes of Ancient Greek Music* (1892). In this groundbreaking work, the professor of Oriel College draws on Aristoxenus's treatise on harmony to give a systematic exposition of the various "scales" or "modes" used to perform lyric or dramatic poetry in classical Greece, demonstrating that they had a complex system of musical notation that distinguished both the pitch and the rhythm of the syllables. In the second chapter of his commentary, Butcher cites a long passage from Monro's work that seeks to establish the unity of rhythm and melody in the performance of Greek poetry, a natural correspondence between duration and pitch that seems to have disappeared from modern poetry: "We have in the keys the same or even the greater command of degrees of pitch; but we seem to have lost the close relation which once obtained between a note as the result of physical facts and the same note as an index of temper or emotion" (cited in Butcher 1895, 124). By comparing the melody of ancient Greek verse to modern languages, such as English, Monro was relying on the scientific work of Hermann von Helmholtz, for the German physicist was the first to devise a reliable method of measuring the natural pitch of the vowels used by the human voice (see Ch. 4). In these ways, it can be seen that the interpretation of classical texts was being informed by the principles of rhythmic science, for scholars such as Westphal, Humphrey, and Monro were seeking to understand the relationship between psychology, rhythm, and music in the poetry of the ancient Greeks.

When Butcher's commentary on the *Poetics* is situated in the context of the scientific discourse of the late nineteenth century, it becomes clear why he attributes such a prominent role to rhythm in the performance of Greek music, because the phenomenon of rhythm had become the subject of research in both the fields of psychology and classics. More specifically, physiological psychologists such as Spencer and Wundt had posited a parallelism between mental and bodily processes that was mediated by the perception and the production of rhythmic patterns.[2] Although Butcher does not cite any of these thinkers in his commentary, he nevertheless posits a parallelism between thought and movement that is mediated by the intuition of rhythm. In the chapter titled "Art as Imitation," Butcher defines the concept of *praxis* or action as "psychical energy moving outwards," a definition which allows him to reduce any physical movement to its psychological correlate. While poetry in general imitates "characters" (*ēthē*), "emotions" (*pathē*), and "actions" (*praxis*), all three regions of human life are reduced to the inner life of the soul, for, as Butcher argues "the common original, then, from which all the arts draw is human life— its mental processes, its spiritual movements, *its outward acts issuing from deeper sources*; in a word, all that constitutes the inward and essential activity of the soul" (118: my italics, WM). As the rhythm and harmony of Greek music seems to reflect the ethical character of the soul, Butcher claims "Music was held by Aristotle, as by the Greeks generally, to be the most 'imitative' or representative of all the arts" (122). In the language of rhythmic science, rhythm and harmony are the external correlates of the inner life, for as Butcher puts it:

> The dominant element in Greek music was the rhythm; the spirit and meaning of any given composition was felt to reside especially here; and the doctrine which asserted the unique imitative capacity of music had for Aristotle its theoretic basis in this, that *the external movements of rhythmical sound bear a close resemblance to the movements of the soul.* Each single note is felt as an inward agitation. The regular succession of musical sounds, governed by the laws of melody and rhythm, are allied to those *praxeis* or outward activities which are the expression of a mental state. (125: my emphasis, WM)

Of course, Butcher does not cite the work of Spencer or Wundt; yet, his account of rhythm reproduces the basic principle of "physiological psychology," for the external movements of the body are held to mirror or reflect the inner life of the soul.

From the account of Greek music in Butcher's commentary, it has now become clear that the concept of rhythm performs a pivotal role in translating the moral character of the dramatic hero into a series of external gestures that possess a rhythmic form. In the entry of the Paris notebook mentioned above (dated to March 27), Joyce goes on to consider whether sculpture is to be considered an art of *repose*, "if by that be meant that sculpture is unassociated with movement" (*CW*, 145). Once again, Joyce appears to be engaged in a silent dialogue with Butcher, for the Greek scholar poses a similar problem in his commentary: "Painting and sculpture working through an inert material cannot indeed reproduce the life of the soul in all its variety and successive manifestations" (1895, 128). When we take into account the pivotal role which rhythm plays in the outward expression of inner thought processes, it becomes clear why the arts of painting and sculpture appear to be impoverished, for they lack the temporal movement of a performed rhythm. Nevertheless, Butcher appeals to the structural rhythms of architecture to legitimate the aesthetic form of painting and sculpture, conceding that the symmetry of the image compensates for the lack of movement:

> Still shape and line and colour even here retain something of their significance, they are in their own degree a natural image of the mind; and their meaning is helped out by the symmetry, *which in the arts of repose answers to rhythm*, the chief vehicle of expression in the arts of movement. (129: my emphasis, WM)

From this passage, it becomes clear that the *symmetry* of the sculpture is strictly analogous to the *rhythm* of poetry. Following this line of argument, Joyce holds that the process of perceiving a visual image possesses a temporal rhythm, for the reason that the movement is performed in the imagination of the spectator: "Sculpture is associated with movement in as much as it is rhythmic; for a work of art must be surveyed according to its rhythm and this surveying is an imaginary movement of space" (*CW*, 145). By reconciling the temporal performance of rhythm with the apprehension of spatial forms, Joyce therefore develops a method of translating the metrical rhythms of poetry into the structural rhythms of drama.

By tracing the definition in the Paris notebook to the discussion of tragedy in Aristotle's *Poetics*, we have discovered that the conception of rhythm as the formal relationship between the parts and the whole is derived from the organic unity and completeness of the "plot" (*mythos*) in classical drama. Nevertheless, to the extent that the *form* of the drama can be perceived in everyday life, it must also be recognized that the completeness (or universality) of the dramatic phenomenon shines forth in fragmentary instances, and shows itself as the incomplete moment that requires the construction of a *mythos* to explain its universal significance. Indeed, Aristotle compares the structure of drama to a portrait, which can be perceived at a single glance, and it is this spatial conception of drama that allows Joyce to devise a theory of aesthetic apprehension, for the organic unity of the whole can be perceived through the fragmentary appearance of a single part. By reconstructing the dramatic whole that surrounds the appearance of each part, Joyce (or Stephen Dedalus) can implicitly perceive the social forces that produce antagonism and conflict in everyday life, for it is precisely the relationship between the part and the whole that determines the relationship between the individual and the social configuration that surrounds and shapes him. As the tragic situation involves a reversal of fate, it expresses the moral contradiction between the ethical character of the hero and the moral norms of society, a contradiction that is marked as a rhythmic inflection. Indeed, it is precisely this rhythmic inflection that is perceived by the artist, for the *part of the drama that shows itself in everyday life is the dramatic reversal of fortune that brings about the sympathetic identification of the spectator with the hero.* The task of Joyce's aesthetic theory is therefore to reveal how the contradiction at the heart of the dramatic moment manifests itself in a rhythmic gesture that is inflected by a strong and a weak element, thereby revealing the political contradictions at the center of modern society.

The Epiphany and the Rhythmic Gesture

Joyce recorded his "epiphanies," a series of short prose poems that were later incorporated throughout *Stephen Hero*, *Portrait*, and *Ulysses*, during his time at University College (1901-2).[3] Pursuing a method of realism pioneered by Zola and Ibsen, two of the modern writers whom Stephen defends in *Stephen Hero*, Joyce recorded a number of the remarkable incidents that he perceived during his daily walks through the Dublin cityscape. According to Stanislaus, Joyce regarded these epiphanies as "little errors and gestures—mere straws in the wind—by which most people betrayed the very things they were most careful to conceal" (*PSW*, 157). As indicated here, Joyce's epiphanies require interpretation, for the surface appearance of these dramatic gestures reveal a deeper significance that is only perceivable to the mind of the aesthete (see Scholes 1973, 10-13).

In chapter XXV, Stephen defines the epiphany as "a sudden spiritual manifestation," drawing on the meaning of the term *epiphaneia* in the New Testament, a word used to describe the appearance of divinity in the figure of Jesus (2 Timothy, 1.10). In an essay on Munkacsy's *Ecce Homo*, Joyce identifies the rhythmic gesture with the figure of Christ on the Cross (*CW*, 36); yet, the divine significance of the term suggests an even closer identification between the "epiphany" and the "rhythmic gesture" in *Stephen Hero*, for the universal meaning of the dramatic gesture is revealed to the mind of spectator in a sudden moment of revelation. Indeed, when Stephen situates the concept of the epiphany within the theory of aesthetic apprehension, it becomes clear that the rhythmic "structure" of the image is synonymous with the "soul" of the object, for "when the relation of the parts is exquisite, when the parts are so adjusted to the special point, we recognize that it is *that* think which it is. Its soul, its whatness, leaps to us from the vestment of its appearance" (*SH*, 213). In psychological terms, therefore, the concept of the epiphany describes the moment in which the meaning of the "whole" emerges from the formal interaction of the "parts," for the "soul" or "structure" of the object shines through the material elements in which it is embodied: "The soul of the commonest object, the structure which is so adjusted, seems to us radiant. The object achieves its epiphany" (*SH*, 213).

In stylistic terms, however, Stephen's qualification that epiphanies may appear "in the vulgarity of speech or gesture or in a memorable phase of the mind itself" (*SH*, 216) reveals that these short prose–poems can be divided into two, distinct literary genres. Even a brief glance at the 40 surviving epiphanies reveals that approximately half record fragments of dialogue, the other half recording the lyrical meditations of the aesthete. As we are concerned with the rhythmic dimension of the dramatic gesture in this chapter, I will focus upon the fragments of dialogue, for the ellipses in the text reveal moments in which the pulse of the conversation breaks down. In my view, these dialogues represents mini-dramas that Joyce perceived in the context of everyday life, dramas whose rhythmic form was revealed to the mind of the aesthete through the play of call and response that governs the interaction of speakers in a conversation. By seeking to preserve the temporal form of these dialogues (including ellipses for pauses, and altered spellings for dialectical features), Joyce anticipates the method of the modern "ethnographer," for he seeks to reveal the social significance of even the most commonplace conversations.

The connection between the rhythmic gesture and the dramatic moment can be perceived in the first epiphany recorded by the young

Joyce, because the rhythmic correspondence between two phrases creates a moral contradiction that remains unresolved. Set in Bray, "in the parlor of the house in Martello Terrace," this conversation reproduces an early trial in the life of the artist, and attempts to reproduce the dialogical rhythms of Joyce's mother conversing with Mr Vance. By using ellipses to mark the gaps in the conversation, Joyce makes it clear that the aesthetic form of this epiphany is determined by the presence of an underlying temporal form, a recurring pulse that remains *unrealized* in the pauses between statements:

> [Bray: in the parlour of the house in Martello Terrace]
> Mr Vance (*comes in with a stick*): O, you know, he'll have to apologise, Mrs Joyce.
> Mrs Joyce: O yes ... Do you hear that, Jim?
> Mr Vance: Or else—if he doesn't—the eagle'll come and pull out his eyes.
> Mrs Joyce: O, but I'm sure he will apologise.
> Joyce (*under the table, to himself*):
> —Pull out his eyes,
> Apologise,
> Apologise,
> Pull out his eyes.
> Apologise,
> Pull out his eyes.
> Pull out his eyes,
> Apologise. (*PSW*, 161)

By including stage directions in parentheses, the literary form of this epiphany reveals that Joyce perceived the presence of dramatic forms in everyday conversations. At the level of "vulgarity," the ethical character of Mr Vance is embodied in his stick, for this stage-prop represents the authority of the father and the threat of punishment. Although his speech lacks any sense of rhetorical flow, Mr Vance forms two phrases that possess a similar metrical form ("pull out his eyes" / "apologise"), and the young boy's perception of the end rhyme creates a poetic correspondence with moral significance. Indeed, *unless* the boy apologizes, he will be punished, and it is this condition that embodies the dramatic reversal at the heart of the situation: "Or else—*if he doesn't*—the eagle'll come and pull out his eyes." By translating this moral contradiction into purely aesthetic terms, Joyce creates an image that is *rhythmically inflected*, because the harmonic correspondence between "pull out his eyes" and "apologise" still maintains a trace of the dramatic alternatives. Indeed, it is the rhythmic correspondence that allows the artist to see both the aesthetic correspondence of the words and the moral contradiction that they are seen to embody.

Joyce's dialogical epiphanies are remarkable for the accuracy with which they capture the accentual particularities of individual characters. In epiphany no. 15, Joyce attempts to capture the dialect of a lame beggar, who is described *"moving his stick up and down,"* a gesture that highlights his tendency to repeat things and insist on making his point. By spelling "you" as "ye," and eliding "of" as "o'," Joyce captures the individual accent of his character, and the repetition of phrases creates a short oral poem:

> The Lame Beggar: Well, if ye call out after me
>   Any more I'll cut ye open with
>   that stick. I'll cut the livers
>   out o' ye … (*explains himself*)
>   … D'ye hear me? I'll cut ye
>   open. I'll cut the livers and
>   lights out o'ye. (*PSW*, 175)

This epiphany contains an ironic reversal, for although the lame beggar threatens to murder the children, he is clearly unable to carry out his threat, and his insistence on cutting "the livers and lights out o'ye" simply serves to reinforce the idleness of his threat. In another epiphany (35), set in a house at Kensington, Joyce captures the sound of the Dublin accent by transcribing the vowel shift in the words "white" (*whoite*), "away" (*awoy*), "times" (*toimes*), and "night" (*noight*). The assonance between these words creates an echo effect that reinforces the underlying rhythm of Eva Leslie's speech. Joyce's focus on the vulgarity of the Dublin accent is here designed to reflect the squalor of Eva's domestic situation in London. Indeed, she appears to be an Irish prostitute, for not only does she seem to be having an incestuous relationship with her brother Fred (who is perhaps her pimp), but she also claims to have slept with the same men ten times in one night: "I told you *someun* went with me ten *toimes* one *noight*" (*PSW*, 195: my italics, WM). Rather than imposing any metrical scheme upon the material hand, Joyce focuses on those prosodic aspects of speech that *spontaneously produce a rhythmic form*. In this way, Joyce not only captures the peculiarities of accent and dialect, but he also points to a wider dramatic situation in which these specific gestures begin to acquire a universal significance.

From this brief analysis of Joyce's dialogical epiphanies, it can be seen that the mind of the artist remains attuned to the prosodic peculiarities of individual characters, and attempts to record the spontaneous emergence of rhythmic forms in the context of everyday life. I will use the term *concrete rhythms* to refer to these emergences, because they cannot be separated from the phonetic material in which they are embodied. When interpreting the short stories of *Dubliners*, I will attempt to link the emergence of these concrete rhythms to the structure of the wider dramatic situation, for it will be seen that the accentual and dialectical features of individual voices must be synchronized with an underlying rhythm that coordinates the speech of different speakers. In the context of Joyce's youthful epiphanies, however, it should be noted that the dramatic significance of these fragments remains largely undetermined. When writing these epiphanies, Joyce may not have been fully aware of the dramatic significance pertaining to each dialogue, but he seems to have used his "esthetic instinct" in determining which incidents to preserve in his notebooks. It is perhaps for this reason that he refers to the artist's faculty of "selection" in *Stephen Hero*. Although he may not have been able to adequately express the principles guiding this so-called instinct, he was acutely aware of the moral and political contradictions running through Dublin society in the early twentieth century.

Beats of Dialogue in "Grace"

According to Neil Murphy, the "modernist" element of Joyce's fiction is revealed through his attitude of self-questioning, a critical perspective that is embodied in the dramatic dialogues in *Dubliners*, for as he argues, "there is a recurring pattern of communicative breakdown" (2004, 197). By recording fragments of conversation, and tracing their dramatic significance to the prosodic features of individual speech-acts (poetic figures, rhetorical rhythms, accentual features), Joyce anticipates the method of modern sociologists, for it has now become accepted that the "beat" or "pulse" of dialogue possesses a normative force that is responsible for both coordinating conversations and socializing individuals (Erickson and Schultz 1982, Ch. 4). While it has been demonstrated that Joyce's theory of the rhythmic gesture was informed by Aristotle's *Poetics* (and Butcher's modern commentary), his representation of rhythmic dialogues constitutes a genuine stylistic innovation that exceeds the scope of his own theoretical description. In order to describe the subtleties of Joyce's *rhythmic practice*, I will draw on some of the concepts developed by contemporary theorists in the fields of sociology and discourse analysis. In pursuing this method, a rigorous distinction must be drawn between the influence of rhythmic science on Joyce's *aesthetic theory* and our contemporary interpretation of his *stylistic practice*. As we will see, the performance of a speech-act in the context of dialogue involves the appearance of "openings" which must be immediately filled if the speaker is to assume his or her place in the interaction (Sacks and Jefferson 1974). In order to fill an "opening," the speaker must anticipate the underlying rhythm of the dialogue and understand the social dynamics that regulate the taking of turns in the conversation. By analyzing delays and gaps in the drama of Joyce's dialogue, we can begin to analyze the points at which social interaction begins to break down, points of silence that symptomatically reveal the causes of social dysfunction that has led to the so-called paralysis of Dublin society in the early twentieth century.

We know from Joyce's "epiphanies" that he recorded fragments of dialogue, but it is also clear that he incorporated a family tradition of storytelling into many of his fictional works. While Joyce was still studying at Belvedere, his family rented a Victorian terrace in North Richmond Street, and it is during this time that John Stanislaus used to take his sons on long walks through the city, expeditions punctuated by anecdotes and stories associated with local Dublin places. According to Jackson and Costello,

> These long walks led to James' own habit of walking the streets, either alone or with a friend or one of his brothers. He had discovered (thanks to his father) that the activity of a *flâneur* could be both cheap and stimulating. These pedestrian whorls laid down the foundations for the recreation of the city in his work. At the same time he was hearing from his father about the buildings, the characters and their histories: stories of public executions, private revenges, and musical and literary greatness achieved in an improbably turbulent history. (1997, 201)

Here we can see that the synchronic activity of transcribing conversations is accompanied by a diachronic history of Dublin folklore that selects fragments of conversations and reproduces them with a surrounding narrative. While John Stanislaus Joyce must have authored many of the anecdotes reproduced in *Dubliners* and *Ulysses*, it is also evident that he was also the protagonist in some of these stories. Indeed, the story of Tom Kernan being found unconscious in "Grace" seems to have been inspired by an actual incident in which the drunken John Stanislaus fell down a flight of stairs at Jon Nolan's public house in Harry Street. According to Richard Ellmann, Joyce primarily modeled Kernan on the figure of Ned Thornton, a teataster who lived in the same neighborhood of Dublin (*JJ*, 43); yet, the story of his father's fall provides the pivotal incident in the narrative. While the fictional character is rescued by a benevolent constable named Power—who shows some "grace" toward the disgraceful behavior of his drunken friend—John Stanislaus was apparently rescued by Tom Devin, "an official in the Dublin Corporation Cleansing department on Wood Quay" (Jackson and Costello 1997, 199).

While the story of John's fall must have circulated around the pubs of Dublin, the actual dialogue in "Grace" was inspired by a real conversation that Stanislaus recorded in his Dublin diary. In the fictional story, a group of Catholic businessmen convince Tom Kernan to attend a retreat at a church in Purdon Street, a venue at which they propose to "wash the pot" (a euphemism for absolution). Once again, Joyce parodies the middle-class aspirations of his Catholic subjects, for by treating the act of confession as a form of monetary exchange, Cunningham, Power, McCoy, and Kernan appear to be indistinguishable from the "Orangemen" they so despise. While Kernan agrees to attend the sermon to maintain his status as a gentleman, he nevertheless maintains a degree of symbolic defiance toward the business of cleansing the soul, for he refuses in advance to light any candles, stating that "I bar the candles." In the version of the conversation recorded by Stannie (Stanislaus), it can be seen from the stage directions that "Pappie" (John Stanislaus) was "very drunk," and this perhaps explains his tendency to repeat phrases, filling the beats of dialogue with expressions that add little or no meaning:

CHANCE: Holy communion on Sunday morning and then at half to go to renew baptismal vows. They'll give you candles—and then all together we'll—

PAPPIE: (very drunk): Oh, I bár the candles, I bár the candles! I'll do the óther job alright, but I bár the candles.

CHANCE: Oh, that'll do all right—only a formality—but what hour'll we call for you tomorrow night to go to confession? Matt Boyd and myself are going at half seven.

PAPPIE: Oh, I don't know. I don't know—I'll—Well, call at half seven then. Will that suit you?

CHANCE: Splendidly. And you'll come then.

PAPPIE: Oh yes! Oh yes! Old fellow, I'll go, never you fear, I'll go— Can you go to whoever you like?

CHANCE: Oh yes! They've all equal power, all the same.

PAPPIE: I don't mind you know. I don't mind you know. I don't care. I'd go to the first telleh that's open. I haven't got much to tell him, you know. D'you think I have much to tell him?

MOTHER: I do. God forbid I had as much.

CHANCE: Oh, that's not the point.
MOTHER: Oh no! That's not the point of course.
CHANCE: It doesn't matter how much you have to tell him, it'll be all
    wiped off; you'll have a clean sheet.
PAPPIE: I don't mind, you know. I'd go in to the first bloody felleh
    that's open and have a little chat with him. (cited in Jackson and
    Costello 1997, 252)

Thanks to Stannie's attention to detail, we have a fairly good record
of John Stanislaus's conversational style. While the repetition of formulaic phrases establishes the rhythm of the social interaction—each
"bar" actualizing an underlying beat—it also works to differentiate
the idiolect of "Pappie" from the other speakers. Indeed, the transcription of the word "fellow" as "felleh" serves to mark the colloquial
nature of his speech, and serves to undermine the authority tradi-
tionally associated with the figure of a Catholic priest. By inserting
the adjective "bloody" in the second version of this formula, Pappie
alters the position of the primary accent, and thereby asserts his own
authority at the very moment of his subordination to the moral law.
While Pappie simulates an eagerness to confess, his moral uncertainty
is reflected by the virtual conversation that he holds with himself:
"I haven't got much to tell him, you know. D'you think I have much
to tell him?" Here we can see that the rhythm of the statement dictates the form of the rejoinder, establishing a higher order pattern of
call and response. In responding to this question, Charlie Chance
employs the same formula, adding "It doesn't matter how much you
have to tell him, it'll be all wiped off; you'll have a clean sheet." It
seems that this statement inspired the comparison between business
and religion in "Grace," for the Priest in Joyce's short story closes
with the moral direction that "I have looked into my accounts. I find
this wrong and this wrong. But, with God's grace, I will rectify this
and this. I will set right my accounts" (D, 174).

While the fragments of conversation recorded by Joyce and his
brother Stannie are remarkable for their fidelity to the transcription
of coordinating expressions and idiolectical features (properties that
allow us to infer the position of the rhetorical accents and the beats
of the dialogue), we can use some of the theoretical insights from
the field of sociolinguistics to explain the role which rhythm plays in
the coordination of communicative action. Based on a study of college
interviews, Erickson and Shultz (1982) have argued that the performance of social roles and the construction of personal identity depend
on the coordination and synchronization of the speakers' utterances

and gestures to the beat of the social interaction. For Erickson and Shultz, rhythm plays a constitutive role in establishing the temporal framework for an interaction, because

> communicative action occurs in a particular moment of actual time, in particular relationships of simultaneity and sequence. These relationships in time, taken together, constitute a regular rhythmic pattern. This regularity in time and timing seems to play an essential, constitutive role in the social organization of interaction. (72)

In the context of the interaction, Erickson and Schultz make a distinction between actions that occur simultaneously (complementarity) and those that occur across turns (reciprocity). With regard to the latter, they point out that:

> Reciprocity refers to the interdependence of actions taken successively across moments in time. One party takes action in account of what another party has just done, and then in the next moment another party takes account of what was done the moment before. (71)

As it can be seen from this definition, the rhythm of dialogue does not necessarily depend upon the duration of the syllables or the periods of prose, but rather upon a slower beat that regulates the exchange of turns. If the alternation does not occur within the rhythm of the interaction, it will often be supplied by gestures, or the speaker will reiterate the point he has just made, paraphrasing for clarification. The category of complementarity, on the other hand, refers to "the interdependence of actions taken simultaneously in the same moment" (71). According to this dimension of the analysis, the gestures and intonation patterns of the speaker can be used to measure the degree of attention and coordination, for "the synchrony among conversationalists seems not to be a matter of stimulus-response organization at microsecond intervals, but of mutual entrainment of all conversational partners within an overall pattern of rhythm" (72). When seeking to apply these categories to the analysis of literary text, it ought to be recognized that the dimension of complementarity is much easier to discern, for it can be assumed that the rhythmic form of the conversation extends for the duration of the reported dialogue. The dimension of simultaneity, on the other hand, can only be described through the inclusion of prose passages (or stage directions) that describe how characters react to the speech-acts of their interlocutors. Nevertheless, these two dimensions provide a spatial–temporal framework to analyze the coordination of turn-taking and the mutual entrainment of the speakers to the underlying pulse of the dialogue.

Erickson and Shultz also make a useful distinction between *kairos* and *chronos* that will allow us to distinguish between the tension of the narrative and the recurring beats of the dialogue. On the one hand, *kairos* (a Greek term borrowed from the New Testament) refers to the "right time" to perform an action, which in the context of communication refers to either the performance of a speech-act or a gesture. The "right time" is not necessarily governed by the rhythm of the interaction, but rather by the logic of the routine or narrative that is being performed. The authors clarify that "the *kairos* organization of discourse defines relationships of appropriateness in sequencing at various hierarchical levels, from pairs of adjacent utterances to pairs of adjacent discourse topics" (73). The meaning of the "right time" is not determined by any quantitative duration, but rather simply by the temporal categories of now, not quite yet, too late, which means that the dimension of *kairos* is simply a matter of causal relationships, referring to the logic of a routine or narrative. On the other hand, *chronos* refers to the continuous duration of the conversation, is measurable by clock-time, and features a regular rhythm in both the speech-acts of the participants and the exchange of turns. In the case of rhythmic alternation, the time of call and response is determined by both *kairos* and *chronos*, for the moment of interchange is determined by both the logic of the narrative and the pulse of the conversation: "When conversation takes place there are rhythmic cycles and wave patterns in verbal and non-verbal behavior that are both intuitively apparent and mechanically measurable. These are durations in *chronos* time" (74). If the chronometric beat of the conversation remains unfilled, then it is usually caused by a disruption to the logical sequence of the narrative. As a consequence, any pause in the conversation must be interpreted as a chronological symptom of a social dysfunction that is revealed at the deeper level of the narrative.

We can apply the concept of *kairos* time to the analysis of the narrative in "Grace," for as the title of Joyce's story suggests, the dialogue is regulated by the convention of "grace" that allows each speaker the "right" amount of time to repay his debts. At the beginning of the story, Mr Kernan is found in the lavatory of a bar, with his eyes closed, and a "thin stream of blood" (D, 150) trickling from his mouth. When the man is brought to the floor of the bar, a young policeman asks the crowd of observers the name and address of the unknown man, and finally revives Kernan by calling for some brandy. Due to Kernan's anonymity and recklessness, he might easily have been arrested by the policeman, but he is saved at the list minute by the appearance of Mr Power, a senior constable with the Royal Irish Constabulary. In deference to his senior officer, the young policeman taps his hat, a gesture which makes clear the significance of the favor that Power has granted Kernan. Due to this act of "grace" on the part of the policeman, Kernan is now in a state of spiritual "debt" toward Power, and this sense of "debt" is only increased on his arrival home, for his wife has nothing to offer the constable in the way of drink. Shifting the blame to the alcoholism of her husband, Mrs Kernan tells Power that: "We were waiting for him to come home with the money. He never seems to think he has a home at all" (*D*, 155). Not only does Kernan owe Power a "debt" for rescuing him from the law, he also owes his wife a "debt" for spending his wages on drink. When questioned by the lawyer, Martin Cunningham, Kernan confesses that he had been drinking with a moneylender named Harford. Although the latter is a Catholic, it is revealed that he is in partnership with Mr Goldberg from the Liffey Loan Bank, and these Jewish associations are reinforced by the description of the narrator:

> Though he had never embraced more than the Jewish ethical code, his fellow-Catholics, whenever they smarted in person or by proxy under exactions, spoke to him bitterly as an Irish Jew and an illiterate, and saw divine disapproval of usury made manifest through the person of his idiot son. (*D*, 159)

From this account, it becomes probable that Harford was seeking the repayment of a loan. When the sum was not forthcoming—presumably because Kernan had spent his wages on stout—Harford administered some form of physical punishment, either in "person" or "by proxy."[4] Kernan's injury has therefore been caused by Harford's lack of "grace" toward him, an unwillingness to grant the man some time to repay his debts. In contrast to the Usurer, the solidarity of the Catholic men is guaranteed by their willingness to grant their friends some grace.

While the Catholic men appear to visit Kernan's house for the purposes of reforming his drunken behavior, it is clear that the solidarity of the group depends on the ritual of drinking rounds, for it is only by simulating a visit to the pub that they can convince Kernan to attend Father Burke's sermon. As Kernan has fallen from grace, and damaged his tongue, he is initially barred from the conversation, and his social exclusion is reinforced by the fact that his wife does not offer him a drink ("Nothing for poor little hubby"). While the other men are drinking freely, they establish a dialogue that alludes to a prior arrangement, a discussion that remains concealed from Kernan, who is effectively a spectator to the dialogue:

C:	On	/ Thursday night, you said
		/ Jack
P:		/ Thursday,
		/ yes.
C:		/ Righto!"
M:	We can meet in	/ McAuley's.
		/ That'll be the most con-
		/ venient place.
P:	But we mustn't be	/ late, because it is
		/ sure to be crammed to the
		/ doors.
M:	We can	/ meet at
		/ half seven,
C:		/ Righto! …
		/ Half seven at
		/ M'Auley's be it![5] (*D*, 162)

By transcribing the dialogue in this manner, I have marked the beats of the conversation, each hyphen indicating the beginning of a period and the position of the underlying pulse. While there is some uncertainty as to the position of the rhetorical accents, the repetition of certain phrases allows a pattern to be established, and the pragmatic function of each speech-act allows a judgment to be made. In the first instance, Power's "Thursday" responds directly to Cunningham's proposal, which in turn points back to a prior agreement ("Thursday night, you said Jack"). The first two utterances taken together constitute a unit of dialogical interaction. In the terminology of Harvey Sacks, the arrangement of two utterances next to each other, with an alternation of speakers, constitutes an "adjacency pair" (Sacks 1995, 521–33). The basic form of adjacency pair is the exchange of question and answer, but in principle, any statement made by a speaker calls for acceptance or denial on the part of the listener. When McCoy proposes that "We can meet at M'Auley's," his statement is supplemented by a reason ("that'll be the most convenient place"), and the use of two accents calls out for a rejoinder with a similar rhythmic form: "We mustn't be late, because it is sure to be crammed to the doors." In both of these interactions, we can see that there is an element of symmetry between statement and rejoinder, a form of equivalence that is reflected in both the periods of prose and the beat of the dialogue.

In order to mark their participation in the dialogue, each speaker marks an affirmation at the right moment, with Cunningham using the expression "righto" to take his place in the conversation, affirming the solidarity of the group and the consensus of the speakers. Just as Kernan remains excluded from the round of drinks, so does he remain silent during this initial phase of the conversation. Despite the triviality of the utterances, and the free substitution of positions in the dialogue—the time and place is repeated by McCoy and Cunningham in virtually the same words—Kernan is excluded from the plan, and this dramatic situation symbolizes his temporary exclusion from the respectable society of the Catholic middle classes. It is therefore only after a considerable silence that he enters the conversation: "There was a short silence. Mr Kernan waited to see whether he would be taken into his friend's confidence. Then he asked: What's in the wind?" (*D*, 162). From Joyce's prose description, we can see that the complementarity of the dialogue has broken down, for there is no longer a regular exchange of turns. As Kernan does not know the underlying meaning of the conversation, he does not feel capable of interrupting the conversation at the right time, and this is why he waits for the rhythmic pulse to pass away.[6] When Cunningham begins to reveal the meaning of the prior agreement, Joyce inserts an ellipse to mark his hesitation, the unrealized beat marking a point of dramatic reversal at the heart of the dialogue: "No, no, said Mr Cunningham, in an evasive tone, it's just a little … spiritual matter" (*D*, 162). In many ways, the dramatic suspense before the word "spiritual" reveals the meaning of the hoax. When Cunningham begins to say "spiritual," Kernan may have interpreted the sound of the word as "spirits." Indeed, it appears that the men have engaged in a highly scripted dialogue designed to arouse Kernan's interest in the appointment. As the form of the dialogue resembles a ritualized agreement to meet at a Dublin bar, Kernan desires to be included, but as the content is concealed from him, and in fact refers to a sermon to be held at the Jesuit Church in Gardiner Street, Kernan has been deceived into attending the retreat.

The ritualized dialogue between the men therefore appears as a highly scripted "drama" designed to persuade Kernan to attend a Catholic retreat with them. Once the fiction has been established—the substitution of "spirits" for "spiritual matters"—Cunningham introduces a metaphor for absolution, the euphemism "wash the pot" alluding to the periodic cleansing of the soul (as if the soul were a glass of porter). The proverb is a shibboleth for the drinkers who are to attend the retreat, and therefore works to secure consensus: "Yes, that's it, …

Jack and I and McCoy here—we're all going to wash the pot" (*D*, 163).
When seeking the conscription of the men to the ritual of washing the
pot, the repetition of the phrase "own up" is distributed among speakers in order to realize the underlying beat of the dialogue:

> C: You see, we may as well
>   all admit we're a nice
>   collection of scoundrels,
>   / one and all. I say,
>   / one and all
>   / (*turns to Power*)
>   / Own up now!
> P: / I own up.
> M: And   / I own up,
> C: / So we're going to
>   / wash the pot to-
>   / gether, (*D*, 163)

With the affirmation of his initial proposal with a slightly different
point of emphasis ("we're áll going to wash the pot" / "so we're going
to wash the pot togéther"), Cunningham marks the beginning and
end of the sequence, and secures the consensus of the group. While
the four men have agreed to "wash the pot," Kernan still remains
excluded from the group, for as the narrator puts it, "Mr Kernan was
silent. The proposal conveyed very little meaning to his mind ... He
took no part in the conversation for a long while, but listened, with an
air of calm enmity, while his friends discussed the Jesuits" (*D*, 163).
Indeed, the significance of the Catholic retreat remains concealed
from Kernan until he can relate the form of the sermon to the content
of his personal experience. Indeed, Kernan only enters the dialogue
when he recognizes the name of Father Burke, but he still remains
hesitant: "I heard him once, I forget the subject of his discourse now.
Crofton and I were in the back of the ... pit, you know ... the—" (*D*,
165). While Kernan can now anticipate the beat of the dialogue, he
lacks the vocabulary to continue his train of thought, the word "pit"
indicating a dramatic rather than a religious space. By inserting the
word "body" into the gap of the dialogue, Cunningham completes
the utterance of his friend, and reintroduces Kernan into the circle of
the conversation. When Kernan finally strings a number of phrases
together, it is significant that he dwells on the subject of oratory, for
his own speech possesses a continuity that it previously lacked:

> Yes, in the back near the door. I forget now what ... O yes, it was
> on the Pope, the late Pope. I remember it well. Upon my word it was

magnificent, the style of the oratory. And his voice! God! hadn't he a voice! The Prisoner of the Vatican, he called him." (*D*, 165)

At the moment when Kernan is accepted into a respectable society, he immediately makes a wrong move, because he cites a Protestant as the source of his knowledge on Catholicism. When he begins an anecdote with the words, "I remember Crofton saying to me when we came out—," he is immediately interrupted by Power, who asserts, "But he's an Orangemen, Crofton, isn't he?" (*D*, 165). By taking the floor of the conversation, precisely at a moment in which it has been claimed by another person, Power is in fact disputing the right of Kernan to speak at all, for he has cited an authority outside the circle of the conversation. Nevertheless, the discourse of this "Orangemen" provides an opportunity for bridging the differences between Protestants and Catholics, a difference that is overcome by their common identification as businessmen. When Kernan cites Crofton's assertion that "we worship at different altars ... but our belief is the same" (*D*, 165), he introduces a proposition that asserts the symbolic equality of all members of the middle classes, Catholic and Protestant alike. In the current context, however, this equality is performed through the ritual of drinking rounds, and the acceptance of Kernan back into a respectable society is announced with the entry of Fogarty, who is described by the narrators as bearing a "certain grace." While this description initially refers to his demeanour, it is soon embodied in a gift that reveals the material basis on which the solidarity of the group is formed:

Mr. Fogarty brought a gift with him, a half-pint of special whisky. He inquired politely for Mr. Kernan, placed his gift on the table and sat down with the company on equal terms. Mr. Kernan appreciated the gift all the more since he was aware that there was a small account for groceries unsettled between him and Mr. Fogarty. (*D*, 166)

Despite the fact that Fogarty has gone out of businesses as a publican, he has nevertheless granted his friend some "grace" in the repayment of his debts. As Fogarty is willing to share his whisky with the other men, he sits down on "equal terms," and this social contract reveals a complex economy of "grace" and "debt" that regulates the exchange of favors and establishes the solidarity of the group. Indeed, the identity of the social group is based upon the common exchange of liquor, a gift economy that allows for the deferred repayment of symbolic obligations. As the conversation of the men is always accompanied by a round of drinks ("Glasses were rinsed and five small measures of whisky were poured out. This new influence enlivened the conversation"; *D*, 166), the symbolic "equality" of the men is the precondition for them participating in the dialogue.

In the final exchanges, Joyce emphasizes the rhythmic pulse of the conversation through the repetition of a pseudo-Latin "motto" that is falsely attributed to Pope Leo XIII. Misquoting the Latin phrase *Lumen in coelo* ("Light in Heaven"), Cunningham mixes Latin diction with English syntax to create a rhythmic motif (*Lux upon Lux*—"Light upon Light"; *D*, 167) in the form of a classical choriamb. According to Fogarty, however, the supposed "motto" was *Lux in Tenebris* ("Light in Shadow"; *D*, 167), an oxymoronic phrase used by the Apostle John (1:5) to illustrate the ignorance of nonbelievers. Despite the ignorance of the men, the choriambic rhythm of the original motif persists throughout the course of the interaction, for when predicated of Pope Pius, the motto is subsequently modified by Cunningham to *Crux upon Crux* ("Cross upon Cross"; *D*, 167). Indeed, by repeating this rhythmic motif in the mouths of Cunningham, Fogarty, and McCoy, Joyce establishes a classical meter that intersects with the beats of dialogue, each choriamb constituting a period of the conversation. For the remainder of the dialogue, Latin phrases such as *ex cathedra* and *Credo* function as rhythmic motifs that maintain the pulse of the conversation and reveal the ignorance of the speakers. Ironically alluding to the structural rhythm that emerges from the correspondence between these metrical phrases, Joyce presents the speakers discussing Pope Leo's poem on the invention of the photograph, a modern machine that suspends the movement of the body as a momentary gesture.

By analyzing these exchanges, and the way in which the rhythmic pulse distributes the turns of speakers, we have seen that Kernan finds it difficult to time his interventions and maintain the pulse of the dialogue. This can be seen as a symptom of his exclusion from the circle of conversation and the economy of debt and grace that determines the "right" time to make an assertion. Until the end of the dialogue, Kernan is a reluctant convert, and his solidarity is assured only through the symbolic rejection of bearing a "candle" at the retreat, a gesture that he is only attending ironically—that is to say, for the sake of conformity. Note how he expresses this resistance, and how his speech regains its rhetorical force after a moment of hesitation:

> No damn it all, ... I draw the line there. I'll do the job right enough. I'll do the retreat business and confession, and ... all that business. But ... no candles. No damn it all, I bar the candles. (*D*, 171)

Here, Joyce marks the presence of an epiphany by his use of ellipses. The double meaning of the word "bar," as both prohibition and public house, makes it clear that Kernan is maintaining his defiance in the very act of conformity. Indeed, the continuous rhythm of his utterance is only restored through an act of blasphemy, exclaiming "damn it all." Furthermore, the act of resistance becomes a refrain at the end of his speech, saying once again that "I bar the candles," and then more vehemently, "I bar the magic lantern business" (*D*, 171). At the end of the dialogue, therefore, we can see that although Kernan has submitted to the rhythm of the conversation, he has nevertheless maintained a form of symbolic resistance that is manifested through the ambiguity of his final gesture.

Cycles of History in "Ivy Day"

Although many of the stories in *Dubliners* contain extended sections of dialogue, most are surrounded by a narrative and are designed to reveal the personality of specific characters or the dramatic significance of particular events. By contrast, "Ivy Day in the Committee Room" can be interpreted as a one-act play, for, with the exception of the opening paragraphs that establish the setting of the story (and can perhaps be read as stage-directions), most of the action consists of a dialogue between a group of Irish Nationalists who are canvassing votes in the council elections, and debating the proper manner in which to commemorate the death of the Irish parliamentary leader, Charles Stewart Parnell. Indeed, as the play is staged on "Ivy Day," an event instituted to commemorate the death of the controversial Irish leader (October 6, 1891), Joyce demonstrates how even the most insignificant fragments of dialogue can participate in the performance of public rituals that embody the recurring cycles of history, expressing the spirit of the political community.[7] Rather than creating a mythic parallel to explain the epic significance of everyday events—a technique that leads to the modernist separation of a transhistorical culture from the finite consciousness of the historical actors—Joyce attempts to show how dramatic forms can spontaneously emerge in the context of everyday life. While each speaker in the conversation contributes to the so-called rhythm of the dialogue, an underlying pulse that serves to structure the social interaction and coordinate the turns of different speakers, Joyce constructs the dialogue in such a manner that the structural unity of the whole begins to emerge. Without the three-act structure of classical drama at his disposal,

Joyce chooses to foreground the performance of a eulogy at the end of the play ("The Death of Parnell"), allowing the underlying rhythm of the dialogue to provide the pulse for a poem that synthesizes the perspectives of the various characters. As this poem draws on popular mythology and contains a number of clichés, it should not be interpreted as the authentic expression of the author himself, but rather as the symbolic expression of the will of the political community. In this way, Joyce attempts to show that the recitation of poetry can be linked to the performance of public rituals that reveal the spontaneous emergence of rhythmic forms in everyday life.

The title of the short story, "Ivy Day in the Committee Room," contains allusions to two significant historical events, and their combination within a single phrase has the effect of superimposing one upon the other. The first of these, "Ivy Day," refers to the annual procession of Dublinites to Glasnevin cemetery on October 8, a public ritual instituted to reenact the work of mourning begun on the day of his funeral (October 8, 1891). The second, "the Committee Room," refers to the protracted debates that took place between members of the Irish Parliamentary Party in December of 1890, at "Committee Room 15" in the British House of Commons. During these debates, which were published in *The Freeman's Journal* on a daily basis, Parnell eventually lost the chairmanship of the party to Justin McCarthy, and was subjected to a number of personal insults by his former protégé, Tim Healy. While most of the discussions were centered around the contradiction between the institutional independence of the Irish party from the Liberals (an argument stressed by Parnell, who rebuked Gladstone for interfering with Irish politics) and the strategic dependence of the Irish party upon the Liberals to pass the Home Rule Bill (stressed by Healy), it was ultimately the divorce scandal surrounding the leader's affair with Kitty O'Shea that caused the rift between Parnell and Gladstone, a rift that was exploited by Healy to ensure that the party split between those supporting and those opposing Parnell (Lyons 1960, 132). By creating a historical parallel between "Committee Room 15" and the "Committee Room" in Wicklow Street, where a number of canvassers working for candidates in the 1903 municipal elections meet to commemorate "Ivy Day,"[8] Joyce symbolically fuses the stage of Parnell's political downfall with the event of his death, thereby creating an "historical drama" that is enacted and reenacted through the form of a public ritual.

The ritual of commemorating Ivy Day is foregrounded at the beginning of the short story, when Mat O'Connor illuminates an Ivy Leaf on his lapel while lighting a cigarette with one of Tierney's "pasteboard cards." In the words of the narrator, "Mr O'Connor tore a strip off the card and, lighting it, lit his cigarette. As he did so the flame lit up a leaf of dark glossy ivy in the lapel of his coat" (*D*, 119). As Anne Fogarty has pointed out, the ritual of commemorating Ivy Day usually involved a public procession to Parnell's grave at Glasnevin cemetery. The symbolism of the Ivy Leaf derives from the first anniversary of his death, when mourners apparently picked twigs and bushes from around his grave as tokens or souvenirs of the event (Fogarty 2006, 110). At various times during the 1890s, the act of wearing an Ivy Leaf was associated with both the Parnellite and anti-Parnellite movements; yet, in this context, the act of wearing the leaf should be interpreted as a gesture of solidarity toward the Home Rule movement, because the Irish party had been reunited under the leadership of John Redmond in 1900. We know that the events in Joyce's story are supposed to take place in 1902, because they precede the visit of King Edward in 1903, and it is precisely the issue of receiving or rejecting the English King that determines whether or not the Nationalists are remaining faithful to the spirit of Parnell (Fairhall 1988, 290). Indeed, after voicing his opposition to the Royal visit, Hynes points to the Ivy Leaf on his hat, and says "If this man was alive ... we'd have no talk of an address of welcome" (*D*, 122). In response, O'Connor simply says "That's true." But the old caretaker is more enthusiastic, voicing in his Dublin accent, "Musha, God be with them times! ... There was some life in it then" (*D*, 122). From the early exchanges of the dialogue, therefore, we can conclude that the symbolic act of wearing an Ivy Leaf provides a source of consensus between the Nationalists, a symbol of identification with Parnell that also implies a rejection of British sovereignty.

Throughout the course of Joyce's dialogue, his characters perform actions that are motivated by the current of energy moving through the play as a whole. In the opening paragraph of the story, Joyce describes the actions of the old caretaker, Jack, who stokes the fire with a rhythmical movement:

Old Jack raked the cinders together with a piece of cardboard and spread them judiciously over the whitening dome of coals. When the dome was thinly covered his face lapsed into darkness but, as he set himself to fan the fire again, his crouching shadow ascended the opposite wall and his face slowly re-emerged in the light. (*D*, 118)

By describing the old man as "crouching," Joyce shows that the old man is involved in the performance of an action that is supposed to continue for the duration of the play. Indeed, as the weather is inclement, and the canvassers can no longer walk the streets, knocking on

doors to secure the support of voters, the maintenance of this fire provides the material conditions in which the spiritual dialogue of the canvassers can unfold. The contrast between the material and the spiritual
(outer and inner) aspects of the scene is symbolized by the difference
between the actions of the caretaker and his shadow upon the wall, a
possible allusion to the myth of the cave in Plato's *Republic*. Although
the canvassers are supposed to be earning their wages by persuading
potential voters, they are in fact engaged in a leisure activity that relies
on the resources of their employer (Richard Tierney) and the labor of
the caretaker. As we will see, the council elections of 1902 involved
the systematic bribery of the electorate that was promised free booze
in exchange for votes. Toward the end of the dialogue, one of Tierney's
agents delivers a dozen of stout that he has promised the canvassers in
exchange for their so-called labor. As there is no corkscrew in hand,
Henchy suggests that they place each bottle of stout near the fire, relying on the expanding liquid to force open the bottle. Here we can see
that the energy of the fire is responsible for both increasing the "tension" of the dramatic situation and releasing it, for when the pressure
reaches a certain point, the lid is sent flying off with a loud "pock." In
the final third of the dialogue, these "pocks" become more frequent,
anticipating the resolution of the conflict and the rhythm of Joe Hynes's
poem. By moving from the actions of the caretaker to the dialogue of
the canvassers, and finally the poetic performance of Joe Hynes, Joyce
relates the rhythm of the action to the beats of the dialogue, and compares the structure of the play to the metrical organization of verse.[9]

The tension of the dramatic situation is related to the set of obligations that regulate the contractual relations between the council
candidate and his canvassers. Just as the Nationalists need to perform
the role of the faithful mourner, identifying with Parnell through the
wearing of an Ivy Leaf, so does Richard Tierney have to deliver on
his promise to pay the canvassers' wages. As Mr O'Connor puts it,
"I hope to God he'll not leave us in the lurch tonight" (*D*, 117). Until
the dozen of stout arrives halfway through the dialogue, this promise remains unfulfilled, and remains a source of dramatic tension.
Assuming Tierney to be a middle-class businessman, the canvassers
believe that he will deliver on his promise. On the other hand, they
do not believe that the Socialist candidate can be trusted, an assertion
that provokes the following response from Hynes:

It is because Colgan's a working-man you say that? What's the difference between a good honest bricklayer and a publican-eh? Hasn't the
wórking-man as good a right to be in the Corporation as anyone else-ay,

and a better right than those shóneens that are always hat in hand before any fellow with a handle to his name? Isn't that so, Mat? (*D*, 121)

According to James Fairhall, Joyce modeled the Socialist candidate, Colgan, on the historical figure of James Connolly, who founded the Irish Socialist Republican Party (ISRP) in 1896 (1988, 293).[10] Although Colgan does not appear in the dialogue, his political views are represented by Joe Hynes, whose idiolect is represented by the repetition of the phrase "working-man." In contrast to the exchanges of dialogue that precede this political rhetoric, Hynes creates a stream of speech by responding to his own statements, instituting a rhythm of call and response that persists for a number of periods. By responding to himself with the simulated affirmations "eh" and "ay," Hynes effectively occupies the position of the interlocutor, and actualizes the beats that would have enabled another speaker to take the floor. By stressing Hynes's use of syntactic inversions ("It is") and Hiberno-Irish ("Shoneen"), Joyce marks the authenticity of Hynes's Dublin accent, an impression that is reinforced by the assonance between "hat" and the "handle," a local proverb that symbolizes the class antagonism between the Nationalists and the Socialists.

In contrast to Hynes, who begins the dialogue as an outsider, and must establish the "working-man" as the legitimate subject of political debate, Henchy is an insider who claims an intimate knowledge of his employer and the electorate as a whole. As soon as the former leaves the room, the latter enters, marking a shift in the pace and tempo of the dialogue. From the initial exchange between Henchy and Mat O'Connor, it is clear that the former is the more senior of the canvassers, for each of his questions calls for an immediate response:

— Did you serve Aungier Street? he asked Mr. O'Connor.
— Yes, said Mr. O'Connor, beginning to search his pockets for memoranda.
— Did you call on Grimes?
— I did.
— Well? How does he stand?
— He wouldn't promise. He said: *I won't tell anyone what way I'm going to vote.* But I think he'll be all right.
— Why so?
— He asked me who the nominators were; and I told him. I mentioned Father Burke's name. I think it'll be all right. (*D*, 122–3)

As can be seen from the order of questions, Henchy moves from the general to the particular, calling upon his interlocutor to give more and more specific information. As O'Connor is unwilling to give an account of his labor, or his ability to persuade voters, he responds with one-word statements, simply conforming to the exchange of turns and the pulse of the dialogue. As it can be seen from his eventual answer, the canvassers must report the content of their conversations in the form of a narrative to demonstrate the utility of their labor. From a dramatic perspective, the relating of anecdotes serves an important narrative function in "Ivy Day," for not only does it give us a panoramic view of Dublin from the committee room in Wicklow Street, but it also provides the agents with an opportunity to prove the value of their labor. As the dialogue unfolds, the external form of the dialogue becomes more and more introspective, for Henchy begins to deliver long speeches that contain stretches of reported dialogue.

A dramatic shift is marked when the phrase "Tricky Dicky Tierney" becomes the refrain by which the canvassers begin to refer to the Nationalist candidate, Richard Tierney. In the first instance, Henchy reports Tierney's promise to pay his canvassers in booze for their labor. Recognizing the corruption at the heart of his election campaign, Hynes labels him "Tricky Dicky Tierny." The rhythm of this refrain leads to the construction of a longer speech in which the deception of the politician becomes more manifest:

> Did you never hear that? And the men used to go in on Sunday morning before the houses were open to buy a waistcoat or a trousers-moya! But Tricky Dicky's little old father always had a tricky little black bottle up in a corner. Do you mind now? That's that. That's where he first saw the light. (*D*, 123)

Once again, Henchy simulates the periods of dialogue in order to maintain the floor for an extended duration. While rhetorical questions work to secure the consensus of his listeners in advance ("Did you never hear that?" / "Do you mind now?"), affirmations are used to reiterate the force of his argument ("moya!" / "that's that"). Each element actualizes a pulse of the dialogue and serves to heighten the rhetorical impact of the speech. Indeed, it is this story that reveals the cause of the conspiracy in "Ivy Day," for it soon becomes clear that Richard Tierney is the owner of a public bar called "Kavanagh's," and is supplying free alcohol to his patrons in exchange for their vote in the coming elections. As Jackson and Costello (1997, 246) have suggested, Richard Tierney was modeled on the historical figure of Richard Cummin, who was elected to the local office but subsequently dismissed for corruption, being convicted of bribing voters with drink under the Corrupt Practices Act of 1873. While this form of persuasion was seen as corruption in British Law, Tierney's canvassers see this as a legitimate way to do business, all expecting to be paid in stout for securing votes. From a dramatic perspective, it is the contract between Tierney and his canvassers that sustains the unfolding action, because it is only the promise of booze that motivates the characters to participate in the dialogue. Later in the play, the dramatic tension caused by this illegal conspiracy is relieved by the appearance of Father Keon, who is comically mistaken for a "dozen of stout."

Henchy's final speeches reveal the extent to which the Home Rule movement has become corrupted by the dependence of Ireland on British capital. Having received the promised stout, Henchy feels the need to prove the value of his labor, and this is achieved by relating anecdotes demonstrating his rhetorical skill. It is significant that he stresses Tierney's status as a Landlord, for it shows the extent to which the voters of the Catholic middle classes aspired to become like their Protestant predecessors:

— Well, I got Parkes for one, and I got Atkinson for two, and got Ward of Dawson Street. Fine old chap he is, too-regular old toff, old Conservative! 'But isn't your candidate a Nationalist?' said he. 'He's a respectable man,' said I. 'He's in favour of whatever will benefit this country. He's a big ratepayer,' I said. 'He has extensive house property in the city and three places of business and isn't it to his own advantage to keep down the rates? He's a prominent and respected citizen,' said I, 'and a Poor Law Guardian, and he doesn't belong to any party, good, bad, or indifferent.' That's the way to talk to 'em.

— And what about the address to the King? said Mr. Lyons, after drinking and smacking his lips.

— Listen to me, said Mr. Henchy. What we want in this country, as I said to old Ward, is capital. The King's coming here will mean an influx of money into this country. The citizens of Dublin will benefit by it. Look at all the factories down by the quays there, idle! Look at all the money there is in the country if we only worked the old industries, the mills, the ship-building yards and factories. It's capital we want.

— But look here, John, said Mr. O'Connor. Why should we welcome the King of England? Didn't Parnell himself ...

— Parnell, said Mr. Henchy, is dead. Now, here's the way I look at it. Here's this chap come to the throne after his old mother keeping him out of it till the man was grey. He's a man of the world, and he means well by us. He's a jolly fine decent fellow, if you ask me, and no damn nonsense about him. He just says to himself: 'The old one never went to see these wild Irish. By Christ, I'll go myself and see what they're like.' And are we going to insult the man when he comes over here on a friendly visit? Eh? Isn't that right, Crofton? (*D*, 131–2)

In his first speech, Henchy begins with a catalogue of the citizens he has persuaded, placing rhetorical accents on "one" and "two." Resembling an oral poet in his use of formulaic phrases, Henchy modifies the same basic sentence ("I got X for Y") to compose his list of supporters. Reflecting on the conservative character of Ward, Henchy composes a number of epithets each of which actualizes a beat of the dialogue, "Fine old chap he is, too—regular old toff, old Conservative." By shifting from the formal style of political rhetoric to the colloquial style of recounting anecdotes, Henchy alters the rhythm of his speech to appeal to different audiences (see Gumperz 1982, Ch. 9). The irony here is that Henchy has convinced a conservative to vote for the Nationalist cause, a shift in opinion that reflects his own willingness to support the reception of King Edward. In the same way that the old caretaker uses the convention of reporting speech to establish the rhythm of the anecdote, Henchy alternates between "said I" and "I said" to emphasize the delivery of each counter-reason. Once he has established himself as the speaker at the center of the floor, Henchy is free to deliver a long speech, his reasoning with Dawson extending into a long argument about the need for British capital in Ireland. By making such a speech, Henchy appears to have become the antithesis of Hynes, for while the former advocates the importation of foreign capital and the reception of an English king, the latter is a staunch supporter of the working classes and remains faithful to the memory of Parnell. By contrasting the political views of his two central characters, and giving them the floor at the beginning and end of the dialogue, Joyce creates an "ideological dialogue" (Bakhtin 1981) that is neither for nor against the Nationalist movement, but remains suspended in its oscillation between the past memory of Parnell and the future reception of King Edward.

As the dialogue comes to a close, it becomes clear that the commemoration of Ivy Day has become an empty ritual, for the canvassers cannot agree on the reasons for remaining faithful to him. Comparing Parnell's adultery with the philandering of King Edward, Mr O'Connor makes it clear that he respects the former Irish Leader only for the reason that he is now dead—"We all respect him now that he's dead and gone" (*D*, 132). The conservative canvasser, Crofton, on the other hand, indicates his superficial support for Parnell by recognizing him as a "gentleman," but this is immediately undermined by Henchy, who parodies the technique of obstructionism that the leader of the Irish Parliamentary Party employed to stall legislation in the House of Commons. Indeed, as there is no substantive basis upon which their allegiance to Parnell can be recognized, the commemoration of Ivy Day loses its ethical character, and is enacted and reenacted simply for the aesthetic forms in which it is embodied. At the end of the story, Joe Hynes is called on to recite a eulogy titled "The Death of Parnell." While most of the Nationalists assent to the sentiments expressed by the poem, Crofton maintains his distance from the emotional content of the poem, conceding only that "it was a very fine piece of writing" (*D*, 135). By stressing the *written* form of the poem, Croften negates the political significance of the oral performance. Indeed, by distinguishing the aesthetic form of the poem from its tragic content, the Conservative figure of Crofton is able to negotiate his political differences from the Nationalists, and his aesthetic distance reveals in turn the ironic manner in which Joyce portrays the performance of Hynes's poem.

Although the symbolism in the poem accords with the allegories used in the 1912 essay titled "The Shade of Parnell"[11]—Parnell is compared with Moses and Jesus Christ—Joyce deliberately mixes the genre of the popular ballad with religious symbolism to create a hybrid poetic artifact. By employing the ballad form, a popular genre that features a strong underlying rhythm of four beats, Hynes's performance must be placed in the tradition of eulogizing Parnell, a piece of writing comparable with Katherine Tynan's "The Green Ivy," Lionel Johnson's "The Wail of Irish Winds," or even Yeats's "Come Gather Round Me, Parnellite" (Fogarty 2006, 109). In order to distinguish his own poetic style from that of Hynes, Joyce mixes elevated symbolism with popular diction, and includes a number of hiatuses to indicate that the poet lacks the technical mastery of his medium. Nevertheless, the underlying rhythm is strong enough to overcome the flaws in its metrical realization, and it is ultimately the intuition of rhythm that leads to the conversion of the audience. In the opening stanza of the poem, Hynes recites:

> He is dead. Our Uncrowned King is dead.
> O, Erin, mourn with grief and woe
> For he lies dead whom the fell gang
> Of modern hypocrites laid low. (*D*, 131)

By describing Parnell as "Our Uncrowned King," Hynes is quoting an epithet coined by Parnell's betrayer, Tim Healy, who mockingly accused Parnell of making Kitty O' Shea the "mistress" of the Irish party. During the debates held in Committee Room 15, Healy made it clear that he was willing to sacrifice Parnell for the greater cause of Home Rule, stating that "Heads of greater leaders have been stricken on the block before now for Ireland ... and the Irish cause remained. The Irish people can put us down, but the Irish cause will always remain" (Lyons 1960, 141). While Joyce initially compared Parnell's betrayal with that of Julius Caesar, casting Healy in the role of Brutus in a youthful poem titled "Et tu Healy," his later essay on the subject invokes the figure of Judas as another archetype of the betrayer. By using quotation marks, Joyce maintains his ironic distance from Healy, stating that "the shade of the 'uncrowned king' will weigh upon the hearts of those who remember him" (*CW*, 228). In the same essay, Joyce also compares Parnell with the tragic figure of Christ: "The sadness that devastated his soul was, perhaps, the profound conviction that, in his hour of need, one of the disciples who had dipped his hand into the bowl with him was about to betray him" (*CW*, 228). Considering that Hynes attributes the fall of Parnell to the "modern hypocrites," it is clear that he also is using the epithet ironically, because the meaning of the phrase derives from the period of history following the betrayal of Parnell.

The ironic manner in which Joyce refers to Parnell as Ireland's "uncrowned king" demonstrates the extent to which he shares the ideological views of Joe Hynes. Indeed, the symbolism contained in "The Death of Parnell" resonates with many of the mythic parallels later used by Joyce to understand the life of the Irish leader in his essay titled "The Shade of Parnell." The most prominent is the image of an Irish stag being torn apart by a pack of English hounds. The image was first used by Parnell in his 1890 manifesto *To the People of Ireland*, a provocative document in which he criticized Gladstone for frustrating the Home Rule movement. Appealing to the Irish people to support him in the scandal over the O'Shea affair, Parnell wrote: "Understand the measure of the loss with which you are threatened unless you consent to throw me to the English wolves now howling for my destruction" (cited in Lyons 1960, 321). Referring to this speech in his essay, Joyce blames Irish Catholics for betraying Parnell, using the image of a fallen deer to describe his downfall: "In his last proud appeal to his people, he implored his fellow-countrymen that they did not fail that desperate appeal. They did not throw him to the English wolves: they tore him apart themselves" (*CW*, 228). Significantly, the same image is used by Hynes in his elegy, for "he [Parnell] lies slain by the coward hounds" (*D*, 134). As the poem progresses, this image of Parnell as a fallen deer is replaced by the image of Christ, for in the sixth stanza, Hynes says: "They smote their Lord or with a kiss | Betrayed him to the rabble-rout | Of fawning priests—no friend of his" (*D*, 134). Through the incorporation of historical and religious material, Joyce dramatizes the social contradiction at the heart of Irish society, for although most Irish Catholics supported the Home Rule movement, they nevertheless placed morality above politics in their judgment of Parnell. At the end of the story, therefore, Joyce suspends the conflict between the various parts of Irish society (Catholics/ Protestants; Irish/English; Liberals/Conservatives) within the symbolism of Hynes's communal poem, a hybrid text that is rhythmically inflected by the public discourse surrounding the downfall of the embattled Irish leader.

Conclusion

From this analysis of the dramatic dialogues in "Grace" and "Ivy Day," we have seen that Joyce relates the *rhythmic form of social interaction* to the political contradictions that left Irish society in a state of paralysis at the turn of the twentieth century. In "Grace," we have seen that the solidarity of the Dublin middle classes was culturally secured through allegiance to the Catholic Church, a form of solidarity that was socially affirmed through the secular ritual of drinking rounds. To the extent that the tradition of Irish storytelling is dependent on this ritual of sharing whisky and porter, the "beats of dialogue" perform a socializing function, for not only do they prescribe the temporal form in which citizens converse with their peers, but they also enable the speaker to participate in the performance of their collective history. In "Ivy Day," the collective history of the Catholic middle classes is symbolically affirmed through dramatic identification with the Ghost of Parnell, a fallen political leader who called for the legislative independence of Ireland from Britain through nonviolent means (the so-called Home Rule movement). As the beats of dialogue are progressively usurped by the rhetoric of Henchy, a political opportunist who regularly contradicts himself, the dialogical nature of the social interaction is progressively reduced to the monological form of the poetic statement. At the end of this play, the structural rhythm of Joe Hynes's poem crystallizes the political tensions between the Irish Nationalists and their Conservative opponents, because Parnell is portrayed as a tragic figure whose ethical character remained at odds with the moral norms of Irish Catholics. By synthesizing the various perspectives of his characters into a set of poetic symbols, Joyce translates the rhetorical rhythm of the dialogue into the structural rhythm of a poem, a political ballad that preserves the political contradictions at the heart of Irish society as a set of rhythmic inflections.

Chapter 4

"The Curve of an Emotion"

Rhythm as Ex-tension in A Portrait of the Artist as a Young Man

Introduction

In the context of Joyce's poems and short stories, there is a continual *tension* between the metrical and structural concepts of rhythm, for while the embodied performance of a rhythm necessarily occupies some duration, the apprehension of the aesthetic image seems to suspend this movement within a set of formal relations. In *Portrait*, the duration of the epic narrative becomes the embodiment of this tension, for the life of the hero is stretched between the immediate intuition of rhythmic forms and the realization of deeper structural patterns. While the prose form of the novel does not possess any metrical properties—the periods of rhetoric rarely possess a *regular* rhythm—the intuition of rhythm nevertheless becomes the explicit subject matter of the modernist novel. Indeed, Joyce's *künstlerroman*[1] represents the biographical development of the lyrical artist from his early participation in musical rituals to the composition of his own verses. As the citation of poetic fragments creates a *dramatic space* in which the rhythmic intuitions of the protagonist are presented directly to the imagination of the reader, the representation of rhythmic experience anticipates the development of the interior monologue technique in *Ulysses*, and leads to the dissolution of traditional narrative categories (as exemplified in the diary entries at the end of the novel). By adapting his theory and practice of rhythm to the novel form, Joyce creates a new type of "rhythmic novel" that reconfigures the tension between the metrical and structural rhythms of lyric and dramatic poetry.

The lyrical prose of Joyce's *Portrait* represents a stylistic break from the naturalism of *Stephen Hero* and *Dubliners*, texts that are both concretely grounded in the reality of modern life around the turn of the twentieth century. The origin of this stylistic departure can be traced to the first draft of "A Portrait of the Artist," an unpublished essay that was composed in January 1904 and submitted to John Eglinton, the editor of *Dana* (*PSW*, 276). Written in the style of a prose poem reminiscent of the French symbolists, this essay provides a description of Stephen's education, religious indoctrination and intellectual development; including a veiled account of his sexual awakening. As it provides a sketch of the longer narrative to be developed in the published novel, the first draft can be interpreted as a *manifesto* for Joyce's aesthetic project, which is outlined in the opening paragraph:

> The features of infancy are not commonly reproduced in the adolescent portrait for, so capricious are we, that we cannot or will not conceive the past in any other than its iron memorial aspect. Yet the past assuredly implies a fluid succession of presents, the development of an entity of which our actual present is a phase only. Our world, again, recognises its acquaintance chiefly by the characters of beard and inches and is, for the most part, estranged from those of its members who seek through some art, by some process of the mind as yet untabulated, to liberate from the personalized lumps of matter that which is their individuating rhythm, the first or formal relation of their parts. But for such as these a portrait is not an identificative paper but rather the curve of an emotion. (*PSW*, 211)

For the sake of measuring the impact of rhythmic science (and empirical psychology more generally) on his prose style, Joyce's allusion to "a fluid succession of presents" is highly significant, for it indicates that the author was at the very least vaguely familiar with the notion of the "stream of thought" in January of 1904. While it is possible that Joyce had read William James's lectures on *The Principles of Psychology* (1890), it is more likely that he gained an understanding of this idea from his general awareness of empirical psychology, including the work of Bain, Spencer, Allen, and Maher. Indeed, the curious expression, "curve of an emotion," would seem to indicate that Joyce was familiar with Herbert Spencer's *The Principles of Psychology* (1873), for the British philosopher uses the physiological concept of rhythm to describe the "waves of emotion" that cause the mind to periodically alternate between states of grief and joy. Whatever the source of these allusions, it is clear from this early essay that Joyce wished to orient his prose style toward the representation of inner, temporal experiences, a stylistic tendency that would only have been reinforced by his subsequent exposure to Bergson's *L'Evolution Créatrice* after its French publication in 1907.

Taking into account the evident impact of these psychological and evolutionary theories on Joyce's aesthetic project, it is important to remember that the Irish author was primarily concerned with transforming the narrative form of the novel. Indeed, it is clear from this first draft that Joyce seeks to represent the *continuously unfolding experience of the hero* in a language that nevertheless makes a set of categorical distinctions between past and present tenses, imperfect and perfect aspects. Although Joyce was writing in a period prior to the refinement of "narratology" as a literary science (Genette 1972), his observation that "we cannot or will not conceive the past in any other than its iron memorial aspect" reveals an awareness of how the grammatical categories of language shape our understanding of past events. Indeed, whenever we use the past simple ("he walked") to describe the performance of a completed action ("he walked to the strand"), the perfect aspect of this verb obscures the continuous nature of the movement, making it difficult to establish any temporal correspondence between the rhythm of the utterance and the movement that it describes. By situating the continuity of the present within the horizon of the past ("Yet the past assuredly implies a fluid succession of presents"), however, Joyce demonstrates an awareness of how the categories of language can be used to represent temporal experience, for the tense of the past continuous ("he was walking along the strand") enables the sentence to represent a movement that is reflected by the rhythm of the utterance itself. As we will see, there is a stylistic tendency throughout Joyce's *oeuvre* toward the synchronization of "story-time" and "narrative-time." Indeed, when the description of sensation is reduced to a series of adjectival phrases and participles, the rhythm of Joyce's prose contains a direct temporal reference to the world of social action.

In this chapter, therefore, I will analyze the impact of rhythmic science on Joyce's aesthetic project, with the important qualification that his stylistic experimentation with narrative form must be attributed to his originality and creativity as a literary author. For the sake of describing these stylistic innovations, I will draw on the concepts of "narratology" as developed by Bakhtin (1975) and Genette (1972), for it is only through the use of precise terminology that we can hope to approach the genuine novelty of Joyce's rhythmic practice. Of course, it should be recognized that the concepts of "chronotope" or "narrative time" do not form part of the rhythmic science of the modernist period, as is evident from their publication dates. Nevertheless, to the extent that Joyce's stylistic practice was shaped by the rhythmic science of the late nineteenth century, there is nevertheless an *indirect* link between the psychology of rhythm and the categories of narrative science; for the representation of rhythmic experiences in the modernist novel *causes* the breakdown of traditional narrative categories. Indeed, with the eruption of the diary entries at the end of the novel, Joyce discards the conventions of syntax and grammar, choosing to represent thoughts at the speed at which they unfold. While it might be objected that I am focusing on the *poetic* elements of Joyce's novel at the expense of its more mundane elements, I would assert that the temporal experience of the lyrical artist constitutes the basic subject matter of the novel, and therefore dominates our attention. Although these diary entries are not rhythmic in the metrical sense of the word, they nevertheless simulate the formation of thought processes, for the rise and fall of the prose period corresponds to the "waves of attention" that structure our experience of time (Bolton 1894).

Rhythm as "Entelechy": Bergson and the Evolutionary Debate

In Joyce's *Portrait*, the structural concept of rhythm becomes synonymous with the "harmony" of the aesthetic image; yet, both terms begin to acquire some of the biological connotations associated with the organic theory of art. From an historical perspective, we can trace the shifting meaning of the terms "rhythm" and "harmony" to the attempts of literary scholars to legitimate their aesthetic principles in terms of evolutionary science. In *Practical Rhetoric* (1896), Quackenbos appeals to Ruskin's theory of "vital beauty" to trace the harmonic composition of the living organism to the performance of its vital function, citing a long passage from *Modern Painters* (1888) in support of his theory. Tracing the meaning of the term to its Greek etymology—"Harmony is derived from a Greek verb meaning 'to fit together,' and therefore literally implies fitness, congruity, the union of related parts in a consistent whole" (1896, 37)—Quackenbos supplements his classical account of harmony with an allusion to the philosophy of vitalism, for he constructs an analogy between divine creation and environmental adaptation:

> Harmony involves the action of God's universal laws on substances
> and forces of his creation to realize in each case some specific purpose
> of his own. In this consists design, the adaptation of means to an end;

in this is comprehended the happy fulfillments of function in living things whereby Ruskin explained vital beauty. (1896, 37)

Although Ruskin seems to reject the Darwinian theory of natural selection, his theory of vital beauty nevertheless posits some form of harmonic correspondence between the animal and the environment, for as he puts it, "Science teaches us that there exists between every organism and its surroundings a certain congruity or accord. The conscious or unconscious apprehension of such perfect congruity gives the pleasurable feeling of true beauty" (cited in Quackenbos 1896, 38). If Joyce had read this passage, he would have been pleased to discover a scientific legitimation for the theory of divine creation, for such an account would have only confirmed his belief in Aristotelian "substances" or "entelechies."[2] Although the narrative of *Portrait* dramatizes Joyce's own disillusionment with the Catholic Church, a rejection most forcefully expressed in Stephen's *non serviam*, he nevertheless uses the model of divine substances to describe the act of aesthetic creation.

From reading the philosophy of Henri Bergson in Trieste (Gillespie 1983, 20–1), Joyce would have gained some familiarity with the competing theories of evolution, including Darwin's theory of "natural selection" and Lamarck's notion of "acquired characteristics." From a philosophical point of view, the adoption of these theories leads to either a mechanistic (determinist) or vitalist (volitional) perspective of the individual in relation to the evolution of the human species. Although the detailed discussion in *L'Evolution Creatrice* (1908) may not have interested Joyce, he nevertheless possessed a summary of the French philosopher's view in Joseph Solomon's commentary on *Bergson* (1911). In the chapter titled "Evolution," Solomon discusses the work of Hans Driesch, a German vitalist who uses the Aristotelian concept of "entelechy" to describe the manner in which the differentiated parts of living organisms grow and develop in harmony with one another. Most famously describing a number of experiments in which the eggs of some sea urchins were divided, Driesch observed that each "part" evolved into a "whole" sea urchin, demonstrating that the whole structure of a living organism is potentially present in the germ of the cell (1908, 59). Although Solomon does not discuss these experiments in any detail, his allusions to Driesch's work enables him to equate the Aristotelian concept of "entelechy" with the teleological theory of evolution, a position that does not differ substantially from Bergson's vitalism. Indeed, in a memorable passage, Solomon writes:

The living world compels us to the admission of a Life-Force (*élan de vie*) wholly unmechanical, for that very reason purposive or teleological, only with a purpose turned in a certain direction, not towards a certain end; immanent in the individual, and yet transcending it so that we must not look for it in some "entelechy" or "psychoid" attached to each individual, (as Driesch does), nor yet must we narrow it to "effort" such as we are conscious of. It must be wider and deeper than any conscious, personal effort, though such personal effort is a form of it, and though Lamarck and the Neo-Lamarckians were, Bergson thinks, undoubtedly on the right track in making effort, and not accident, the agent of evolution. (1911, 71)

Although Solomon ultimately rejects the teleological theory, the mere mention of Driesch's work serves to legitimate the Aristotelian notion of "entelechy" as a valid contribution to the scientific discourse on evolution. As Joyce was already steeped in the philosophy of Aristotle and Aquinas, the discussion of the teleological theory would have provided a classical framework within which to understand Bergson's own notion of the *élan vitale*. Considering that Joyce equates the structural conception of rhythm with the *entelechy* of a living organism, Solomon's account of the evolutionary debate would have only strengthened his belief that the process of artistic production could be compared with the physical growth of living organisms.

Joyce's critics have frequently applied the structural conception of rhythm to describe the spiritual development of Stephen Dedalus in *Portrait*. In an influential article on the organization of the novel, Sidney Feshbach (1967) has argued that the sections of Joyce's *Portrait* correspond to the five types of soul listed by Aristotle in the *De Anima*, allowing him to interpret Stephen's spiritual growth as a transition from the psychic power of plants (nutrition) and animals (locomotion) to the soul of human beings (rationality), before approaching the divine powers of angels (intellect) and God (creation). In *The Empirical Strikes Back* (2004), John Gordon has taken the argument a step further, suggesting that Joyce modeled the development of his protagonist upon the biogenetic law first formulated by Ernst Haeckel: Phylogeny recapitulates ontogeny. According to this interpretation, Stephen's material growth recapitulates the evolution of the human species from the simplest form of bacterial life, an account that accords with the concept of "entelechy" developed by Hans Driesch. While it is clear that Joyce approached Stephen's spiritual development from an evolutionary perspective, such accounts tend to provide an overly mechanistic explanation for his biographical development, and fail to adequately distinguish between the "development" of the individual and the "evolution" of the human species as a whole. Indeed, if Joyce had read Bergson closely, he would have encountered a dialectical solution to the question of individual freedom, for as Solomon puts it, "the life-principle asserts itself in individuality, that the individual alone is truly living since self-creation, adaptation to self, requires an individual self and yet that it transcends any single individual or succession of individuals" (1911, 59–60). When applied to the analysis of Joyce's narrative, the evolutionary perspective would appear to suggest that the composition of the rhythmic structure provides a genetic blueprint for the development of the artist; yet, the individual speech and action of the hero (the metrical rhythm) constitute a process of self-creation that continually modify the deeper significance of the structural rhythm.

In the aesthetic dialogue of *Portrait*, Stephen Dedalus compares the "mystery of esthetic creation" to the act of material creation, claiming that "the [dramatic] artist, like the God of the creation, remains within or behind or beyond or above his handiwork, invisible, refined out of existence, indifferent, paring his fingernails" (*P*, 215). While this account is no doubt steeped in the transcendental philosophy of St. Thomas Aquinas, the association between aesthetic and material creation allows us to compare the process of individual development with the concrete realization of a dramatic structure. Indeed, as the dramatic author writes the *script* that determines the fate of the hero, the structural rhythm of the play can be compared with an "entelechy," for it is an immanent end that is expressed through the actions of the dramatic actor. In the second section of *Portrait*, Stephen performs the leading role in a play at Belvedere College to commemorate Whitsunday (the seventh Sunday after Easter). Although the play is not named in the novel, we know that this scene is based on Joyce's own performance of the teacher in Anstey's *Vice Versa*, for the narrator tells us that Stephen played the "chief part, that of the farcical pedagogue" (*P*, 73). According to Richard Ellmann, the young Joyce exploited the role of the teacher in Anstey's play to parody the mannerisms of Father Henry, the Rector at Belvedere College, and this comic experience would have communicated to Joyce the power of drama to transform art into life, and vice versa (*JJ*, 56). Although Stephen feels slightly "humiliated" for having to perform the part of the teacher, an occupation that seems to contradict his artistic vocation, his resolve to perform the role is strengthened by the presence of Emma Cleary in the audience, for "he saw her serious alluring eyes watching him from among the audience and their image at once swept away his scruples, leaving his will intact" (*P*, 85). While the fate of the hero appears determined by the structural rhythm or entelechy of the plot, this incident nevertheless demonstrates that the life of the dramatic spectacle is derived from the empathetic identification between the actor and audience.

In his description of the dramatic performance, Joyce makes it clear that the rhythm of music is the medium that ensures the sympathetic identification of the actors and the audience, a temporal movement that lends "life" to the dead letter of the script. Prior to the performance of the play, Stephen hears the school band playing the prelude to a waltz, and the rhythm of the tune provides an external realization to the feeling of longing that he feels for Emma Cleary. Listening to the "faint rhythm of the music" from outside the theatre, "the sentiment of the opening bars, their languor and supple movement, evoked the incommunicable emotion which had been the cause of all his day's unrest and of his impatient movement of a moment before" (P, 75). As Stephen's thoughts are filled with the memory of touching Emma Cleary's hand on a tram earlier in the day, the rhythm of the music provides some cathartic relief for the unrest gathering in his loins. Prior to the performance of the play, Stephen hears the band playing *The Lily of Killarney,* and the sound of this aria marks the transition from life into art, for it provides the cue for raising the curtain. When Stephen finally goes on stage, the rhythmic power of the music is transferred to the harmonious manner in which actors participate in the realization of the dramatic plot:

> It surprised him to see that the play which he had known at rehearsals for a disjointed lifeless thing had suddenly assumed a life of its own. It seemed now to play itself, he and his fellow actors aiding it with their parts. (P, 85)

As we know from the *Poetics*, Aristotle compares the structure of a play to the picture of a living organism, and this theory is reflected in Joyce's description of the troupe, for each actor contributes a "part" to the organic "whole." At the end of the play, however, this heightened sense of reality is shattered, for when the curtain falls, Stephen hears the applause, and "saw the simple body before which he had acted magically deformed" (P, 85). As this incident demonstrates, the empathetic relationship between an actor and audience creates an aesthetic space in which the various parts (actors) of the body (play) are animated with a "vital force" that resembles the miracle of divine creation.

From Joyce's account of classical poetry, it is clear that he equates the energy of drama with the creative "Life-Force" of Bergsonian evolution, for the creative power of the artist is transmitted to the audience via the actors' participation in the drama. In the aesthetic dialogue, Stephen Dedalus compares the spiritual growth of the artist to the evolution of the poetic genres, from the humanity of the lyrical and epical forms to the quasi-divine status of drama. At the origin of this process lies the embodied performance of rhythm, for Stephen traces the origin of lyric poetry to the phenomenon of the *clamor concomitans* described by Max Müller in his lectures on Science of Language: "The lyrical form is in fact the simplest verbal vesture of an instant of emotion, a rhythmical cry such as ages ago cheered on the man who pulled at the oar or dragged stones up a slope" (*P*, 214). Considering that the rhythmic movement of lyric poetry can be traced to the physical energy of social labor, which gives the performance of poetry some of kind of lived "reality," it would appear that Joyce's account of the evolution of the poetic genres is dialectical, for this kinetic energy is passed from one genre to the next. Indeed, when it comes to describing the epic genre, the rhythmic energy is passed to the rhapsodist, for the "inspiration" of the epic narrator is conceptualized as a "vital force" that is mimetically transferred to his characters:

> The simplest epical form is seen emerging out of lyrical literature when the artist prolongs and broods upon himself as the centre of an epical event and this form progresses until the centre of emotional gravity is equidistant from the artist himself and others. The narrative is no longer purely personal. The personality of the artist passes into the narrator itself, flowing round and round the persons and the action like a vital sea. This progress you will easily see in that old English ballad *Turpin Hero* which begins in the first person and ends in the third person. The dramatic form is reached when the vitality which has flowed and eddied round each person fills every person with such vital force that he or she assumes a proper and intangible esthetic life. (*P*, 214–15)

By using the adjective "vital" to describe the "vital sea" and the "vital force" of the narration, Joyce makes an explicit allusion to the evolutionary debate between mechanicists and vitalists, suggesting that the artist possesses a creative power that is not wholly determined by the evolution of the human species. As the biographical development of Stephen Dedalus is presented to the reader in the form of an epic narrative, it can be argued that this "vital force" is nothing other than the current of life that motivates the individuation of the artist as both a reflection of the creator's will and the realization of his own personality. As the epic form is a mixed mode of narration and imitation, the "vital force" of Joyce's novel emerges from the tension between the metrical rhythm (lyric) and the structural rhythm (drama), a tension that is embodied in Stephen's stream of consciousness. While the concrete performance of the metrical rhythm gives us some access to the lived reality of the central protagonist, the structural rhythm provides us with an intellectual scheme for understanding the significance of the critical events that determine the fate of his biography.

The stylistic form of Joyce's *Portrait* is therefore constituted by a fundamental *displacement* of the metrical rhythm by the grammatical categories of the fictional narrative, for the energy of physical movement is transformed into the psychological stream of consciousness ("a fluid succession of presents") that is only indirectly represented by cognitive verbs. Despite the displacement of this metrical rhythm, the flexible periods of Joyce's prose nevertheless maintain the concrete sensation of rhythm as a *trace*, for isolated words and phrases emerge to recall the embodied performance of rhythmic movements. In the opening sentence of the novel, for example, the father personifies the mother as a moocow that is coming down the road to meet the young boy:

> Once upon a time and a very good time it was there was a moocow coming down along the road and this moocow that was coming down along the road met a nicens little boy named tuckoo ...
> His father told him that story: his father looked at him through a glass: he had a hairy face. (*P*, 7)

Through the enunciation of the speech-act, "Once upon a time," the father establishes the absolute division between the present (discourse) and the past (story), which is nevertheless filled by the *continuous* movement of the cow coming down the road. As the son is *named* through the performance of this speech-act ("a nicens little boy named tuckoo"), his subjectivity is *stretched* between the absolute past (mother) and the present (father), a continuous form of temporal experience that is ordered by the sensation of rhythm. Although written in prose, the repetition and displacement of the phrase "*there was a* moocow coming down along the road" as "*this* moocow *that* was coming down along the road" create a rhythmic echo that draws attention to the temporal experience of reading the sentence. Indeed, to the extent that this phrase contains two clauses, each possessing a primary and a secondary accent (there was a móocow còming | dówn along the ròad), the regular recurrence of the stresses contains a temporal reference to the movement of the cow as it continues down the road.

The Synchronization of "Story-Time" and "Narrative-Time"

In the first chapter of Joyce's *Portrait,* the tension between the metrical rhythm (lyric) and the structural rhythm (drama) is configured as the symbolic opposition between the maternal and paternal spheres, for the prose narrative of Stephen's biographical development is formed from the tension between lyrical and dramatic modes of imitation. On the one hand, the musical dimension of language is associated with the maternal sphere, for Stephen's mother (May Dedalus) provides his musical education, and becomes the archetype for the multiple female *personae* that inspire his youthful poems. On the other hand, the intellectual dimension of language is associated with the paternal sphere, for Stephen's father is thematically associated with Stephen's separation from the home and his education at Clongowes Wood and Belvedere. For the majority of the narrative, the narrator maintains the distance between the metrical and structural dimensions of rhythm; yet, the haunting presence of these rhythmic forms is always felt, for Joyce develops a flexible prose style that features both rhetorical rhythms and symbolic associations. As we shall see, the distance between the plot of the drama and the rhythm of the poetic utterance collapses at certain points in the novel, for, through the dramatization of lyrical experiences, Joyce fuses the duration of the "narrative-time" and the "story-time," achieving the point of "zero-degree narrative" described by Genette in *Narrative Discourse* (1980). When the act of telling the story is synchronized with the experiences of Joyce's central character, the generic distance between lyric and drama is shattered, and the stream of consciousness emerges as the direct psychological correlate of the epic narrative.

In the opening scenes of the novel, the personality of the child is formed from the intersection between music and discourse, for the sensuous dimension of maternal music (accent, intonation, and rhythm) is united with the intellectual dimension of paternal discourse (word, concept, and symbol). Thus, the dramatic presentation of "baby tuckoo" singing his song combines the sensuous colours of Dante's nursery with the political alliances upheld by Simon Dedalus: "*O, the wild rose blossoms | On the little green place*" (P, 7).

As it soon becomes clear, the association between red and green symbolizes the political alliance between Michael Davitt (the Land league) and Charles Stuart Parnell (the Irish Parliamentary Party), an alliance that at one time promised to reconstitute the Irish Parliament (the so-called Home Rule movement). With the death of Parnell in the second section of the novel, however, and the fracture of the Irish Parliamentary Party, the innocence of this primal scene is shattered, a conflict between Irish Nationalism and Catholic morality that is dramatized in the Christmas Dinner scene. The death of Parnell therefore constitutes a highly traumatic episode in the context of Stephen's biographical development, for it not only marks the decline of the Home Rule movement, but it also symbolizes the ascent of Catholic morality in Ireland, a discursive regime that will dominate his education at Belvedere College. Considering that Parnell is associated with Stephen's musical education, it is significant that the return of his body to the port at Dun Laoghaire (Kingston Pier) is apprehended through the rhythms of visual and aural sensations, for Stephen compares the light of the fire and the cries of the mourners with the rise and fall of the waves:

> How pale the light was at the window! But that was nice. The fire rose and fell on the wall. It was like waves. Someone had put coal on and he heard voices. They were talking. It was the noise of the waves. Or the waves were talking amongst themselves as they rose and fell. (*P*, 27)

As we have seen, the rhythmic science of the late nineteenth century is founded on the principles of "physiological psychology," for the perception of rhythmic forms is linked to the phases of tension and relaxation that coordinate the periodic movements of the body. Incorporating the psychology of rhythm into his modern account of English prosody, Derek Attridge describes the motor responses associated with the perception of auditory rhythms:

> The most powerfully rhythm-inducing events, some kinds of sound, for instance, appear to be those which involve discharges of energy that can be directly interpreted in terms of muscular activity. The natural response to rhythmic sound is muscular participation, whether in the movement of a finger or the movement of the whole body in dance. (1982, 7)

At the beginning of the novel, Stephen begins to develop his *rhythmic* competence by participating in musical rituals, and these are enacted through the related activity of listening and dancing, for his mother "played on the piano a sailor's hornpipe for him to dance" (*P*, 7). Significantly, Joyce represents this dance as a nonsense song, highlighting the temporal correspondence between the syllables, the underlying rhythm and the motor patterns of the body:

Tralala lala,
Tralala tralaladdy,
Tralala lala,
Tralala lala. (*P*, 7)

Nowhere in the text does Joyce indicate that a song is being sung. The nonsense verse simply marks Stephen's intuition of the melody. Through the use of differing consonants ("tra" is accented and aspirated, "la" is light and liquid), typography, and lineation, Joyce creates an intonation pattern with a distinct rhythm and melodic contour. This passage demonstrates that the perception of a rising and falling rhythm must be linked to the muscular patterns of the body (that are programmed to *produce* rhythms), thereby creating a sensorimotor network between the associated processes of hearing and dancing.

When Stephen goes to a boarding school at Clongowes Wood, the paternal sphere is embodied in an institution that is physically separated from the home. Nevertheless, Stephen constantly imagines the return to the home, and his desire to return to his mother is condensed into the physical gesture of a kiss. On his departure, the kiss of the mother is associated with the pain of separation, for as the narrator puts it: "she had put up her veil double up to her nose to kiss him: and her nose and eyes were red" (*P*, 9). Here, the mother's kiss is more a sundering than a coming together, for it is only granted as a way of saying goodbye. Subsequently, the love of the mother is replaced by the law of the father, for on his departure to Clongowes Wood, Simon tells his son "never to peach on a fellow" (*P*, 9). Yet, this contract between Stephen and his schoolmates is only signed when he has undergone the rites of initiation. In response to Wells's question, "do you kiss your mother before you go to bed?" (*P*, 14), Stephen oscillates between saying "I do" and "I do not," and this uncertainty captures an intellectual and moral problem that he is unable to understand: "Was it right to kiss his mother or wrong to kiss his mother? What did that mean, to kiss?" (*P*, 14–15). Stephen's moral dilemma therefore highlights the manner in which he oscillates ambivalently between the maternal and paternal spheres.

In contrast to the musical nature of the maternal sphere, the paternal sphere is associated with the hierarchies of theological discourse

and the construction of geometrical forms. In an early geography lesson, for example, Stephen learns to locate his name and situation by
listing a number of geographical categories that contain the preceding
elements within them:

> *Stephen Dedalus*
> *Class of Elements*
> *Clongowes Wood College*
> *Sallins*
> *County Kildare*
> *Ireland*
> *Europe*
> *The World*
> *The Universe (P, 15)*

As each element of the list is a "part" that is contained within the
"whole" of the universe, this list represents the awakening of Stephen's
spatial imagination and the rudimentary construction of a "structural rhythm." As the concept of "the universe" causes Stephen to
meditate on the *limits* of the sensible world, he begins to perceive
the intellectual relationship between words and concepts. Thus,
the sensible word "God" comes to signify the "Nothing" that limits the extension of the universe; yet, the intellectual meaning of the
word emerges from the realization that there are different words for
God in English and French.

As Stephen's education progresses, he becomes increasingly capable of intellectual abstraction, but the capacity to make *connections*
between ideas remains dependent on the synthetic power of the
imagination. In one lesson, the appearance of a mathematical equation becomes a pulsating image of the universe, the harmony of the
spheres reflected in a poetic fragment from Shelley:

> The equation on the page of his scribbler began to spread out a widen-
> ing tail, eyed and starred like a peacock's; and, when the eyes and stars
> of its indices had been eliminated, began slowly to fold itself together
> again. The indices appearing and disappearing were eyes opening and
> closing; the eyes opening and closing were stars being born and being
> quenched. The vast cycle of starry life bore his weary mind outward
> to its verge and inward to its centre, a distant music accompanying
> him outward and inward. What music? The music came nearer and
> he recalled the words, the words of Shelley's fragment upon the moon
> wandering companionless, pale for weariness. The stars began to
> crumble and a cloud of fine stardust fell through space. (*P*, 102–3)

Stephen's capacity to abstract is shaped by his instruction in mathematical and scientific discourse; yet, his ability to assimilate the equation is still dependent on the sensuous intuition of both word and image. With the momentary emergence of the two rhyming phrases from Shelley's verse, "wandering companionless" and "pale for weariness," Stephen highlights the symmetry between the two lines, and contrasts the constancy of this rhythmic structure with the temporal movement of the imagination. Thus, the mathematical conception of planetary motion is infused with the rhythm of Shelley's "To the Moon," the poetic fragment capturing the tension between the geometrical image and the physical movement.

As we have seen, the maternal and paternal spheres are geographically dislocated from one another; yet, the train journey from Bray to Clongowes Wood provides an experience of continuous movement and duration that allows Stephen to reduce this structural rhythm to a metrical pattern. Indeed, when Stephen is immersed in the daily rituals of the classroom and the chapel, he can only imagine home as another form of experience, for he does not perceive a *continuous* alternation between the two. Yet, Stephen's memory of the train journey allows him to simulate the alternation between home and school, creating a continuous rhythm that dramatizes the structural rhythm as the opposition between two poetic symbols:

> First came the vacation and then the next term and then vacation again and then again another term and then again the vacation. It was like a train going in and out of tunnels and that was like the noise of boys eating the refectory when you opened and closed the flaps of your ears. Term, vacation; tunnel, out; noise, stop. (*P*, 17)

In this passage, Joyce uses the technique of symbolic substitution to synchronize three rhythms with differing periods of recurrence. On the one hand, term and vacation represent two discrete periods that are spatially and temporally dislocated from each other. On the other hand, the alternation between noise and silence (open and closed ears) constitutes a continuous rhythm controlled by the movements of the body. As the alternating noise and silence of the boys in the refectory resembles the movement of the train in and out of the tunnel, the continuous rhythm allows ones form of experience to be transformed into another. The effect of this transformation is the creation of a symbolic correspondence between term and noise, vacation and silence. Indeed, the mind of the young artist reduces three symbolic oppositions to a single rhythmic schema: "Term, vacation; tunnel, out; noise, stop."

The preceding term stages the withdrawal of pleasure—the creation of tension, the latter enacts the relaxation of the tension—the passage from desire to fulfillment.

It is not simply through the construction of metrical rhythms that the dramatic structure of the narrative is translated into concrete images. Through the use of refrains, Joyce creates a technique for highlighting the emergence of poetry from within the periods of his prose. In another scene, Stephen is depicted walking from his dormitory to the chapel for evening prayers. He distinguishes the holy smell of the chapel from the smell of the peasants who attend mass on Sundays: "There was a smell of air and rain and turf and corduroy" (*P*, 18). This train of images moves from the medium of smell (air) to the physical basis for the smell (turf) and expresses the symbolic opposition between the sacred and the profane. As Stephen associates the pastoral scene with his family home in Bray, the train of images functions as a symbolic substitute for the return home, and henceforth provides an artistic mode of mediating between the sensory immediacy of the maternal and the distanced authority of the paternal. This movement is paralleled by the creation of a dramatic scene in which the refrain is repeated: "It would be lovely to sleep for one night in the cottage before the fire of the smoking turf, in the dark lit by the fire, in the warm dark, breathing the smell of the peasants, *air and rain and turf and corduroy*" (*P*, 18). The refrain serves to transform the mere smell of a physical object into a concrete scene in which the peasants appear as an *image* in the mind of the hero. The act of literary creation, which here stages the wish of the young artist to return home, is constituted by this act of rhythmic citation that distinguishes the reference to an external object from the novelistic image of the object.[3] Yet, it is precisely the stylization of the "air and rain and turf and corduroy" that serves to make the association between the scenes, in both the memory of the young child and reader. The use of the connective "and" creates an iambic rhythm that prolongs the pleasure associated with the scene. Each "and" marks the tension of an offbeat that is relaxed by the arrival of a corresponding beat.

There is a stylistic tendency in Joyce's "rhythmic-novel" (my term: WM) toward the condensation of temporal experiences that exhibit a rhythmic pattern. While there remain a number of deep structural oppositions that determine the underlying significance of symbols in the narrative (maternal/paternal; rhythmic/linguistic; vacation/term; kiss/parting), these oppositions are coordinated and synchronized through the creation of rhythmic correspondences. At critical moments of the narrative, Stephen's experience of time is condensed around a single rhythm that synthesizes these conflicting forces. As he lies in bed at Clongowes Wood, Stephen imagines the end of term. Anticipating "Going Home for the Holidays!," Stephen imagines the "Cheers for the Rector!" and conjures an iambic schema that is constituted by the repetition of a single word: "Hurray! Hurray! Hurray!" (*P*, 20). In the next scene, the cheers of the excited boys resonate and reflect off each other, a movement toward *continuous* experience that is completed with the recapitulation of the earlier refrain. In addition to the echoes of the cheers, the first paragraph features the intermingling of different refrains, causing the "wintry air" to be fused with the "air and rain and turf and corduroy" to form the hybrid expression, "rain and wintry air and turf smouldering and corduroy":

> The cars drove past the chapel and all caps were raised. They drove merrily along the country roads. The drivers pointed with their whips to Bodenstown. *The fellows cheered.* They passed the farmhouse of the Jolly Farmer. *Cheer after cheer after cheer.* Through Clane they drove, *cheering and cheered.* The peasant women stood at the halfdoors, the men stood here and there. The lovely smell there was in the wintry air: the smell of Clane: *rain and wintry air and turf smouldering and corduroy.*
>
> The train was full of fellows: a long long chocolate train with cream facings. The guards went to and fro opening, closing, locking, unlocking the doors. They were men in dark blue and silver; they had silvery whistles and their keys made a quick music: click, click: click, click. (*P*, 20: my italics, WM)

It is significant that both passages are structured around the continuous movement of machines that accelerate the tempo of everyday life. In the former, the boy receives recognition from his peers as he travels in a horse-drawn carriage—it is precisely the differentiation of the artist's own rhythm that is the source of pleasure. In the latter, the subjectivity of the artist is merged with the collective consciousness of all the boys sitting in the train, the uniformity of time marked by the authority of the guards. Finally, the locking and unlocking of the doors (another symbol of transition between states) provides a rhythmic schema for the coordination of these different horizons of experience, for the monotonous periodicity of each "click" marks the beat of an underlying rhythm common to all. At this point of the novel, rhythm is no longer merely a means of *representing* temporal experience; it becomes the psychological *schema* that orders the experience of time in the consciousness of the hero.

The representation of rhythmic experience in Joyce's *Portrait* challenges the orthodoxies of contemporary "narratology," for rhythm is not reduced to a mere *means* of poetic expression, but is represented as a fundamental category of temporal experience. In *Narrative Discourse*, Genette makes a distinction between the "story time" (the duration of the events recounted in the story) and the "narrative time" (the duration of the act of storytelling); but this category collapses at certain points of Joyce's "rhythmic-novel," because the perception of the underlying rhythm fuses the duration of the story-time with the narrative-time. The act of reading is therefore synchronized with the perception of rhythmic forms. This is what Genette calls the "zero degree" of narrative, in which there "would be a condition of perfect temporal correspondence between narrative and story" (1980, 36). When Joyce immediately represents the rhythmic experience of Stephen Dedalus—"click, click: click, click."—the speed of the narrative is identical to the speed of the story, and this temporal fusion of narrative and story has ramifications for the dramatic structure of the novel as a whole. Indeed, if the ironic separation of the author from the hero depends on the use of the third-person voice, and the hierarchy of verbal tenses, then this distance is overcome by the immediate presentation of rhythmic experience.[4] Dislocated from any grammatical or syntactical structure, the temporal structure of the ticking is marked by the use of *punctuation*, for Joyce differentiates the identity of successive periods through the use of a semicolon. Without this semicolon, the perception of the clicking might remain homogeneous, each successive "click" marked by the metronomic repetition of an antecedent "click"; yet, the orthographic distinction between semicolon and full stop marks the position of the cadence, illustrating the manner in which the mind of the artist synthesizes the recurring intensity of each beat within an overarching rhythmic schema.

The abstraction of the psychological rhythm in the context of Joyce's epic narrative calls for an interrogation of the concept of the "chronotope." In *The Dialogic Imagination* (1981), Bakhtin argues that specific genres of the novel are formally constituted by the manner in which they use space to represent historical time. He gives "the name *chronotope* (literally, 'time space') to the intrinsic connectedness of temporal and spatial relationships that are artistically expressed in literature" (1981, 84). While a full summary of Bakhtin's theory is beyond the scope of this chapter, it will be useful to give a brief account of what he calls the "idyllic" chronotope, for it connects the rhythms of nature with the cycles of human experience. For Bakhtin, the idyllic chronotope is an organic expression of the form of time characteristic of the collective life of the folk, whose battle against nature is embodied in collective labor, and symbolized in the cycles of nature and human life. It is characterized by unity of place (a single town or family home), continuity of family history (genealogy), and the limitation of life to a few basic realities (love, birth, death, marriage, labor, food and drink, stages of growth, and so on). The concept of rhythm plays an important role in integrating the cycles of private experience with the cycles of nature, because the idyll represents "the conjoining of human life with the life of nature, the unity of their rhythm, the common language used to describe phenomena of nature and the events of human life" (1981, 226). In the context of Joyce's *Portrait*, we have already seen that Stephen experiences the oscillation between term and vacation according to the logic of the idyllic chronotope; yet, the immediate perception of rhythm orients the experience of the hero toward the concrete realization of historical time.

For Bakhtin, the integration of personal education with the unfolding of historical processes is the characteristic chronotope of the *bildungsroman*, a genre that he links to the industrialization of agricultural society and the development of capitalism:

> Here the issue is primarily one of overturning and demolishing the world view and psychology of the idyll, which proved increasingly inadequate to the new capitalist world ... We get a picture of the breakdown of provincial idealism under forces emanating from the capitalist center. We see the breakdown, the hero's provincial romanticism, which is in no way idealized; the capitalist world is also not idealized, its inhumanity is laid bare, the destruction within it of all ethical systems ..., the disintegration of all previous human relationships (under the influence of money), love, the family, friendship, the deforming of the scholar's and the artist's creative work and so forth—all of these are emphasized. The positive hero of the idyllic world becomes ridiculous, pitiful and unnecessary, he either perishes or is re-educated and becomes an egotistic predator. (1981, 235)

We can see, therefore, that the *bildungsroman* (along at least one line of development) is associated with the destructive forces of capitalism, a chronotope that is characterized by the lack of coordination between public time and private rhythms. Nevertheless, in the context of Joyce's *künstlerroman*, the rhythmic experience of Stephen Dedalus serves as a supplement for the loss of the idyllic chronotope, for the perception of the recurring beat becomes a psychological schema synthesizing the opposition between the home (idyllic) and the school (historical development). Although Stephen is alienated from the twin

institutions of state and church, the discovery of his artistic vocation provides an alternative path of biographical development, for the
rhythmic patterns embodied in the composition and performance of
verses provide an alternative source of value.

Primary and Secondary Rhythms

In the first section of *Portrait*, Joyce represents the spiritual "birth"
of the artist through the performance of a number of musical rituals
that foreground the relationship between the organic rhythms of the
body and the temporal structures of mental experience. In the initial phase of Stephen's development, Joyce places particular emphasis on the production of rhythms; yet, this is soon surpassed by the
mere perception of rhythmic forms in the context of everyday life (the
sound of water dripping, the clang of the train tracks, and so on). As
Stephen begins to master the English language, he begins to formu-
late words and phrases that fill out the beats of these basic rhythms,
improvising prayers and poems to reflect his changing moods. There
are a number of passages in *Portrait* that indicate a general familiarity with Sidney Lanier's distinction between "primary" and "secondary" rhythms. By eliding the distance between the discourse of the
narrator and the idiolect of Stephen Dedalus at specific points in the
novel, Joyce reveals the rhythmic sensations of the artist as he learns
to separate the temporal form of the rhythm from the words of the
poem. Placed in the historical context of the late nineteenth and early
twentieth centuries, the abstraction of the *rhythmic intuition* from
the wording of the literary text can be interpreted as symptomatic of
the rise of a scholarly discourse on rhythm that sought to distinguish
the *psychological perception of rhythmic forms* from the prosodic
conventions of classical and modern poetry.

Joyce's *Portrait* employs the distinction between the primary and
secondary rhythms in the scene where Stephen accompanies his
father on a train journey from Dublin to Cork. The purpose of the
journey is to auction off one of the family's remaining Cork properties. As he listens to the sound of the train tracks passing beneath
him, Stephen composes a prayer that "ended in a trail of foolish
words which he made to fit to the insistent rhythm of the train; and
silently, at intervals of four seconds, the telegraph poles held the galloping notes of the music between punctual bars" (*P*, 87). Here we
can see that the intuition of the rhythmic form precedes the attempt
to compose the prayer, such that the choice of diction (and its order)

is predetermined by the perception of the metrical pattern. Although Stephen is attempting to compose an oral prayer, the periodic appearance of the telegraph poles creates a *visual rhythm* that is coordinated with the aural rhythm of the prayer. In *The Science of English Verse* (1880), Lanier expands his definition of the primary rhythm to include the perception of recurrent patterns in nonmusical contexts, arguing that:

if equal or proportionate intervals of time be marked off to any of our senses by recurrent stresses of similar events, we may be said to perceive a primary rhythm through that sense. *Thus, if a rose be waved before the eyes once every second, we may be said to have a perception of primary rhythm through the sense of sight.* (Lanier 1880, 62)

It is significant that Lanier extends the perception of rhythm to the sense of sight, because it enables the auditory rhythms of poetry and music to be represented via a graphic notation that is itself perceived to be rhythmic.

Yet, the so-called primary rhythm is never perceived without the fundamental alternation between strong and weak elements, for as soon as the mind begins to participate in the production of the rhythm, it is motivated to form a second-order pattern that distinguishes between strong and weak beats. As Lanier argues in *The Science of English Verse*, the mind tends to order the perception of rhythmic beats into metrical groups, for by placing emphasis or stress on the first element of each period, a higher-order or "secondary rhythm" begins to emerge that embodies the aesthetic form of the perception:

A clock which ticks seconds may be said to set up a primary rhythm for the ear which hears each recurrent tick. These ticks are exactly alike: they fulfill the definition of primary rhythm, which describes it as a conception resulting from a similar event recurring at equal (or simply-proportionate) periods of time. But everyone who has been in a room alone with a ticking clock must have observed that every other tick seems to be different, somehow, from its fellow, as if it said, "Tick-*tack*, tick-*tack*," &c.; and the effect of this difference is to arrange the whole series into groups, of two ticks in each group. Now, this grouping is secondary rhythm. The ear not only goes on comparing each tick with tick as a *primary* unit of rhythmic measure; but it proceeds to compare each group of two ticks with its fellow-group of two ticks, thus constituting a *secondary* unit of rhythmic measure. These processes, and several extensions of them which must presently be detailed, are precisely what are carried on in verse. (1880, 63)

As the altered spelling of the word "tack" (or "tock") implies, the mind tends to mark the recurrence of each strong element with a change in pitch, such that the first beat of the primary rhythm is heard to possess an "accent," despite the fact that the metronome beats with a monotonous tone. In Joyce's *Portrait*, we can see the emergence of a secondary rhythm in the scene where Stephen observes his classmates practicing cricket. Each "pick" of the ball hitting the bat is altered by a descent in the pitch of the following vowel sound, causing the four beats of the series resemble a musical cadence: "The fellows were practicing long shies and bowling lobs and slow twisters. In the soft grey silence he could hear the bump of the balls: and from here and from there through the quiet air the sound of cricket bats: pick, pack, pock, puck: like drops of water in a fountain falling softly in the brimming bowl" (*P*, 59). Here we can see that the altered spellings reflect the consciousness of the aesthete (and not the objective sound of each "pick"), such that the language of the narrator begins to express the rhythmic perceptions of the central protagonist.

It is clear that Joyce associated the perception of the primary rhythm with the ticking of a clock, for the third section of the novel depicts a "Fire Sermon" in which Father Arnall constructs a rhetorical conceit that links the opposition between heaven and hell to the alternation between the "tick" and the "tock" of a great clock. Modeled on Pinamonti's *Hell Opened to Christians, to Caution Them from Entering It* (1688), Father Arnall's sermon is structured in four parts, dealing with the subjects of death, judgment, hell, and heaven respectively. For Stephen, however, it is the description of hell that has the highest impact on his consciousness, for not only does it provide a fund of images to understand and interpret the daily torments haunting his soul, but it also provides moral certainty in a time of doubt. In practical terms, Stephen learns to subordinate his experience of historical time to a hermeneutic scheme that reduces all temporal events to a reflection of the divine order. This transition from historical time to eternity is achieved through the performance of Father Arnall's speech, for the periods of his prose seem to stretch into eternity as he describes the continuous ticking of a great clock:

—A holy saint (one of our own fathers I believe it was) was once vouchsafed a vision of hell. It seemed to him that he stood in the midst of a great hall, dark and silent save for the ticking of a great clock. The ticking went on unceasingly; and it seemed to this saint that the sound of the ticking was the ceaseless repetition of the words—*ever, never; ever, never. Ever* to be in hell, *never* to be in heaven; *ever* to be shut off from the presence of God, *never* to enjoy the beatific vision; *ever* to be eaten with flames, gnawed by vermin, goaded with burning spikes, *never* to be free from those pains; *ever* to have the conscience upbraid one, the memory enrage, the mind filled with darkness and despair, *never* to escape; *ever* to curse and revile the foul demons who gloat fiendishly over the misery of their dupes, *never* to behold the shining raiment of the blessed spirits; *ever* to cry out of the abyss of fire to God for an instant, a single instant, of respite from such awful agony, *never* to receive, even for an instant, God's pardon; *ever* to suffer, *never* to enjoy; *ever* to be damned, *never* to be saved; *ever, never; ever, never.* (*P*, 132–3: my italics, WM)

Here the periodic alternation between "ever" and "never" embodies the primary rhythm of the ticking clock and also expresses the symbolic opposition between hell and heaven. By punctuating the periods with alternating commas and semicolons, Joyce makes explicit that Stephen perceives the refrain as two groups of two: "ever, never; ever, never." Once the audience has been entrained to the beat of the primary rhythm, Father Arnall uses the opposition between "ever" and "never" to structure the duration of his periods, each thesis (the eternal experience of hell) balanced by a corresponding antithesis (the exclusion from heaven), as the extended duration of the sermon begins to embody the eternal ticking of hell's clock. While the meaning of this speech is fairly emphatic, Father Arnall's image retains some ambiguity in the mind of the artist, for the ticking of hell's clock embodies the continuous experience of time. Indeed, the monotonous repetition of the period also *signifies* the duration of eternity, causing the intuition of rhythm to possess both a temporal (continuity) and an atemporal (eternity) aspect. The concrete intuition of rhythm always possesses two aspects, therefore, for the repetition of the period must occupy some duration; yet, it also creates an aesthetic form that seems to be suspended from the experience of historical time.

Narrative Tension and the Rhythmic "Chronotope"

We know that Joyce was familiar with Henri Bergson's critique of the scientific method, for he uses the term "cinematographic" in the Trieste notebook to describe the manner in which photographs of the body can stimulate the reflex actions of the body: "Pornographic and cinematographic images act like those stimuli which produce a reflex action of the nerves through channels which are independent of esthetic perception" (Scholes and Kain 1965, 96). From this entry, it is clear that Joyce was also familiar with Bergson's notion of the "sensori-motor" system, a network of *afferent* and *efferent* nerves that automatically translates sensations into movements, and vice versa.[5] In *L'Evolution Créatrice* (1908), the French philosopher contrasts the embodied performance of a continuous movement to the analytical (or divisive) power of the intellect, using the metaphor of the "cinematograph" to describe the manner in which the intellect dissects the *duration* of the original act into a series of discrete images (or photographs). In a memorable passage, Bergson describes the filming of a marching regiment and its subsequent projection on the screen, suggesting that the original movement is *simulated* by the motion of the film rolling through the projector:

> In order that the pictures may be animated, there must be movement somewhere. The movement does indeed exist here; it is in the apparatus. It is because the film of the cinematograph unrolls, bringing in turn the different photographs of the scene to continue each other, that each actor of the scene recovers his mobility; he strings all his successive attitudes on the invisible movement of the film ... Such is the contrivance of the cinematograph. And such is also that of our knowledge. Instead of attaching ourselves to the inner becoming of things, we place ourselves outside them in order to recompose their becoming artificially. (Bergson 1911, 331)

In the context of Joyce's aesthetic theory, the pornographic effect of the cinematograph is associated with the *kinetic emotions*, for the representation of the nude figure in motion causes the body of the spectator to *pursue* the pleasurable object. To the extent, however, that the cinematographic method divides the physical movement into a discrete number of images (or photographs), the analytical power of the intellect would seem to be associated with the structural rhythm of Joyce's *Portrait*, for the book as a "whole" is divided into a number of "parts." Indeed, through the division of the novel into a number of distinct sections, Joyce constructs a narrative that presents the pivotal episodes of Stephen's biographical development (home, schooling, religious indoctrination, sexual awakening, aesthetic sublimation, and so on). Nevertheless, the structural rhythm can be animated through the performance of the metrical rhythm: Just as the movement of the film through the projector supplements the lost motion of the marching regiment, so does the metrical rhythm simulate Stephen's temporal experience as he walks through the city.

We can use the hyphenated term "ex-tension" to describe the manner in which Joyce represents the rhythmic experience of Stephen Dedalus in *Portrait*, as it captures the opposition between the fluid movement of the imagination and the divisive power of the intellect. In a section of *Creative Evolution* (1911) that describes the interpretation and performance of poetry, Bergson contrasts the "extension" of the spatial form to the "tension" of the temporal movement that inspired the composition of the poem:

> Now, I need only relax my attention, let go the *tension* that there is in me, for the sounds, hitherto swallowed up in the sense, to appear to me distinctly, one by one, in their materiality ... In proportion as I let myself go, the successive sounds will become the more individualized; as the phrases were broken into words, so the words will scan in syllables which I shall perceive one after another ... I shall then admire the precision of the interweavings, the marvelous order of the procession, the exact insertion of the letters into the syllables, of the syllables into the words and of the words into the sentences. The farther I pursue this quite negative direction of relaxation, the more *extension* and complexity I shall create. (1911, 228–9: my italics, WM)

According to Bergson's account, the "rhythm" of the poem is simply a spatial form that *simulates* the original movement, the "flux" or "flow" of the voice that maintains the organic unity (or vitality) of the poem as a whole. When applied to the narrative form of Joyce's *Portrait*, this oscillation between the "tension" of the movement and the "extension" of the intellect can be used to theorize the relationship between the metrical and structural concepts of rhythm. Indeed, as the composition of a longer work involves a "relaxation" of the mind's attention, the biographical development of the hero progresses in proportion to the "extension" of the work as a whole. In the second half of the novel, Stephen Dedalus self-consciously adopts a literary vocation in order to transform the kinetic impulses of his sensory experience into poems and essays that possess a spatial form. While the "extension" of the structural rhythm describes the intellectual development of the artist and the deeper significance of the narrative, the "tension" of the metrical (or rhetorical) rhythm is the vital force that maintains the organic unity of the work as a whole.

In both *Stephen Hero* and *Portrait*, Joyce compares the activity of walking through the city with the process of composing a literary work, a metaphor that allows us to extend the concepts of "tension" and "extension" to the development of narrative forms. According to the artistic economy outlined in *Stephen Hero*, the young artists perform

the locomotive rhythm of walking through the city in order to compose
lines of rhetoric and verse, for as the narrator puts it:

> In this manner he had his whole essay in mind from the first word to
> the last before he had put any morsel of it on paper. In thinking or
> constructing the form of the essay he found himself much hampered
> by the sitting posture. His body disturbed him and he adapted to the
> expedient of appeasing it by gentle promenading. Sometimes during
> his walk he lost the train of thought and whenever the void of his mind
> seemed irreclaimable he forced order upon it by ejaculatory fervours.
> His mornings were critical, his evening walks were imaginative and
> whatever seemed plausible in the evening was always rigorously exam-
> ined in the light of day. (*SH*, 74)

The rhythmic activity of walking through the city enables Stephen
to achieve a periodic balance between the intellectual and imaginative
activity, for the morning is dedicated to criticism and the evening to
the creation of poetry. The composition of such verses contributes to
the sublimation of Stephen's sexual instincts, for his "body disturbed
him," a feeling of stored energy that requires physical and intellectual
activity to be expended. In *Portrait*, Joyce makes explicit the correspondence between the rhythm of walking and the meters of verse,
for Stephen paces across the city as he waits for his father to return
with information:

> From the door of Byron's public-house to the gate of Clontarf Chapel,
> from the gate of Clontarf Chapel to the door of Byron's public-house
> and then back again to the chapel and then back again to the public-
> house he had paced slowly at first, planting his steps scrupulously in
> the spaces of the patchwork of the footpath, then timing their fall to
> the fall of verses. (*P*, 164)

By comparing the zig-zag movements of Stephen's walk to the
structures of verse, Joyce constructs an analogy between the extension of the narrative and the spatial outline of the city.

As Brandon Kershner (1989) has shown, *The Count of Monte
Cristo* is a pivotal intertext in Joyce's novel, for the romantic narrative
functions as a dramatic script that programs the actions of the young
reader. Initially, the novel provokes the child with an imaginary sense
of the setting that makes up the fabric of a novel, for "At night he built
up on the parlour table an image of the wonderful island cave out of
transfers and paper flowers and coloured tissue paper and strips of the

silver and golden paper in which chocolate is wrapped" (*P*, 62). More significantly, however, the hero of Dumas's novel provides Stephen with a figure of authority, a source of psychological identification that maps out in advance the future biography of the artist:

> In his imagination he lived through a long train of adventures, marvelous as those in the book itself, towards the close of *which there appeared an image of himself, grown older and sadder*, standing in a moonlit garden with Mercedes who had so many years before slighted his love. (*P*, 63)

While Stephen apprehends the narrative as a series of adventures—that is to say, the biography of the hero is determined by the outcome of a number of discrete episodes—he also perceives the *telos* of the novel. By imagining a more mature version of himself at the end of the book, Stephen realizes that the narrative of the romance novel is driven by the ongoing desire to possess the heroine, a desire that is manifested in affective terms as a *continuous source of tension*. Although the discrete episodes of the romance narrative cannot directly represent the progressive development of the hero, the experience of reading creates a feeling of expectation or "tension" that is only realized when the hero possesses the beloved at the end of the novel. In order to prolong this tension, Stephen's refusal to kiss Mercedes demonstrates that he wishes to transform the romance into a tragedy ("Madam, I never eat muscatel grapes"), and therefore sublimates his desires for the sake of attaining a new stage of maturation.

With the transition from the first to the second sections of the novel, the image of the mother (associated with the performance of music) is substituted for the fictional beloved of Stephen Dedalus (the heroic desire for the beloved at the end of the tale), causing the continuous *tension* of the underlying rhythm to become fused with the *extension* of the hero's biographical development. At this stage of the novel, Stephen begins to feel the terror of carnal desires that cannot be satisfied physically, but can only be sublimated through the composition of verses: "As he brooded upon her image," says the narrator, "a strange unrest crept into his blood" (*P*, 64). From this moment onward, Joyce uses images of fluidity to symbolize the carnal longings of the artist; yet, this sense of continuity is also registered at the level of the novel's *chronotope*, for Stephen is no longer content to act out discrete adventures, but begins to search for the continuous experience of modernity in the city. In order to express this underlying sense of tension, Stephen begins to walk through the streets of Dublin, for this mode of exploring the city provides a unique mode of access to the continuity of historical time:

> Dublin was a new and complex sensation. Uncle Charles had grown so witless that he could no longer be sent out on errands and the disorder in settling in the new house left Stephen freer than he had been in Blackrock. In the beginning he contented himself with circling timidly round the neighbouring square or, at most, going half way down one of the side streets but when he had made a skeleton map of the city in his mind he followed boldly one of its central lines until he reached the customhouse. He passed unchallenged among the docks and along the quays wondering at the multitude of corks that lay bobbing on the surface of the water in a thick yellow scum, at the crowds of quay porters and the rumbling carts and the ill-dressed bearded policeman. The vastness and strangeness of the life suggested to him by the bales of merchandise stocked along the walls or swung aloft out of the holds of steamers wakened again in him the unrest which had sent him wandering in the evening from garden to garden in search of Mercedes. And amid this new bustling life he might have fancied himself in another Marseille but that he missed the bright sky and the sun-warmed trellises of the wineshops. A vague dissatisfaction grew up within him as he looked on the quays and on the river and on the lowering skies and yet he continued to wander up and down day after day as if he really sought someone that eluded him. (*P*, 66)

By constructing a "skeleton map of the city," Stephen links the extension of his intellect to the tension of the temporal movement. In narrative terms, the walk through the city serves as a modern substitute for the episodic adventures of the romantic chronotope. The fluidity of the river, the movement of bodies, and exchange of commodities opens up a new horizon of temporal experience that is filled with a stream of new and changing impressions. Although Joyce has not yet perfected the technique of representing the stream of consciousness, he nevertheless gives a precise description of the dominant impressions that enter Stephen's mind, each phrase containing an image that paints a picture of the scene. It is significant, however, that the realism of Joyce's prose style is explicitly contrasted with the imagination of Stephen Dedalus, who superimposes Dumas's narrative on the unfolding scene in an attempt to discover a symbolic substitute for Mercedes. As this section progresses, it soon becomes clear that this elusive "someone" is none other than a prostitute, whose "parting kiss" haunts Stephen with the pain of his original separation from the mother. Although the stroll through the city provides relief and expression for the sense of unrest that is gathering in his loins, it nevertheless remains an incomplete expression of this underlying tension, and needs to be transformed into the material of poetry (or art) to be properly purged.

It is significant that Stephen's first genuinely erotic encounter with Emma Cleary occurs on a tram, because this scene serves to identify the rapid movement through the city with the release of "sexual" tension. After a children's party at Harold's Cross, at which Stephen has apparently "sung his song," he leaves the party with Emma and feels the heat of her breath as they walk together toward the tram. After boarding the tram, Emma flirts with Stephen by periodically moving from the lower step to the upper step. When describing the scene, Joyce makes it clear that the rhythm of the dialogue is paralleled by the alternating position of Emma's body, because

> She came up to his step many times and went down to hers again between their phrases and once or twice stood close beside him for some moments on the upper step, forgetting to go down, and then went down. His heart danced upon her movements like a cork upon the tide. (*P*, 69)

Here we can see that Stephen has perceived Emma's movements according to a rhythmic schema, because he notices the interruption of the rhythm, and those moments when she is supposed to descend, but forgets "to go down." The image of the tide symbolizes the movement that periodically brings Stephen and Emma together and pulls them apart. Perceiving that this is in fact a game, Stephen compares the scene with a former encounter with Eileen Sheehy, an association that reveals the romantic narrative behind the actions of the characters: "He heard what her eyes said to him from beneath their cowl and knew that in some dim past, whether in life or revery, he had heard that tale before" (*P*, 69). Once again, the hero becomes self-consciously aware that his actions are determined by the outline of a narrative form. While there is no explicitly rhythmic refrain that embodies this movement up and down the steps of the tram, the continuous alternation brings to the surface the deeper currents that motivate the development of the artist, and the tension of the narrative begins to exhibit itself at an experiential level.

In order to make this tension fully manifest, Stephen then begins to compose a book of verses that he titles in the manner of Lord Byron: "To E— C—." Here, Joyce makes explicit the fact that Stephen's prosaic experiences have been transmuted into poetry, for the verse retains the mood at the heart of the scene: "there remained no trace of the tram itself nor of the trammen nor of the horses: nor did she or he appear vividly. The verses told only of the night and of the balmy breeze and the maiden lustre of the moon" (*P*, 70). Although Stephen's verses lack any element of realism, they still capture the mood of the erotic encounter, the essence of which is captured in the image of a parting kiss: "Some undefined sorrow was hidden in the hearts of the protagonists as they stood in silence beneath the leafless trees and when the moment of farewell had come the kiss, which had been withheld by one, was given by both" (*P*, 71). Just as the original encounter only simulates the states of nearness and farness, so does Stephen's poetry simulate an erotic encounter that ends with a parting kiss. Yet this "parting kiss" is not unproductive in the life of the artist, for it signifies that the fulfillment of desire is only the temporary compensation for an absolute loss that cannot be regained. The "parting kiss" therefore announces the *end* of one stage of the artist's development and the *beginning* of the next.

The "Esthetic" Concept of Rhythm

In the past, Joyce's critics have frequently used the concepts contained in his aesthetic theory to interpret the *style* of his prose works, and the concept of rhythm is no exception, for scholars such as Stuart Gilbert (1963), Clive Hart (1990), Thomas Connolly (1966), and Bryan Reddick (1969) have all attempted to interpret the *narrative structure* of Joyce's novels through the lens of this concept. While there is, doubtless, some validity to this approach, such critics fail to distinguish the aesthetic theory of the young Stephen Dedalus, who draws on the classical authorities of Aristotle, Aquinas, Coleridge, and Shelley, from the mature prose style of James Joyce, who seems to have been more influenced by the evolutionary theories of Bergson, Darwin, and Spencer. More recently, Sandra Tropp (2008) has suggested that the aesthetic dialogue in *Portrait* contains allusions to Charles Darwin's *The Descent of Man* (1871), Alexander Bain's *Mental and Moral Science* (1872), and Grant Allen's *Physiological Aesthetics* (1877). In an important passage, Stephen criticizes the view "that every physical quality admired by men in women is in direct connection with the manifold functions of women for the propagation of species" (*P*, 208), criticizing Darwin's account of female beauty for constructing a science of eugenics rather than aesthetics. While Stephen prefers a more idealistic explanation for the origin of beauty—the theory of aesthetic apprehension is mapped on to the Thomistic qualities of *integritas*, *consonantia*, and *claritas*—the inclusion of these scientific sources reveals an alternative point of view that reflects the ironic perspective of the author. Indeed, Joyce reveals his own ironic perspective through the comic figure of Lynch, who undermines the idealism of Stephen through his jokes and references to the material world.

There is evidence to suggest that Joyce incorporated the insights of rhythmic science when he began to reflect on his own method of sublimating his repressed sexual instincts into the "rhythm" of his verses. Indeed, in the first draft of "A Portrait of the Artist," Joyce writes "a portrait is not an identificatory paper but rather the curve of an emotion" (*PSW*, 11), alluding to Spencer's concept of "emotional waves." In the *Principles of Psychology* (1873), Spencer develops a theory that relates the degree of emotional excitement to the amount of blood circulating in the body. In a chapter titled "Aestho-Physiology," Spencer holds that the intensity of emotional states are altered in direct proportion to physiological processes occurring in the body, for "Emotions, like sensations, may be increased or decreased in intensity by altering either the quantity or quality of the blood" (121). As the circulation of blood is used by the body to replenish the energy of organs, muscles, and nerves that have been overstimulated, the "quality or quantity" of the blood can be used to measure the intensity of the emotions experienced by the subject. Just as the contraction of any muscles causes the onset of fatigue that temporarily prevents any further activity, so does the experience of intense emotion require a corresponding period of relaxation:

> Be it in grief, or joy, or tenderness, there is always a succession of rises and falls of intensity—a paroxysm of violent feeling with an interval of feeling less violent, followed by another violent paroxysm. And then, after another succession of these comparatively quick alternations, there comes a calm—a period during which the *waves of emotion* are feebler: succeeded, as it may be, by another series of stronger waves. (1873, 122: my emphasis, WM)

Considering that the alternation between emotional states possesses the rhythmic form of a wave, it is probable that Joyce's allusion to "the curve of an emotion" refers directly to Spencer's theory.

In "A Portrait of the Artist," Joyce relates the poetic state of inspiration to an increase in the amount of blood circulating in the body. In that section of the prose poem that focuses on Stephen's beloved—a heroine modeled on Dante's Beatrice, and named only as "Lady of the Apple Trees, Kind Wisdom, Sweet Flower of Dusk" (*PSW*, 217)—Joyce describes a feeling of increasing sexual excitement that is sublimated through the creation of poetic phrases. Initially, Joyce hints at sexual intimacy between Stephen and his beloved, the "central torrents of life" referring to the state of sexual tension that begins to inhabit his body: "In ways of tenderness, simple, intuitive tenderness, thy love had made to arise in him the central torrents of life" (*PSW*, 216). Rather than having to imagine the physical possession of his beloved, Stephen thanks her "for that enrichment of soul by thee consummated," and suggests that the excess of nervous energy has been released through action in the external world: "His way (abrupt creature!) lies now to the measurable world and the broad expanse of activity. The blood hurries to gallop in his veins; his nerves accumulate an electric force; he is footed with flame. A kiss: and they leap together, indivisible, upwards, radiant lips and eyes, their bodies sounding with the triumph of harps! Again, beloved! Again, thou bride! Again, ere life is ours!" (*PSW*, 217). Although the physiological dimension of this experience is quickly superseded by a train of religious metaphors, Joyce makes an explicit connection between the quantity of blood in the central nervous system and the electricity that transfers and multiplies the wave of emotion throughout the body. By alluding to the "galloping" of horses, and the state of being "footed" with flame, furthermore, Joyce suggests that the emotion accompanying the sexual act possesses a rhythmic form that communicates its aesthetic dimension.

In the aesthetic dialogue of *Portrait*, Stephen introduces the concept of rhythm when discussing the emotions of terror and pity that characterize the experience of the dramatic spectacle, indicating that the sensation of rhythm is associated with the psychological transformation of life into art:

> Beauty expressed by the artist cannot awaken in us an emotion which is kinetic or a sensation which is purely physical. It awakens, or ought to awaken, induces, or ought to induce, an esthetic stasis, an ideal pity or an ideal terror, a stasis called forth, prolonged and dissolved by what I call the rhythm of beauty. (*P*, 206)

As indicated by the word "prolonged," Stephen conceives the proper experience of drama as a feeling of *stasis* (rest) that nevertheless possesses some *duration*, for the perception of rhythm maintains at the very least a *temporal correspondence* to the physical movement that caused the sensation. In the fourth section of the novel, Stephen encounters a girl during a walk along Dollymount Strand, and the periodic movement of her feet gives rise to the apprehension of an aesthetic image: "Long, long she suffered his gaze and then quietly withdrew her eyes from his and bent them towards the stream, gently stirring the water with her foot *hither and thither*" (P, 171). According to his own terminology, Stephen's carnal desire for the girl must be classified as one of the kinetic emotions ("Desire urges us to possess, to go to something"); yet, the periodic nature of the movement allows him to reduce the image to its purely intellectual aspect: "The first faint noise of gently broken water broke the silence, low and faint and whispering, faint as the bells of sleep; *hither and thither, hither and thither*: and a faint flame trembled on her cheek" (P, 171: my italics, WM). Despite the physical desire connoted by the girl's blush, the repetition of the phrase "hither and thither" marks the rhythmic form of the physical movement, allowing the aesthete to perceive the harmonic correspondence between the recurring temporal pattern and the spatial outline of the movement. As a consequence, Stephen is able to distinguish his "ideal pity" for the girl from the physical desire of attraction that urges him to go toward her, and it is precisely the *rhythmic form of the movement* that enables him to pass from the real world to its ideal reflection in the shape of the poetic phrase.

In the aesthetic dialogue of *A Portrait*, Stephen claims that the "whatness" (*quidditas*) of a thing is perceived by the artist in the act of creation, for "this supreme quality is felt by the artist when the esthetic image is first conceived in his imagination" (P, 215). Rather than linking the act of creation to the actual composition of the literary text, a task that is laborious, and does not come to fruition in an instant, Joyce identifies the act of creation with the act of apprehension, borrowing an image from Shelley to describe its transitory nature: "The mind in that mysterious instant Shelley likened beautifully to a fading coal" (217). The image is taken from the "Defense of Poetry," an essay in which Shelley elevates the intuitions of poetry above the rationalization of science, stating that

> the mind in creation is as a fading coal, which some invisible influence, like an inconstant wind, awakens to transitory brightness: this power arises from within, like the colour of a flower which fades and changes as it is developed, and the conscious portion of our natures are unprophetic of its approach or its departure. (Shelley 1965, vol. 7, 135)

In practice, Joyce uses the image of a fading flower to describe the lyrical movement of Stephen's imagination, for after the appearance of

Stephen's muse, her movement is transformed into a pulsating image: "*Glimmering and trembling, trembling and unfolding,* a breaking light, an opening flower, it spread in endless succession to itself, breaking in full crimson and unfolding and fading to palest rose, *leaf by leaf and wave of light by wave of light,* flooding all the heavens with soft flushes, every flush deeper than the other" (*P*, 187: my italics, WM). In the italicized passages, Joyce uses the techniques of inversion and repetition to create musical periods, illustrating the manner in which the act of aesthetic apprehension gives birth to the poetic image.

When called upon by Lynch to clarify the meaning of rhythm, Stephen modifies an entry first made by Joyce in the Paris notebook (March 25, 1903), stating that "rhythm ... is the first formal esthetic relation of part to part in any esthetic whole or of an esthetic whole to its part or parts or of any part to the esthetic whole of which it is a part" (*P*, 206). In contrast to the more mature Joyce's presentation of the girl on Dollymount Strand, whose waving foot embodies the physical production of a periodic movement, Stephen's definition places more emphasis upon the spatial form of the aesthetic image, and the harmonic structure that emerges from the mutual reflection and interaction of the elements. As Joyce was reading Aristotle's *Poetics* during his first stay in Paris, it is likely that this structural conception of rhythm is based upon the Greek philosopher's conception of *mythos*, for as we have seen, he specifies that the tragic "plot" must have an order and magnitude that allow the parts (beginning, middle, and end) to be integrated into the order of the whole (see Ch. 2). When incorporated into Stephen's theory of aesthetic apprehension, which corresponds to the three qualities of Beauty outlined by St. Thomas Aquinas (*integritas, consonantia,* and *claritas*), the structural conception of rhythm is linked to the synthetic movement of the imagination, for Stephen explains:

> You pass from point to point, led by its formal line; you apprehend it [the esthetic image] as balanced part against part within its limits; you feel the rhythm of its structure ... Having felt that it is *one* thing you now feel that is a *thing.* You apprehend it as complex, multiple and divisible, separable, made up of parts, the result of its parts and their sum, harmonious. (*P,* 212)

As Stephen is here discussing the Thomistic quality of *consonantia,* a term that can be translated as "harmony," it can be seen that the structural conception of rhythm becomes loosely synonymous with the classical conception of "harmony," which might refer to the simultaneous sounding of music tones, the symmetry of architecture or the spatial form of sculpture.

In the context of Joyce's *Portrait*, the structural conception of rhythm is used to describe the second stage of aesthetic apprehension, an act of perception that is also used to describe the rhythmic and thematic correspondences that structure the composition of Stephen's verses. It is now clear why Joyce writes in *Stephen Hero* that "the rhythm is the esthetic result of the senses, values and relations of the words thus conditioned" (*SH*, 31), a fragment that has hitherto remained difficult to interpret due to the missing pages of the manuscript. When placed in the context of Stephen's theory in *Portrait*, it becomes clear that the apprehension of the structural rhythm is *conditioned* by the temporal experience of the metrical rhythm, a relationship of dependence that correlates to the distinction between kinesis and stasis. In the section that depicts the composition of "The Villanelle of the Temptress," the perception of musical echoes between the rhyming words elucidates how the structural rhythm begins to emerge from the metrical correspondence between lines. In this instance, the phenomenon of rhyme translates the kinetic rhythm into a static image:

> *Are you not weary of ardent ways,*
> *Lure of the fallen seraphim?*
> *Tell no more of enchanted days.*

> The verses passed from his lips and, murmuring them over, he felt the rhythmic movement of a villanelle pass through them. The roselike glow sent forth its rays of rhyme; ways, days, blaze, praise, raise. (*P*, 222)

Although the process of composing the villanelle unfolds in time, Stephen nevertheless possesses a spatial view of the whole, because the "roselike" image of the muse is seen through the lens of each rhyming word. It is significant that the list of these rhymes precedes the composition of the complete verse, because it maps out in advance the structure of the poem as a whole, creating a set of rhythmic correspondences that need to be filled out by connecting phrases. According to the rhyme scheme (ABA ABA), there is a structural correspondence between the first and third lines of each tercet, creating a mirror effect within each stanza. On the other hand, the correspondence between the middle line of each tercet allows the imagery to be connected between stanzas, providing the momentum for the poem to develop. As the villanelle superimposes the carnal longings of the poet on the ritual of the Catholic mass, the cycle of the sacrificing and resurrecting Christ provides a temporal schema for the phases of desire and satisfaction that structure the life of the artist. In this way, the process of artistic development, which unfolds in a linear manner, and is oriented toward the completion of a poetic product, can be superimposed on the recurring cycles of religious ritual.

Conclusion

As the metrical and structural concepts of rhythm are reconciled with the composition of Stephen's "Villanelle," it would appear that Joyce's novel achieves the ideal of classical unity attributed to tragedy by Aristotle in the *Poetics*. With the inclusion of the diary entries at the end of the novel, however, Joyce shatters the illusion that the complexity of modern experience can be suspended by a set of formal relations, for these prose fragments provide a more immediate index of the thought and emotions passing through Stephen's mind. Although these entries are "reflections" on earlier experiences, they nevertheless anticipate the synchronization of narrative-time and story-time that characterizes the interior monologues of *Ulysses*.

By choosing to end his novel with a series of diary entries, Joyce achieves the ultimate parody of the poetic genres, for the style of each entry differs according to the content of the thought. Thus, Stephen reflects on conversations with his friends at University College, encounters with Emma Cleary, and memorable words and phrases from books. Although the ironic distance between the epic narrator (Joyce) and the hero (Stephen) is elided by the *dramatic* style of these entries—the lyrical artist becomes the author of his own autobiography—Stephen nevertheless reflects on his experiences in the past tense, using the grammatical categories of a narrative to order his thoughts. Thus, Stephen records a past conversation as a prose narrative:

> Met her today pointblank in Grafton Street. The crowd brought us together. We both stopped. She asked me why I never came, she said she had heard all sorts of stories about me. This was only to gain time. Asked me, was I writing poems? About whom? I asked her. (*P*, 252)

When Stephen enters thoughts in a more poetic style, however, the tense of the verb is dropped, and a rhythmic correspondence is established between the sound of the words and the train of images: "The spell of arms and voices: the white arms of roads, their promise of close embraces and the black arms of tall ships that stand against the moon, their tale of distant nations" (*P*, 252). By dislocating his train of thoughts from the grammatical categories of a narrative, Stephen develops a fragmentary style of recording passing thoughts. The eruption of these diary entries therefore announces the arrival of a distinctly "modernist" tendency in Joyce's stylistic development, for Stephen's thoughts are now directly *presented* in a language that is freed from the hierarchies of grammar and syntax that characterize traditional narrative forms.

Chapter 5

"Acatalectic Tetrameter of Iambs Marching"

Rhythm as Movement in Ulysses

With the development of the "interior monologue" technique in *Ulysses*, Joyce makes the literary fragment the basis for a modernist aesthetic that reflects the changing reality of life in the industrial city. In this chapter, I will not analyze the "encyclopedic" dimension of Joyce's novel as typified by the catalogues of "Ithaca" or the stylistic parodies of "Oxen of the Sun," but rather focus on the *representation* of rhythmic experiences in the interior monologues of Stephen and Bloom. In the preceding chapter, it was argued that the narrative form of Joyce's *Portrait* tends toward the synchronization of "story-time" and "narrative-time," for with the dramatization of lyrical fragments and the presentation of the diary entries at the end of the novel, the epic distance between the discourse (present) and the story (past) of the narrative begins to disappear. While there is some stylistic similarity between the form of these diary entries and the fragments of the interior monologue, the phrases of the latter do not *reflect* on past experiences, and do not derive their material existence from the literary text, but rather they directly embody thought processes as they float freely in the minds of Joyce's characters. As we will see, the spontaneous emergence of rhythmic forms in the "stream of consciousness"[1] provides a temporary means of *ordering* the chaos of modernity, providing an alternative to the so-called mythic method at the level of the individual phrase.[2] Although rhythmic forms tend to structure the experience of time in the *psychological* stream of consciousness, the emergence of such order should not be interpreted as the product of a rational, willing subject, but rather as a *physiological* response to the physical vibration of colors, sounds, and the movements of machines in the modern metropolis.

Although the ever-changing stream of words and phrases passing through the interior monologue seems to represent a purely "psychological" dimension of experience, I will argue in this chapter that the *form* of such thought processes are motivated by the reception of physical rhythms, the production of physiological rhythms, and the imagination of psychological rhythms. In "Sirens," an episode that has often been interpreted as a catalogue of Wagnerian *leitmotifs*, I will suggest that Joyce simulates the production of musical tones through his stylistic experimentation with the "tone-colour" of the various vowels. As the ear can itself be conceived as a musical instrument, the "sympathetic vibration" among the tuning fork, the piano, and Bloom's inner ear at the Ormond Hotel provides a model of creative transformation that is integrated into the "musical" style of the narrator's prose. With the development of the interior monologue in "Proteus," furthermore, we will see that the rhythms of poetry and walking provide a temporal schema for ordering the relationship between vision and touch, a set of "kinesthetic" feelings that motivate the orientation of the visual field and order the series of impressions striking the mind. In "Lotus Eaters" and "Lestrygonians," finally, we will see that the mind of the modern subject is entrained to the circulation of commodities and money through his or her participation in the movement of the city. As the synchronization of subjectivity to the movements of the city is achieved at a physiological level, the legitimation of the capitalist order is achieved through the habitual memorization and performance of advertising jingles that secure consensus at a subconscious level. In all of these ways, we will see that the production and performance of rhythms not only determine the *form* of the "interior monologue" but also provide an *aesthetic* means of ordering the apparent chaos of modernity as reflected in the psychological stream of consciousness.

Sympathetic Vibrations in "Sirens"

In an article titled "Good Vibrations" (2009), Plock has argued that Joyce's musical experimentations were influenced by the acoustic theory of the German physicist, Hermann von Helmholtz, whether it be through the publication of his groundbreaking *On the Sensations of Tone as the Physiological Basis for the Theory of Music* (1895), more general accounts such as John Tyndall's *Sound* (1875), or popular summaries in the *Freeman's Journal*. Indeed, it is possible that Joyce gleaned the Homeric correspondence between mechanical and mythic

"Sirens" from Tyndall's lectures on *Sound*, for the Irish physicist describes the construction of a "Siren" that produces musical tones through the rotation of a disk containing a number of perforations. Just prior to Ben Dollard's inspired performance of the *Croppy Boy*, Bloom meditates on the mundane significance of the word "chambering," suggesting that Molly's urination in her chamber pot might be considered a kind of music:

> Chamber Music. Could make a kind of pun on that. It's a kind of music I often thought when she. Acoustics that is. Tinkling. Empty vessels make most noise. Because the acoustics, the resonance changes according as the weight of the water is equal to the law of falling water. (*U*, 11:979–83)

By comparing Molly's chamber pot to the resonating box of a musical instrument, Bloom argues that the stream of urine generates a series of musical tones, for the pitch alters in direct proportion to the amount of liquid added. Of course, Joyce is alluding ironically to the title of *Chamber Music*. Yet, Bloom's meditation on the laws of acoustics and the natural resonance of physical objects introduces the discourse of acoustic science into "Sirens," suggesting in turn that the rhythmic science of the late nineteenth century may have influenced the style of the episode (and the novel as a whole). In a section describing the transmission of sounds through liquids, Tyndall writes "The Siren has received its name from its capacity to sing under water," describing the immersion of the disk into a vessel of water. Explaining that the disk is caused to rotate rapidly or slowly in proportion to the strength of the current let in by the "cock," Tyndall concludes: "Thus, by alternately opening and closing the cock, the song of the siren is caused to rise and fall in a melancholy manner. *You would not consider such a sound likely to woo mariners to their doom*" (1875, 77). Considering the erotic overtones pervading Tyndall's description, it is possible that Joyce also drew on it when describing the "chambering" of Molly and Boylan.

Although Plock was the first critic to identify the possible allusions to Tyndall's lectures in *Sirens*, she perhaps underestimates the authority of this source, for she is unable to identify the exact textual source of Bloom's mental calculations. As he listens to Simon Dedalus singing "Love's Old Sweet Song," Bloom constructs a primitive harp using a string of gat-cut as a source of vibration, and his four fingers as a bridge: "Bloom wound a skein round four forkfingers stretched it, relaxed, and wound it round his troubled, double, fourfold, in octave, gyved them fast" (*U*, 11:682–4). By halving the length of the string to produce an octave higher, Bloom is employing the method of tuning first invented by the Greek mathematician, Pythagoras. According to this practice, the mathematical relationship between consonant sounds can be determined by comparing the lengths of string (of equal tension and density) to produce musical tones. In *Sound* (1875), Tyndall describes the process in the following terms:

> By placing a movable bridge under the middle of the string, and pressing the string against the bridge, it is divided into two equal parts. Plucking either of those at its centre, a musical note is obtained, which many of you recognize as the octave of the fundamental note. In all cases, and with all instruments, the octave of a note is produced by doubling the number of its vibrations. It can, moreover, be proved, both by theory and by the siren, that this half string vibrates with exactly twice the rapidity of the whole. In the same way it can be proved that one-third of the string vibrates with three times the rapidity, producing a note a fifth above the octave, while one-fourth of the string vibrates with four times the rapidity; producing the double octave of the whole string. In general terms, the number of vibrations is inversely proportioned to the length of the string. (88)

By punning on the words "trouble" and "treble," Joyce suggests that Bloom constructs the intervals of an octave, a fifth, and a double octave by reducing the length of the string by ratios of 2, 3, and 4, a description that parallels the process of tuning described by Tyndall. When Bloom later "teases" the string in sympathetic vibration with Simon Dedalus's performance, he reflects on the mathematical relations that govern the sensation of harmonic intervals: "Numbers it is. All music when you come to think. Two multiplied by two divided by half is twice one. Vibrations: chords those are. One plus two plus six is seven" (*U*, 11:830–2). When Bloom reflects on the mathematical "symmetry" between the processes of doubling and halving—a term that is thematically associated with Molly kissing a lover under the "cemetery" wall at Gibraltar—he is perhaps echoing Tyndall's observation that "this half string vibrates with exactly twice the rapidity of the whole." In this manner, Bloom intuitively perceives the relationship between frequency and pitch, for a string that vibrates at twice its original speed will sound an octave higher. Such musings demonstrate that Joyce was familiar with the mathematical ratios governing the production of musical tones.

One of the founding principles of physiological acoustics is the idea that the human ear is itself a musical instrument whose various nerve endings are tuned to vibrate sympathetically with sound waves of a certain pitch. More specifically, Helmholtz compares the nerve fibrils in the cochlea to the strings of a piano, for if "every such appendage is tuned to a certain tone like the strings of a piano, then the most recent experiments with a piano show that when (and only when) that tone is sounded the corresponding hair-like appendage might vibrate, and the corresponding nerve-fibre experience a sensation" (quoted in Plock 2009, 484). In order to dramatize the comparison between the ear and the piano, Joyce introduces a blind piano tuner who has returned to the Ormond Hotel to collect a tuning fork left behind earlier in the day. At the beginning of the episode, the tuner's motif is stated as "and a call, pure, long and throbbing. Longindying call" (*U*, 11:12). On his return to the bar room, the tuner conducts a quick test of the piano, the narrator comparing the body of the instrument to a coffin: "Upholding the lid he (who?) gazed in the coffin (coffin?) at the oblique triple (piano!) wires. He pressed (the same who pressed indulgently her hand), soft pedalling, a triple of keys to see the thickness of felt advancing, to hear the muffled hammerfall in action" (*U*, 11:291–4). Alluding to Bloom's idea that there should be a "telephone in the coffin" (*U*, 6:868–9) to prevent the dead from being buried alive, the resonance of the chord ("a triple of keys") on nine strings of the piano ("triple ... wires") creates a vibration that evokes his sympathy for Paddy Dignam. The sounding of the tuning fork here acts a medium to enable the tuner to balance the pitch of the strings against their temperament as heard by the ear, a complex process of mediation that links the sensations of the ear to the specific strings of the piano. As the decaying sound resembles the death of his friend, the vibration of the tuning fork evokes a corresponding emotion in Bloom's mind: "From the saloon came a call, long in dying. That was a tuning fork the tuner had that he forgot that he now struck. A call again. Call again. That he now poised that it now throbbed. You hear? It throbbed, pure, purer, softly and softlier, its buzzing prongs. Longer in dying call" (*U*, 11:313–16).

There is also textual evidence to suggest that Joyce was familiar with the acoustic explanation for the sounding of the "harmonics" that accompany the sounding of a fundamental tone. According to Helmholtz (1895), the human ear is capable of perceiving different musical tones at the same time, so long as each tone issues from a separate sound source. Indeed, the unique sound of each instrument is determined by the form of the sound wave and the vibration of "harmonics" or "upper partials"—that is to say, a series of overtones that are generated in addition to the sounding of the fundamental tone—possessing a frequency in proportion to the primary tone. When listening to a symphony, for example, the human ear can distinguish the reed of the clarinet from the bowing of the violin, for each instrument possesses a unique "timbre," and usually performs a musical line that is differentiated in pitch and rhythm. According to Helmholtz, however, the human ear has difficulty distinguishing between the sound of the "fundamental tone" and the "upper partials," because both tones are produced simultaneously from the same source, and the sound waves interfere with one another to produce a compound wave. In "Sirens," Richie Goulding reminisces about Joe Maas, a tenor who once performed an aria titled "All is Lost" from Bellini's opera *La Somnambula*. As he imitates the performance, Bloom observes that the bird-like sound of Goulding's voice is produced from the sonic interference between two notes:

> Richie cocked his lips apout. A low incipient note sweet banshee murmured: all. A thrush. A throstle. His breath, birdsweet, good teeth he's proud of, fluted with plaintive woe. Is lost. Rich sound. *Two notes in one there.* Blackbird I heard in the hawthorn valley. Taking my motives he twisted and turned them. All most too new call is lost in all. Echo. How sweet the answer. How is that done? All is lost now. Mournful he whistled. Fall, surrender, lost. (*U*, 11:630–6: my italics, WM)

In this monologue, Bloom compares the simultaneous sounding of harmonics ("two notes in one there") with the creative process of imitation whereby the human voice imitates the sound of a bird and vice versa. Via an allusion to Thomas Moore's "Echo," the interference of sound waves is traced to the physical processes of reflection and refraction that caused the original "motive" (*motif?*) to be "twisted and turned." As the "Rich" sound of Goulding's voice can be traced to the manner in which it is produced ("lips apout") and the interference of the fundamental tone with the upper partials, it would appear that Joyce was familiar with the acoustic explanation for the "timbre" or "tone-colour" of different sound sources.

It is significant that Joyce was aware of harmonics, for Helmholtz also demonstrates that the difference between the various vowel sounds is determined by the particular combination of overtones produced by alterations to the shape of the vocal cavity. When Joyce describes the shape of Goulding's mouth uttering the syllable "all," he is stressing the relationship between the shape of the vocal cavity and the quality of the vowel, for as the German physicist writes, "the more this cavity is narrowed, either by the lips or the tongue, the more distinctly marked is its resonance for tones of determinate pitch, and the more therefore does this resonance reinforce those partials in the compound tone produced by the vocal chords, which approach the favoured pitch, and the more, on the contrary, will the others be damped" (1875, 104). Due to this phenomenon of reinforcement, the vowels of the human voice will tend to approach a pitch in which the fundamental tone resonates and interferes with its upper partials, allowing the physicist to measure the natural tones of the various vowel sounds. While the account in Helmholtz's treatise might have been too scientific for Joyce's needs, a simple summary is contained in Tyndall's lectures on *Sound* (1875), for the Irishman there recounts the experimental method of verifying the harmonics associated with each vowel:

> In the organ of voice, the reed is formed by the vocal chords, and asso-ciated with this reed is the resonant cavity of the mouth, which can so alter its shape as to resound, at will, either to the fundamental tone of the vocal chords or to any of their overtones. With the aid of the mouth, therefore, we can mix together the fundamental tone and the overtones of the voice in different proportions. Different vowel sounds are due to different admixtures of this kind. Striking one of this series of tuning-forks, and placing it before my mouth, I adjust the size of that cavity until it resounds forcibly to the fork. (197)

As the human ear cannot easily distinguish between the sound of the fundamental tone and the upper partials, a tuning fork is needed to identify the specific pitch of the harmonics, because it will vibrate sympathetically if tuned to the same frequency. In the context of Joyce's *Sirens*, the harmonics contained in the various vowel sounds overcome the formal distance between music and speech, because each vowel can be analyzed as a "compound rhythm" that contains one or more tones to form a virtual chord.

In the context of nineteenth-century aesthetics, this scientific expla-nation for the relationship between vowels and harmonics provided a legitimation of the Wagnerian ideal of reuniting the arts of music and poetry, as it could now be demonstrated that the "tone-color" of each vowel sound was determined by a specific combination of tones and overtones. In *Sound*, Tyndall translates the German *klangfarbe* literally as "clang-tint" (a more conventional translation would be "timbre"), and thereby institutes an analogy between sound and color that is based on their common origin in rhythmic phenomena:

> We may blend in various ways the elementary tints of the solar spec-trum, producing innumerable composite colours by their admixture. Out of violet and red we produce purple, and out of yellow and blue

we produce white. Thus also may elementary sounds be blended so as to produce all possible varieties of clang-tint. (1875, 199)

When integrated into the rules of prosody, the concept of "clang-tint" or "tone-color" therefore provides a scientific explanation for the theory of correspondences developed by Baudelaire and Rimbaud, for the "tone-color" of each vowel will depend on the particular combination of tones and overtones employed by the speaker. In *The Science of English Verse* (1880), Lanier includes "tone-color" as one the four variables of sound production (the other three being duration, intensity, and pitch), a dimension that accounts for the phenomenon of rhyme and alliteration in the context of English verse. Alluding explicitly to the work of Helmholtz and Tyndall, he writes:

> It is this analogy between processes belonging to sound and processes belonging to light which has originated the very expressive term "tone-color" in acoustics. And inasmuch as vowels and consonants are phenomena of tone-color, the present system of verse acquires a safe and sure basis of classification by referring all those effects of English verse which depend directly upon vowels and consonants to this fact and assembling all such effects under the term 'the colors of English verse." (Lanier 1880, 281)

Of course, the convention of rhyme is the most obvious manifestation of this aspect of color in verse, but Lanier also applies it to the distribution of vowels (assonance) and the repetition of consonants (alliteration).

Taking into account the analogy between the quality of each vowel sound and its corresponding "tone-color," it now becomes clear why the two barmaids in *Sirens* are each associated with a specific color. In the first sentence of the episode (excluding the list of *motifs*), Joyce associates Miss Douce and Miss Kennedy with bronze and gold respectively, the colour of their hair standing metonymically for their personhood: "Bronze by gold, Miss Douce's head by Miss Kennedy's head, over the crossblind of the Ormond bar heard the viceregal hoofs go by, ringing steel" (*U*, 11:64–5). The concept of "clang-tint" is here foregrounded through the allusion to the "ringing" sound the horses' hooves, the specific tone color determined by the impact of the "steel" upon the road. Joyce evidently communicates the "ringing" sound through the repetition of three high "ee" vowels that simulate the sound of the hooves. From the description of the Vice-Regal cavalcade in "Wandering Rocks," it is clear that the barmaids have heard the carriage of Earl Dudley and his wife, with Miss Douce catching a glimpse of Gerald Wald, "the fellow in the tall silk" that follows in the second carriage. By highlighting the correspondence between the sound of the horses' hooves and the train of images seen through the slats of "cross blind" of the Ormond hotel, Joyce reveals that the *rhythm* of the musical motif provides a temporal schema for the perception of a sequence of spatial images. As the mere sight of the Siren is potential death for the passing sailor ("He's killed looking back," *U*, 11:77), Joyce associates the sound of Miss Kennedy's hair with the production of musical tones: "Miss Kennedy sauntered sadly from bright light, twining a loose hair behind an ear. Sauntering sadly, gold no more, she twisted twined a hair. Sadly she twined in sauntering gold hair behind a curving ear" (*U*, 11:81–3). By comparing the color of Miss Kennedy's "gold" hair to the strings of a harp or violin, Joyce makes it clear that her "sauntering" body is to be considered a sounding board that amplifies the tone color of these "gold" strings that are wound around the ear. As Miss Kennedy passes in and out of the light, the color of her hair changes from "bright light" to "gold no more," two epithets whose tone color is determined by the repetition of similar vowel sounds, the sequence concluded by the return to "gold hair behind a curving ear."

At the beginning of *Sirens*, the visual appearance of the two Sirens is translated into music by the rhythmical language of the narrator, an effect that is reinforced by the play of call and response that punctuates their dialogue. As Joyce wishes to characterize the two barmaids as relatively simple souls, their discourse remains banal, the height of its sophistication realized with the bawdy expression, *Sonnez la cloche* (a French phrase that refers to the sound of a garter resonating on an exposed thigh). When reading "Sirens," it is frequently difficult to distinguish the voice of one barmaid from the other, for each interjection seems to be a reflection of the other; yet, this confusion has the positive effect of creating a form of "consonance" or "harmony" between the two voices. When the two Sirens laugh over the "goggle eye" of an "old fogey" from Boyd's chemist, the bright sound of their voices blend into a chord that is suspended by the paratactic style of the narrator's prose: "In a giggling peal young goldbronze voices blended. Douce with Kennedy your other eye. They threw their heads back, bronze gigglegold, to let freely their laughter, their screaming, your other, signal to each other, piercing high notes" (*U*, 11:155–61). As the narrator's prose is mixed with Bloom's interior monologue, the phrase "douce with your other eye" indicates that Bloom is trying to perceive a siren with each eye, causing the sound of their voices to be frozen in stereoscope. As their laughing and shrieking reaches a *crescendo*, Joyce highlights the relationship between the resonance of vowels and the primitive emotions of animals, for the open "O" sound is associated with the mere expiration of air:

> Shrill, with deep laughter, after bronze in gold, they urged each other to peal after peal, ringing in changes, bronzegold goldbronze, shrill deep, to laughter after laughter. And then laughed more. Greasy I knows. Exhausted, breathless their heads shaken they laid, braided and pinnacled by glossycombed, against the counterledge. All flushed (O!), panting, sweating (O!), all breathless. (*U*, 11:174–8).

While the overall effect of this description is a feeling of aesthetic *stasis*, the physical movement that underlies the vibration of sound is highlighted by the repetition of similar vowel sounds, such as "peal after peal" and "laughter after laughter." As the sonic reverberations are reinforced by the visual appearance of the Sirens, furthermore, the narrator inverts the order of "bronze" and "gold" to demonstrate that the two can be mixed to produce a compound tone color.

As we have seen, the concept of tone color provides Joyce with a means of associating the visual and aural dimensions of the text, for the "bright" timbre of the Sirens' voices can be reflected by the choice of vowel sounds with a high pitch (i/ee). At the level of auditory rhythm, however, the relationship between color and sound is dramatized through the characters of the deaf waiter and the blind tuner, who are exclusively associated with seeing and hearing. On the one hand, deaf Pat uses the sense of sight to perceive the difference between the present and the future, for the anticipation of objects at a distance indicates the future movement of his body in space. Although Pat's disability prevents him from talking ("Talk. Talk. Pat! Doesn't. Settling those napkins. Lot of ground he must cover in the day," *U* 11:912–13), he is nevertheless associated with the literary dimension of the text, for he delivers a pen and paper for Bloom to write a letter: "Bald deaf Pat brought quite flat pad ink. Pat set with ink pen quite flat pad. Pat took plate dish knife fork. Pat went" (*U*, 11:847–8). Through the use of only monosyllabic words, Joyce creates a temporal correspondence between walking and speaking. For the reader, the "ground" covered by the deaf waiter is measured by the rhythm of the text, which in the passage cited above is measured by the sound of Bloom laughing "hee hee hee hee." On the other hand, the blind tuner cannot perceive the difference between the present and the future through the sense of sight, and therefore must tap his cane in order to anticipate any obstacles and measure the distance traversed. As the episode progresses, the solitary "tap" of the tuner increases in duration, to the point at which a series of eight "taps" are heard. At one point, a series of four taps ("Tap. Tap. Tap. Tap," *U*, 11:1185) reproduces the rhythm of Bloom's interior monologue ("Far. Far. Far. Far," *U*, 11:1186), a train of thought that highlights the association between sound and the measurement of distance in steps.

By creating a primary rhythm through the repetition of the word "Tap," Joyce may have been alluding to the account of "Musical Sounds Produced by Taps" in Tyndall's lectures on *Sound*, for the Irishman there describes an instrument called a gyroscope that produces a musical tone through a rapid sequence of taps: "The production of a musical sound by taps is usually effected by causing the teeth of a rotating wheel to strike in quick succession against a card" (1875, 50). The fact that a series of taps can produce a musical tone when struck in quick succession is highlighted by Joyce when he alters the vowel of the word "tap" to create a variety of different tone colors:

> Bloom. Flood of warm jimjam lickitup secretness flowed to flow in music out, in desire, dark to lick flow, invading. *Tipping her tepping her tapping her topping her.* Tup. Pores to dilate dilating. Tup. The joy the feel the warm the. Tup. To pour o'er sluices pouring sushes. Flood, gush, flow, joygush, tupthrop. Now! Language of love. (*U*, 11:705–9: my italics, WM)

In the italicized passage, Bloom constructs a descending melody by altering the vowel of the word "tap," the high "I" proceeding to the low "U" in the following order: I, E, A, O, U. Through the transformation of the discontinuous "tap" into a series of verbs that signify the act of copulation, Joyce highlights the difference in tempo between the discrete perception of an auditory rhythm and the continuous sensation of a tone, for the sound of each vowel must resonate in a stream of sound. It is clear therefore that the "language of flowers" that Bloom uses to communicate with Martha Clifford is in fact a kind of musical language, for the "flow" of the language is maintained only by the resonance of the vowels.

In contrast to the classical account of sensation, in which the sense organ is the passive recipient of an impression from the physical world, the physiological account of hearing emphasizes the fact that the nerve fibers in the cochlea are themselves producers of vibrations, transforming the phenomenon of hearing into an active, creative process.

In "Sirens," Joyce continually plays on the pun between the words "ear" and "hear," suggesting that the linguistic transformation of the one into the other parallels the process by which the sound waves outside the ear are reproduced as minute vibrations within the inner ear. At one point, Lydia Douce holds a seashell ("a spiked and windy seahorn," 11:923–4) to the ear of the solicitor, George Lidwell, and the narrator seamlessly elides the difference between the two words in the stream of sound: "Ah, how he heard, she holding it to his ear. Hear! He heard" (*U*, 11:930). In this instance, the transference of the vibrations from the shell to the ears of Lidwell and Douce sets up a train of sympathetic vibrations in the bar room, for the interaction brings another siren near: "She held it to her own and through the sifted light pale gold in contrast glided. To hear" (*U*, 11:931–2). Overhearing the commotion, Bloom now sees the "shell held at their ears" and "heard more faintly that they heard, each for herself alone, then each for the other, hearing the plash of the waves, loudly, a silent roar" (*U*, 11:934–6). As Bloom understands the basic laws of acoustics, and realizes that the ear is itself a source of sound production, he makes explicit the symbolic correspondence between the "sea-horn" and the ear: "Her ear too is a shell, the peeping lobe there" (*U*, 11:938). While it might appear to each of these listeners that the seashell is itself the *source* of the sound, Bloom sees through the illusion, musing: "The sea they think they hear. Singing. A roar. The blood it is. Souse in the ear sometimes. Well, it's a sea. Corpuscle islands" (*U*, 11:945–6). Explaining the origin of the sound in the shell as the resonance of the blood being circulating through the body, Bloom posits a symbolic correspondence between the blood and the ocean, the white cells of the blood becoming "Corpuscle islands" in a red sea.

As Jackson Cope (1962) has pointed out, the sea functions as a point of symbolic correspondence between the Telemachiad and the Bloomiad, for while the sound of the sea-horn amplifies the circulation of the blood in *Sirens*, the endless movement of the ocean provides a source of poetic inspiration for Stephen Dedalus in *Proteus*. Indeed, we learn in *Sirens* that Miss Lydia Douce has been "lying out on the strand all day" (*U*, 11:198–9), an image that not only anticipates Gerty MacDowell's indecent exposure to Bloom in *Nausica*, but also recalls the "cocklepickers" that Stephen sees during his walk along Sandymount Strand. The shell is therefore a symbol that stands for the manner in which the ear receives and amplifies the vibrations of the outer world, translating them into words and signs that have meaning within the inner world of the mind. According to

Cope, the flow of rhythmic language mirrors the flow of nature in *Ulysses*, for as he puts it:

> The sea within encircles and recreates the sea without, and at this meeting of the waters the creative moment of the artist 'flowing round and round the persons and the action like a vital sea' becomes one with the moment of knowing one's relationship with the universe. (1962, 82)

Citing Stephen's definition of the epic narrator in *Portrait*, Cope identifies the energy of the epic narrator with the motion of the sea, pointing toward the aesthetic reduction of external nature to the inner movements of the soul. While the vibration of sound waves motivates the form of the thoughts passing through Bloom's stream of consciousness in *Sirens*, it is the endless movement of the sea that fills the vessel of Stephen's mind in *Proteus*, and the sensations of movement that accompany the rhythm of walking which impose a temporal order on the chaos of impressions continually striking the mind.

The Ontology of Flux and the Rhythm of Walking in "Proteus"

In "Scylla and Charybdis," Stephen Dedalus constructs an analogy between artistic production and natural generation that is based on the principles of biological and physiological science, for he compares the artistic conception of the image with the process of nutrition that continually alters the molecular structure of the body: "as we, or mother Dana, weave and unweave our bodies ... their molecules shuttled to and fro, so does the artist weave and unweave his image" (*U*, 9:376–8). More specifically, Stephen alludes to the "Conclusion" of Pater's *The Renaissance*, the manifesto of "decadence" that reduces the phenomenon of life to the physical interaction and transformation of the elements. Citing a fragment from Heraclitus—*Legei pou Herakleitos hoti panta khorei kai ouden menei* ("Heracleitas says that all things are moving and nothing remains")—Pater constructs an ontology of flux that is legitimated by the science of physiology, for as he puts it:

> What is the whole physical life in that moment but a combination of natural elements to which science gives their names? But those elements, phosphorus and lime and delicate fibres, are present not in the human

body alone: we detect them in places most remote from it. Our physical life is a perpetual motion of them—the passage of the blood, the waste and repairing of the lenses of the eye, the modification of the tissues of the brain under every ray of light and sound—processes which science reduces to simpler and more elementary forces. (1893, 186)

Although Pater does not refer to any specific source, his allusion to our "physical life" and the knowledge of "science" reveals the extent to which the aestheticism of the late nineteenth century was informed by the developing sciences of physics, chemistry, biology, and physiology. Indeed, when Pater refers to "the passage of the blood" or "the waste and repairing of the lens of the eye," he is alluding to the phenomena of nutrition and fatigue described in medical textbooks such as Johannes Müller's *Elements of Physiology* (1838). As Pater wishes to exploit this scientific knowledge for his own aesthetic purposes, he constructs a metaphor of weaving to describe how the image of the body emerges from the momentary arrangement of the elements, arguing that the "clear, perpetual outline of face and limb is but an image of ours, under which we group them—a design in a web, the actual threads of which pass out beyond it" (186–7). When Stephen describes the Goddess of nature weaving and unweaving the image of the artist, the metaphor of "weaving" refers directly to the physiological process of generation and decay that underlies both the formation of the body and the literary text.

As we have already seen, Joyce develops a formal conception of rhythm in the Paris notebook that becomes synonymous with the classical conception of "harmony," a term that is metaphorically used to describe the organic structure of living animals. Although it is unlikely that Joyce ever read Johannes Müller's *Elements of Physiology* (1838), it is probable that he was familiar with the basic principles of physiology from his university education and his preparation for a medical degree in Paris. In *Stephen Hero*, Joyce compares the analysis of modern society to the surgical operation of "vivisection" (*SH*, 190–1), identifying the movement of the intellect with the controversial process of dividing the living body into its constitutive elements. With regard to the scientific legitimation of the organic theory of art, it is important that Müller appeals to the notion of a "final cause" (1838, 25) to explain the harmonious growth and adaptation of the animal, for it reconciles the modern doctrine of the vital force with the Aristotelian concept of the "soul" or "entelechy." It is perhaps more significant, however, that he traces the molecular reproduction of the body to the "action of the vital stimuli," for it demonstrates that the shape of the body is maintained through a continual process of change. Discussing the process of nutrition, Müller writes that

> the external conditions that are necessary to life—caloric, water, atmospheric air and nutriment, at the same time that they maintain life, induce constant changes in the composition of the organized body, while certain old components are again decomposed and cast off. (1838, 29)

Regardless of whether Joyce had read Müller's account of the nutritive process, the aesthetic theories of Ruskin and Pater were influenced by the science of physiology, and Joyce's own notion of "structural rhythm" becomes synonymous with the woven outline of the living organism. Indeed, when Stephen compares the creation of the aesthetic image with the molecular processes of nature, he uses the "outline" or "image" of the body to impose some kind of order on the eternal flux of nature.

In the library episode, Stephen appeals to the principle of nutrition to escape his spiritual and material debt to the Irish poet and theosophist, George William Russell. As a proponent of the Irish Literary Revival and friend of W. B. Yeats, the esoteric figure of AE (George William Russell) represents Stephen's spiritual debt to the lyrical poetry of the so-called Celtic Twilight. Indeed, on his entry to the National Library, AE is heard reciting a line from his own *Deirdre*: "Flow over them with your waves and with your waters, Mananaan, Mananaan MacLir" (*U*, 9:191–2). This allusion to the Irish God of the sea causes Stephen to reflect on his debt to the poet, musing: "How now, sirrah, that pound he lent you when you were hungry?" (*U*, 9:192). Although Stephen formerly had the money to repay Russell, he has already spent the money visiting a whore ("you spent most of it in Georgina Johnson's bed"; *U*, 9:195); and justifies his irresponsible behavior via an appeal to the changing molecular structure of the human body: "Wait. Five months. Molecules all change. I am other I now. Other I got pound" (*U*, 9:205–6). With the return of his moral consciousness, however, embodied in the medieval phrase *agenbite of inwit*, Stephen asserts the unity of his personality as it moves through time, musing: "But I, entelechy, form of forms, am I by memory because under everchanging forms" (9:208–9). Perhaps drawing on the Vitalism of Bergson, Stephen now equates the Aristotelian notion of "entelechy" with the automatic memory of the body, for the memory-image of the self seems to underlie these changing impressions. Yet, it would seem that the sense of self is nothing other than the unity of a poem or a literary text, for Stephen's sense of moral responsibility emerges from the composition of a tone poem to Russell: "A.E.I.O.U" (*U*, 9:213). Significantly, Stephen reduces the temporal structure of his personality to a series of alphabetic "elements" that parallel the motion of nature.

When Stephen composes a tone poem, he posits an analogy between the movement of nature and the production of literature that depends on the metaphysical belief in the existence of atoms. From a classical perspective, the origin of this doctrine can be traced to the atomistic philosophy of Leukippus and Democritus, for the Ionian philosophers argue that the atoms or "elements" (*stoicheia*) are generated from the dialectical interaction of the "full" and the "void" (*Metaphysics*, 985b5). According to Aristotle's summary in the *Metaphysics*, the elements of nature can be analyzed as modifications to the material substratum that are received as an "outline" or "schema" (985b11). Significantly, Aristotle also points out that the Attic term "schema" is a translation of the Ionian word *rhysmos*:

> Things are differentiated by *rhysmos*, by *diathigē*, and by *tropē*; the *rhysmos* is the *schēma* ("form"), the *diathigē* ("contact") is the *taxis* ("order"), and the *tropē* ("turn") is the *thesis* ("position"). (985b15)

As is evident from this passage, the original sense of the Greek word "rhythm" was the "form" or "shape" of a material element as received in the material substratum. According to the French linguist Émile Benveniste (1951), however, the Ionian word *rhysmos* is etymologically derived from *rhein*, a verb meaning "to flow" that exemplifies the Heraclitan ontology of flux. He translates the Ionian word *rhysmos* as "the particular manner of flowing," for the visual aspect of the rhythm maintains a trace of movement that underlies it. Significantly, the term *rhysmos* is also used by Herodotus to describe the forms of the letters of the alphabet, indicating that the Ionian philosophers compared the elemental composition of nature with the production of a literary text. Considering that the Greek word *stoicheia* refers to both the "elements" of nature and the "letters" of the alphabet, it is clear that there was a classical tradition of comparing the generation of nature to the production of writing.

In the philosophy of Plato, the concept of rhythm becomes synonymous with "meter," for it there refers to the "order" (taxis) of the fast and slow movements that regulate the gestures of dance. Within the context of classical drama, the meters of poetry reflect the order of the gestures, demonstrating that the visual aspect of the dance suspends the movement of the voice as an ordered sequence of fast and slow steps. In the *Laws*, Plato posits a correspondence between the fast and slow movements of the dance and the high (short) and low (long) syllables of poetry, for he writes:

> This order (*taxei*) in the movement (*kineseōs*) has been given the name rhythm, while the order in the voice (*phonē*) in which high (*oxeos*) and low (*bareos*) combine is called harmony, and the union of the two is called the choral art. (665a)

Considering that the fluid motion of the dancer underlies the appearance of the rhythmic gesture or "schema," it would appear that the motion of human body is "flowing" beneath the surface of things. Yet, the concept of "flux" could also apply to the motion of the voice, for the Greek conception of *rhēsis* refers to the flowing utterance of the epic narrator or orator. The Platonic concept of rhythm qua *meter* therefore posits a temporal correspondence between singing and dancing that is mediated by the "order" of the fast (short) and slow (long) movements. Of course, the concept of *taxis* is subsequently employed in Aristotle's *Poetics* to describe the "order" of the events in Attic tragedy (beginning, middle, and end), a sequence that enables the whole of the play to be perceived in a single glance. Considering that Joyce defines the structural rhythm as the formal relations between the parts and the whole of an aesthetic image, a definition that derives from the description of classical tragedy in Aristotle's *Poetics*, we can discern a genealogical relationship between the modernist writer and the classical doctrines of Leukippus and Democritus. Significantly, Joyce claims to have read the *Metaphysics* during his time in Paris, and due to his interest in etymological dictionaries, it is also likely that he was aware of the etymological relationship between "rhythm" and the Heraclitan ontology of flux.

In the context of the Irish literary revival, Joyce's knowledge of the "elements" would have been derived from the esoteric knowledge of George William Russell, for the theosophist seems to have had a profound influence on Joyce during his time at University College. According to Richard Ellmann, the young Joyce called on the mystical poet at ten o'clock one August night in 1902, walking up and down the street until Russell arrived at midnight (*JJ*, 99). After being admitted, the two apparently spent the entire night talking about poetry and theosophy, an encounter that would have exposed Joyce to the principles of Eastern philosophy and the work of luminaries such as Madame Blavatsky. In 1918, Russell published an obscure book titled *The Candle of Vision*, in which he reflects upon the process of meditation, empathy, and dreaming which enabled him to create an imaginary world of poetic symbols that he supposed paralleled the divine forms of nature. At times, Russell criticizes the knowledge of modern "psychology" for trying to reduce the workings of the imagination to the preservation of memory traces in the brain, for as he puts it: "One writer talks about light being a vibration, and the vibration affecting the eye and passing along the nerves until it is stored up in the brain cells. The vibration is, it appears, stayed or fixed there" (1920, 44). Nevertheless, this description of light waves becoming states of consciousness is incorporated into his theory of the poetic imagination, for the light waves vibrate sympathetically with all the molecules of the body: "Yet I know that every movement of mine, the words I speak, the circulation of my blood, cause every molecule in my body to vibrate. How is this vibration in the cells unaffected?" (1920, 44). Indeed, Russell cites the work of the Scottish physicist, Balfour Stewart, to support the notion that the form of each element reflects the order of nature within itself, the memory of the earth preserved in the history of its physical transformations. To the extent, therefore, that the body of the artist partakes of the motion of nature, and vibrates sympathetically with waves of light and sound, the molecules of the body constitute a microcosm that reflects the macrocosm of the universe. "But what is matter?" asks Russell, "Is it not pregnant every atom of it with the infinite? Even in visible nature does not every minutest point of space reflect as a microcosm the macrocosm of earth and heaven?" (1920, 105).

Based on the belief that the poetic imagination can reconstruct the order of the universe from the sympathetic vibration of the natural elements, Russell outlines a method of poetic intuition whereby the so-called Language of the Gods can be deduced. According to Russell, the meaning of words can be traced to the particular manner in which the elements of language are combined, for he compares the composition of words to the molecular compounds of the chemist:

> If I interpreted rightly that dweller in the mind, the true roots of human speech are vowels and consonants, each with affinity to idea, force, colour and form, the veriest abstractions of these, but by their union into words expressing more complex notions, as atoms and molecules by their union form the compounds of the chemist. (1920, 121)

Describing a process of "murmuring" the letters of the alphabet (or the "roots" of divine speech) until he discovered "the innate affinities of sound with idea, element, force, colour and form" (1920, 115),

Russell lists a number of letters and outlines their symbolic correspondences. For example: "The first root is A, the sound symbol
for the self in man and Deity in the cosmos. Its form equivalent is
the circle O" (1920, 121). In the "Circe" episode of *Ulysses*, Russell
appears on the dream-stage of Dublin's night-town district in the
guise of Mananaan MacLir, the Irish God of the Sea, uttering the
words "Aum! Hek! Wal! Ak! Lub! Mor! Ma!" (15:2268). According
to Gifford and Seidman, the first of these words means "the beginning and the end," because Russell also tells us that the letter "M ...
is the close, limit, measure, end or death of all things" (1988, 125).
Indeed, by combining the meaning of each element in the manner
of a chemist, the annotators of *Ulysses* have provided the inquisitive
reader with a translation of these cryptic symbols, suggesting that the
sequence of words parallels the process of sexual intercourse. If this
interpretation is correct, then it would seem that Joyce is comically
undermining the divine status of Mananaan MacLir, for Joyce's allusion to the process of material generation undermines the equation of
the Irish sea-God with the state of eternity in *The Candle of Vision*:
"We have first of all Lir, an infinite being, neither spirit nor energy
nor substance, but rather the spiritual form of these, in which all the
divine powers, raised above themselves, exist in a mystic union or
trance" (1920, 155). Similarly, by casting Russell in the role of the
Irish sea-God, Joyce satirizes the theosophist for his distance from the
reality of the material world.

In "Proteus," Stephen attempts to translate the sound of the ocean
into a series of primitive words that reflect the order of the sensations
passing through his mind. As the waves of sound vibrate sympathetically with the molecules of his body, the elements of nature are translated into the elements of speech:

> Listen: a four-worded wave-speech: seesoo, hrss, rseeiss, ooos.
> Vehement breath of waters amid seasnakes, rearing horses, rocks. In
> cups of rocks it slops: flop, slop, slap: bounded in barrels. And, spent,
> its speech ceases. It flows purling, widely flowing, floating foampool,
> flower unfurling, (*U*, 3:456–60)

In this passage, the rocks provide a container to capture the flowing
water of the ocean, just as words capture the stream of sound issued
from the mouth. Considering that the sound of the wind upon the
waves makes a "hissing sound," it comes as no surprise to discover
that Stephen's wave-speech is composed largely of "s" sounds; but
it is interesting to note that Russell lists "impregnation, inbreathing

or insouling" as the divine significance of the letter S. As Lir represents the state of eternity, prior to all material generation, the act of
"impregnation" or "inbreathing" must represent the beginning of creation. Indeed, the act of creation arises from the interaction between
eternity and nature, for as Russell argues: "just as Mananan is the
root of all conscious life, from the imperial being of the gods down to
the consciousness in the ant or amoeba ... So is Dana also the basis of
every material form from the imperishable body of the immortals to
the transitory husk of the gnat" (1920, 158). Here Russell configures
the classical opposition between Heaven and Earth as the relationship
between Lir and Dana, and traces the act of creation to the emergence
of Angus, a Celtic hero who translates the power of Lir into the multiple branches of the "Hazel Wand." Considering that Stephen carries
an ashplant, and is named "Wandering Ængus" (*U*, 10:1066–7) by
Buck Mulligan, a title that is also associated with Yeats's "The Song
of Wandering Angus," it is fairly clear that Joyce modeled his young
protagonist on the figure of the Celtic hero. Just as Russell traces
the act of creation to the emergence of Angus, Stephen Dedalus captures the "breath" of the sea in the womb of his mouth, and translates
the divine form of Lir into the sounds of articulate speech: "His lips
lipped and mouthed fleshless lips of air: mouth to her womb. Omb,
allwombing tomb. His mouth moulded issued breath, unspeeched:
ooeeehah, roar of cataractic planets, globed, blazing, roaring, way-
awayawayawayawayaway" (*U*, 3:401–4). As the sound of the wind
and the waves resolves itself into an iambic pattern, the repetition
of the word "away" creates a rhythmic form that both reflects the
thought patterns of Stephen Dedalus and parallels the periodic movement of the sea.

From the foregoing reconstruction of the elemental philosophy of
Pater and Russell, it is clear that Stephen derives his belief in the ontology of flux from a tradition of esoteric philosophy that can be traced
to the metaphysics of Heraclitus and the atomism of Democritus. Yet,
Stephen's meditation on "the ineluctable modality of the visible" in
Proteus should not simply be interpreted as an attempt to reduce the
motion of nature to a set of poetic symbols, but rather as an elaborate
thought experiment in which belief in the reality of divine forms or
spiritual essences is tested by the materialism of Aristotle and the
skepticism of Bishop Berkeley.[3] Although the atomism of Democritus
describes the impression of "rhythmic" elements on the material substratum of nature, the concrete experience of temporality is related to
the production and perception of metrical rhythms, aesthetic forms
that relate the sound of the voice to the movements of the body. As the

episode progresses, therefore, Stephen progressively works through a number of classical authorities in the search for a theory of rhythm that can account for the manner in which the mind orders the sequence of visual impressions via the parallel sounds of the voice and movements of the body. As we will see, it is the emergence of poetic phrases in the stream of consciousness that performs this synthesizing operation, for the rhythms of poetry provide a temporal means of ordering the relationship between vision and touch.

In the opening paragraph of *Proteus*, Stephen compares the changing sequence of colors parading before his eyes with the words or signs of a literary text, as the "Signatures of all things that I am here to read" could refer to either colors or letters. Alluding to either Berkeley's theory of vision or Boehme's *The Signatures of All Things* (1926), a mystical treatise that posits a symbolic correspondence between concrete images and spiritual essences, Stephen approaches the sensible appearance of the world from the perspective of the skeptic:

> Ineluctable modality of the visible: at least that if no more, thought through my eyes. Signatures of all things I am here to read, seaspawn and seawrack, the nearing tide, that rusty boot. Snotgreen, bluesilver, rust: coloured signs. Limits of the diaphane. But he adds: in bodies. Then he was aware of them bodies before of them coloured. How? By knocking his sconce against them, sure. Go easy. Bald he was and a millionaire, *maestro di color che sanno.* Limit of the diaphane in. Why in? Diaphane, adiaphane. If you can put your five fingers through it is a gate, if not a door. Shut your eyes and see. (*U*, 3:1–9)

As Joyce wishes to represent the colors in the order that they actually appear to Stephen's eyes, he must alter his syntax to reflect the ineluctable movement of the visible world. By dividing Stephen's interior monologue into a number of distinct phrases, Joyces captures each "wave of attention" as it is translated into a set of linguistic symbols. By alternating between "seaspawn and seawrack ," for example, Joyce creates the impression of Stephen's eyes gazing from left to right, the changing orientation of the visual field indicated via the transition from the article to the demonstrative: "*the* nearing tide, *that* rusty boot." Dislocated from any grammatical structure, Stephen names a series of colors that retain an elemental connection to the substances that underlie them: "Snotgreen, bluesilver, rust: coloured signs. Limits of the diaphane. But he adds: in bodies." By arranging these names in the form of a list, Joyce depicts the changing appearance of the material world as a discrete series of impressions that are comprehended by the mind in distinct pulses of attention.

As we have seen, the timbre of various vowel sounds can be associated with specific tone colors, for light vibrates to produce colors in the same way that the air vibrates to produce musical tones. In "Proteus," however, Stephen is seeking to establish a causal relationship between the motion of the physical world and the appearance of color, and therefore meditates on the status of the "diaphanous" medium that communicates the existence of external bodies to his mind. Rather than quoting the full definition of color from Aristotle's *De Sensu*, Stephen simply abstracts the most significant element of the definition, "limits of the diaphane," allowing the phrase to merge seamlessly into the flow of his thoughts (Livorni 1991). The "diaphane" here refers to Aristotle's concept of the visible medium, a diaphanous substance that becomes transparent when activated by light. As the diaphanous substance is said to inhere in the surface of bodies ["It is therefore the Translucent, according to the degree in which it subsists in bodies (and it does so in all more or less), that causes them to partake of colour," *De Sensu*, 439a: cited in Gifford and Seidman 1988, 45], Stephen lists a series of colors that are formed from the chemical reaction between the substance and the transparent medium of visibility. Hence, rust is formed from the chemical reaction between iron and oxygen, just as "blue-silver" is formed from silver and oxygen. Despite the substantial foundation for each of these colors, both are ultimately deceptive, for the "rust" refers to the leather of a boot and the "blue-silver" to the reflection of the water on the sand of Sandymount Strand. Indeed, as soon as the visible sign is translated into language, it becomes overdetermined by a set of symbolic connotations and correspondences. As we know from *Telemachus*, "snot-green" is an epithet coined by Mulligan to describe the sea, but it is also the ironic symbol of Irish art.

In the second paragraph of the episode, Stephen traces the order of the impressions to the alterations of perspective caused by the movement of his body. As each change to the orientation of the visual field can be correlated with the periodic movements of the body, the intuition of rhythm becomes an *aesthetic* means of coordinating the sensation of space and time:

> Stephen closed his eyes to hear his boots crush crackling wrack and shells. You are walking through it howsomever. I am, a stride at a time. A very short space of time through very short times of space. Five, six: the *nacheinander*. Exactly: and that is the ineluctable modality of the audible. Open your eyes. No. Jesus! If I fell over a cliff that beetles o'er his base, fell through the *nebeneinander* ineluctably! I am getting on

nicely in the dark. My ash sword hangs at my side. Tap with it: they do. My two feet in his boots are at the ends of his legs, *nebeneinander*. Sounds solid: made by the mallet of Los Demiurgos. Am I walking into eternity along Sandymount strand? Crush, crack, crick, crick. Wild sea money. Dominie Deasy kens them a'. (*U*, 3:10–20)

In this sequence, Stephen uses the rhythmic activity of walking to coordinate the spatial images of painting (colors) with the temporal sounds of poetry (words). Alluding to the terminology of Lessing's *Laocöon*, Stephen devises an aesthetic solution for correlating the temporal and spatial dimension of his sensible experience, for the German dramatist makes a distinction between the "successive" (*nacheinander*) sounds of poetry and the "coexistent" (*nebeneinander*) parts of the painted image. Indeed, as the signs of speech must follow each other in time, poetry is more suited to the narration of actions than the description of images, for as Lessing reasons:

> If it be true that Painting, in its imitations, makes use of entirely different means and signs from those which Poetry employs; the former employing figures and colors in space, the latter articulate sounds in time ... then co-existent signs can only express objects which are co-existent, or the parts of which co-exist, but signs which are successive can only express objects which are in succession, or the parts of which succeed one another in time. (1874, 148)

As Lessing argues, the medium of poetry can only describe the various aspects of an image via the temporal medium of speech, for the poet can only present one action at a time. When Stephen alludes to the "ineluctable modality of the visible," he is therefore referring to the spatial medium of painting, the "ineluctable modality of the audible" referring to the temporal medium of poetry.[4]

Despite the different media of painting and poetry, Stephen here discovers that the appearance of the visual field is altered with each stride, such that the *difference* between two aspects of the same image can be temporally coordinated with the *difference* between two metrical stresses. When he asserts, "I am, a stride at a time," he not only announces the length of the period that he will use to coordinate his sensation of space and time, but he also establishes an iambic rhythm that persists in his subsequent train of thought: "A vèry short spáce of tíme through vèry short tímes of spáce. Five, six: the *nacheinander*." Assuming that the first phrase contains an iambic rhythm that persists for six beats, we can assume that the second phrase reflects on the underlying rhythm of the first phrase. The naming of beats "five" and "six" indicates that the syntax of the chiasmus is informed by the rhythm of walking and thinking. By demonstrating the reversibility of the relationship between time and space, Stephen shows that the intuition of a spatial form can be derived from the synthesis of a temporal series, and therefore discovers that the intuition of rhythm provides an aesthetic means of mediating between time and space, poetry and painting. Considering that the structural concept of rhythm pertains to the *formal relations between the parts and the whole of an aesthetic image*, the concepts of "succession" and "co-existence" provide an aesthetic means of translating a temporal process into a spatial image, and thereby reconcile the metrical and structural concepts of rhythm.

When Stephen closes his eyes to play the role of the blind man ("I am getting along nicely in the dark"), he is alluding to both the skepticism of Berkeley and his theory of vision. In "A Treatise Concerning the Principles of Human Knowledge" (1910a), the Irish philosopher argues that Locke's notion of the "material substance" is simply an "abstract" or "general" idea that has no real existence inside or outside the mind. Attributing this false belief in the material substratum to the misuse of words, Berkeley argues that words do not signify general ideas, but rather indicate particular ideas that stand as *signs* for universal ideas. For Berkeley, words do not signify concepts, but rather refer to the sensation of things. While this *semiotic* conception of the relationship among words, ideas, and sensations leads to an extreme form of skepticism—most famously expressed in the maxim *esse* is *percipi* ("to be is to be perceived")—it also clears the ground for a phenomenological reconstruction of the constitution of spatial forms through the immediate sensation of visible ideas. Indeed, Berkeley's "Essay towards a New Theory of Vision" (1910b) can be interpreted as a complement to his metaphysics to the extent that the analysis of vision provides a psychological explanation for the perception of objects at a distance, that is to say, objects that are presumed to exist *beyond* the mind. When Stephen reasons that Berkeley was "aware of them before being coloured," he is alluding to Dr Johnson's refutation of the *esse* is *percipi* principle, for he apparently proves the existence of material objects by simply "knocking his sconce against them." When Johnson knocks his foot against a rock, however, he is ironically confirming Berkeley's thesis that visible ideas signify tangible ideas.[5] As the existence of corporeal objects can only be confirmed through the actualization of the sense of touch, the visual perception of an object in space only *signifies* the possibility of moving toward the object and touching it. The confirmation of vision in the present therefore depends on the anticipation of touch in the future.

In the empirical psychology of the middle to late nineteenth century, Bishop Berkeley's theory of vision still retained much of its currency, and it is perhaps for this reason that Stephen alludes to the *Essay towards a New Theory of Vision* when reflecting on the process whereby the mind judges the shifting distance between the eye and objects in space. In *Mental and Moral Science* (1884), for example, Alexander Bain includes an entire section on Berkeley's theory of vision, summarizing his basic position in the following terms: "Berkeley held that distance is not seen, but felt by touch, and that we learn to connect our tactile experiences with the accompanying visible signs" (189). Significantly, Bain includes a section on objections to Berkeley's theory, where he refers to the invention of the stereoscope by Wheatstone, an instrument designed to prove that distance perception is based on the difference of aspect perceived by the dominant and recessive eyes. As Bain puts it, "The picture of the object is received by one eye; the other merely extending its compass, and giving the dissimilarity of aspect that is a sign of distance" (1884, 192). Considering that Stephen alludes to the "stereoscope" in *Proteus*, it is possible that he consulted Bain's "compendium" when formulating his own conception of Berkeley's theory. If he had done so, he would have been interested by a passage in which Bain compares the ideas associated with the perception of colors to the melody that accompanies the text of a song, for he writes: "As in reading our mental picture is not confined to a visible word, but involves the feeling of articulation and melody on our ear, together with the suggested meanings—so in vision, the mind supplies far more than the sense receives" (1884, 193). Although Berkeley himself constructs an analogy between visual signs and linguistic signs in his essay, the allusion to the "melody" behind the written word is unique to Bain's account, and may have motivated Joyce's own attempts to synthesize the ideas of vision and touch through the embodied performance of poetic rhythms.

In contrast to the classical account of visible sensation, which had been based on the science of optics, and the assumption that the perception of distance is automatically derived from the angle of optic axes, Berkeley argues that the mind learns to associate the activity of focusing with the possible movement of the body through space. When someone sees something at a distance, Berkeley reasons that "what he sees only suggests to his understanding, that after having passed a certain distance, *to be measured by the motion of his body,*

which is perceivable by touch, he shall come to perceive such and such
tangible ideas which have been usually connected with such and such
visible ideas" (§45: my emphasis, WM). Stephen will later reconstruct
this process of associating visible signs with tangible signifieds, for he
thinks to himself:

> The good bishop of Cloyne took the veil of the temple out of his shovel
> hat: veil of space with coloured emblems hatched on its field. Hold
> hard. Coloured on a flat: yes, that's right. Flat I see, then think dis-
> tance, near, far, flat I see, east, back. Ah, see now! Falls back suddenly,
> frozen in stereoscope. (*U*, 3:416–19)

Here, the image of the "veil" from the Old Testament (*Exodus*, 26.31–5)
points to the divine significance of tangible experience behind the tap-
estry of visual signs, a screen that separates the public space of the
temple from the "holiest of holies" (Brivic 1990, 738–9). By moving
his pupils and changing the focus of his vision, Stephen shifts his gaze
from the foreground to the background, and associates the activity
of moving his eyes and head with the *future* movement of his body in
space. While the judgment of distance is an intellectual act that takes
place in an instant, the tangible significance of vision derives from the
memory of past movements and the anticipation of future movements.
As a consequence, the spatial analysis of distance perception must be
replaced by a more dynamic theory that takes into account the *continuous* movement of the body through space and the "sensations of
movement" that accompany the alteration of the visual field.

As Berkeley remains concerned with the phenomenon of distance
perception, he assumes that the perceiver and perceived remain station-
ary, situated at a constant distance from one another. Nevertheless,
his description of aural sensation suggests that the distance between
the perceiver and the perceived might be measured by the *duration*
and *speed* of the movement, for as he notes:

> Sitting in my study I hear a coach drive along the street; ... By the vari-
> ation of the noise I perceive the different distances of the coach, and
> know that it approaches before I look out. Thus by the ear I perceive
> distance, just after the same manner as I do by the eye. (§46)

While Berkeley cites this example to demonstrate that the ideas of
vision, touch, and sound remain distinct from one another, it nevertheless serves to show that distance can be measured by the rhythm
and tempo of the movement. In this instance, the increasing volume

and pitch of the coach indicates that it is approaching the ear. We know from Joyce's epiphanies that he had meditated on the association between hearing and movement, for in 27, he hears "the sound of hoofs upon the road," and observes that they beat "Not so faintly now as they come near the bridge" (*PSW*, 187). Similarly, when Stephen closes his eyes in *Proteus*, he measures the movement of his body in space by counting the number of steps, and in this way, he develops a method of translating spatial distance into temporal duration. As each "step" occupies a constant duration and length, it can be effectively used as a measurement of time and space. Rather than assuming a fixed distance between the eye and the surface of the tangible object, Stephen uses the sense of hearing to develop a dynamic model of visual perception, for the rhythm of his poetry provides a temporal schema for measuring the movement of his body. Indeed, if the "steps" of the body can be translated into the "feet" of poetry, then the tangible significance of the world can be reinterpreted as the embodied performance of poetry.

By shifting the theoretical framework of our analysis from the static relationship between words and ideas (or images and objects) to the dynamic relationship between sounds, we should be able to uncover a rhythmic dimension of the interior monologue that facilitates the coordination of visible and tangible ideas. As Derek Attridge (2004, Ch. 5) has shown, onomatopoeia performs an important stylistic function in Joyce's text, for it mediates between the mere perception of sound and the insertion of the sound into the differential structure of the linguistic system. As Stephen walks along Sandymount Strand, he marks the difference between each "step" as an alteration of tone color, forming a cadence from the combination of four steps: "Crush, crack, crick, crick." While the difference between vowels indicates the dynamic alteration of the intonation pattern, and the movement of his body through the space, the combination of the four beats also indicates a completed cadence of thought. Referring to the shells as "wild sea money," Stephen improvises a series of phrases that fit the underlying rhythm of the "crush" cadence ("Dominie Deasy kens them a'."), and forms a line of poetry that alludes directly to the rhythm of walking:

> *Won't you come to Sandymount,*
> *Madeline the mare?*

Rhythm begins, you see. I hear. Acatalectic tetrameter of iambs marching. No, agallop: *deline the mare.* (*U*, 3:21–4)

By using the convention of lineation, Joyce here indicates that the rhythm has assumed the regular form of a four-beat pattern, which Stephen correctly identifies as a "tetrameter of iambs marching." By distinguishing between his *seeing* and *hearing* selves ("you see. I hear"), Stephen suggests that his sensations remain irreconcilable; yet, the *performance* of this rhythm provides a temporal schema for the coordination of vision and sound. By transferring the sense of touch from the external position of the distant object to the "sensations of movement" associated with the activity of walking, Stephen uses the rhythm of his poem to coordinate the movement of the body with the changing appearance of the visual field.

The cryptic allusions in Stephen's short poem also indicate a symbiotic relationship between the artist and nature, for the sea is personified as a Mother Goddess who is the creator of all matter and life on earth. While the name "Madeline" may refer to the biblical figure of Mary Magdalene, it also contains a pun on the construction of verse (made-line), for as Stephen's next thought makes clear, the "made-line" can be "delined." As the rhythm of the iambic feet brings to mind the sound of a galloping horse, Stephen glosses "Madeline" as "the mare," a name that also contains a pun on the French words for "mother" (*mere*) and "sea" (*mer*). Considering that Mulligan addresses the sea as "the great sweet mother," an epithet borrowed from Swinburne, the entire phrase might be interpreted as an image for the waves crashing upon the sand. As this couplet takes the form of a question, it implies that the poem remains incomplete, and this is reinforced by the conscious act of stopping the rhythm: "No, agallop: *deline the mare.*" Indeed, it is only the imagined return of the Tuatha de Danaan on the steeds of Mananaan (the Irish God of the Sea) that will complete the intuition of this rhythm, for the image is now realized in a prose form that more accurately represents the cadences of Stephen's thought: "They are cóming, wáves. The whítemaned séahorses, chámping, bríghtwindbridled, the stéeds of Mánanaan" (*U*, 3:55–7). By using punctuation to separate each image, Joyce demonstrates that each cadence of thought is embodied in a rhetorical accent that parallels the rhythm of the waves beating upon the sand. While the intuition of rhythm provides a temporal means of coordinating the changing impressions of the visual field with the sensations of movement felt by the body, it also provides a schema for perceiving the order of natural processes, for the phases of Stephen's thought now begin to correspond to the rise and fall of the waves.

The Circulation of Commodities in "Lotus Eaters"

In the rhythmic science of the late nineteenth century, writers often appealed to images of the waves to illustrate their theories, in particular, the interference of waves to form compound rhythms of varying amplitude and frequency. In his chapter titled "The Rhythm of Motion," for example, Herbert Spencer writes "the whole outline would show a complication like that of a vast ocean-swell, on whose surface there rise large billows, which themselves bear waves of moderate size, covered by wavelets, that are roughened by a minute ripple" (1896, 278). While it might appear that Spencer is describing a natural phenomenon, the image of the waves is used here to illustrate the complex interaction of forces that dictate the evolution of society, including factors such as demography, health, economics, law, and poverty. Among these, economics possesses a privileged status in Spencer's theory, for the circulation of money provides a quasi-natural means of achieving equilibrium between supply and demand and fixing the prices of commodities. Indeed, Spencer uses the concept of exchange to differentiate the extent to which traditional societies have become integrated with the capitalist mode of production, linking the project of modernity to the accelerated tempo of exchange:

> Exchange during early times is almost wholly carried on at fairs, held at long intervals in the chief centres of population. The flux and reflux of people and commodities which each of these exhibits, becomes more frequent as national development leads to greater social activity. The more rapid rhythm of weekly markets begins to supersede the slow rhythm of fairs. And eventually the process of exchange becomes at certain places so active, as to bring about daily meetings of buyers and sellers—a daily wave of accumulation and distribution of cotton, or corn, or capital. (1896, 278–9)

Extending his rhythmic analysis to the changes in supply (production) and demand (consumption) that determine the oscillation of prices, Spencer demonstrates that the continuous process of exchange on a daily basis has longer-term effects that can be measured in terms of the periodic alternation between extremes.[6] Considering that the aesthete possesses the capacity to perceive rhythmic forms in everyday life, the concrete process of exchange can be interpreted as a *sign* or *symptom* of these larger social forces, for the price of any commodity will reflect the relationship between the forces of production and consumption. While Stephen uses the periodic movements of his body to impose order on the changing forms of the sea, Bloom reflects on the circulation of commodities, and tries to perceive the deeper significance of the cycles that inform the superficial appearance of commodities in the modern, industrial city.

In the context of Bloom's interior monologue, the so-called stream of life is associated with the exchange of commodities and the flow of money in the marketplace. In an encyclopedic book titled *The Economy of Ulysses* (1995), Mark Osteen has analyzed the role that advertising plays in translating the system of economic relations into a system of signs, suggesting that the consumption of commodities also involves the "ingestion" of messages with their associated ideologies:

> Just as money functions as a host enabling the transubstantiation of one commodity into another (C-M-C), and just as commodities mediate the transformation of exchange into surplus value (M-C-M), so ads function as a host that changes purchase into consumption through an exchange of messages and signs. (115)

As indicated by Osteen's argument, the Marxist critique of surplus value implies a shift in perspective from the circulation of commodities (C-M-C) to the circulation of money (M-C-M), a substitution that in practice causes the use value of the object to be mistaken for its exchange value. Significantly, the circulation of money that motivates the generation of surplus value can also be analyzed in terms of its rhythm, for the amount of money in the system is measured in terms of the *velocity* of exchange. Assuming that the sum total of prices is known, as well as the average number of exchanges, Marx writes that "the number of moves or the rapidity of circulation of money is in its turn determined by or expresses the average rapidity with which commodities go through the different phases of their metamorphoses, the rapidity with which these metamorphoses succeed one another, and with which those commodities that have gone through their metamorphoses are replaced by new commodities in the process of circulation" (1904, 132). While this conception of the velocity or "rapidity" of exchange is determined by an abstract mathematical calculation, it also reveals the *intuitive* basis on which the mind of the modern subject passes from the perception of the concrete act of exchange to the generalized system of exchange (the circulation of money and the determination of prices), for it is only by perceiving the velocity of circulating capital (which *symbolizes* the circulation of money) in the modern metropolis that the mind gains an awareness of the total number of exchanges.

In "Calypso," Bloom meditates on the wealth generated by the brewing industry in Dublin, attempting to link the total number of exchanges to the circulation of barrels around the cityscape. In the early twentieth century, Ireland possessed an agricultural mode of production, for with the exception of the shipping industry in Belfast, the sale of livestock still provided the major source of income for Irish landlords and tenants. One major exception to this trend was the growth of the alcohol industry in Dublin, centered on the brewery owned by Arthur Guinness. According to Joseph Lee, "the number of public houses [in Ireland] increased from 15,000 in 1850 to nearly 20,000 by 1911, when about £15 million per annum was spent on liquor" (1989, 14). In contrast to other commodities such as tea or coal, which were imported from overseas, local brewers were able to supply the wants of the Irish public. Observing a shift from the consumption of whisky to beer, Lee notes that "Beer consumption *per capita* increased four-fold, from 40 to 160 pints per annum, while whisky and poteen consumption probably fell about fifty percent" (1989, 14). Taking into account this massive increase in the consumption of beer (or "porter"), it comes as no surprise to discover that Bloom associates the value of bank deposits with the total consumption of beer by the Irish public. Noting that one of the Guinness brothers "once cashed a sevenfigure check for a million in the bank of Ireland" (*U*, 4:304–5), Bloom performs an elaborate calculation in which he attempts to determine the number of gallons of porter needed to generate such a sum: "A million pounds, wait a moment. Twopence a pint, fourpence a quart, eightpence a gallon of porter, no, one and fourpence a gallon of porter. One and four into twenty: fifteen about. Yes, exactly. Fifteen millions of barrels of porter" (*U*, 4:307–10). While Bloom's mental calculations are dependent on certain units of measure that enable the quantity of porter to be determined, these units need to be named and perceived as something meaningful in the context of everyday life. On the side of consumption, the "pint" stands as a unit of measure, for Bloom is no doubt familiar with the taste and satisfaction associated with a pint. On the side of production, however, it is the "barrel" that becomes the object of Bloom consciousness, for it is the means by which the porter is distributed. Mistaking an abstract quantity ("a gallon") for the intuition of a concrete object ("a barrel"), Bloom identifies a false step in his calculation: "What am I saying barrels? Gallons. About a million barrels all the same" (*U*, 4:311–12). Ironically, Bloom's calculation returns in the form of a circle, for it turns out that a barrel is worth approximately one Irish pound.

In practical terms, Bloom perceives a barrel of porter as a standard of value, for not only does it represent the actual consumption of beer in Dublin's pubs, but it also turns out to be loosely equivalent to an Irish pound. Comparing the circulation of money with the distribution of beer, Bloom notices the sound of a train carrying bottles of porter: "An incoming train clanked heavily above his head, *coach after coach*. Barrels bumped in his head: dull porter slopped and churned inside" (*U*, 4:312–13: my italics, WM). After the narrative description of the train, the phrase "coach after coach" embodies the rhythm of the wheels clanging over the sleepers, for it temporarily establishes a dactylic meter in Bloom's mind. Indeed, it is only the sound of the train that explains how these barrels are transferred from the carriages to the inside of Bloom's head. In historical terms, the movement of the train can be associated with the expansion of markets and the growth of the reading public, for the expansion of the Irish railway network not only reduced the cost of transporting consumer goods, but also accelerated the spread of information from urban to rural areas. As Lee notes,

> Ireland, one of the first European countries to rail-roadise, had 65 miles of track in 1845, 1,000 in 1857, 2,000 in 1872 and, with 3,500 by 1914 boasted one of the densest networks in the world. The railway permitted far greater diffusion of information through the tele-post and the rapid distribution of newspapers. (1989, 13)

As we know from *Portrait*, Joyce associates the movement of the train with Stephen's stream of consciousness, and the same image is used in "Penelope" to describe the descent of Molly's memory into the past.[7] When Bloom hears the sound of the barrels clanging in his head, however, the rhythm of the coaches leads to a fantasy of free-flowing porter: "The bungholes sprang open and a huge dull flood leaked out, flowing together, winding through mudflats all over the level land, a lazy pooling swirl of liquor bearing along wideleaved flowers of its froth" (*U*, 4:313–16). In contrast to the concrete existence of the barrel, which separates out a standard quantity of porter as a unit of measure, the image of the flowing porters leads to the dissolution of the differences between all things, and conjures up the fantasy of land entirely covered by liquor. The "flowing-together" of this porter might therefore be interpreted as a metaphor for the general metamorphosis of commodities and the circulation of money in the modern metropolis.

In "Lotus Eaters," Joyce foregrounds Bloom's perception of commodities, highlighting the tendency of the material object to be replaced by its image. At the beginning of the episode, Bloom halts before the shop window of the Belfast and Oriental tea company, and reads the labels on the packets of tea: "choice blend, finest quality, family tea" (*U*, 5:18–19). As he reads, Bloom follows the spatial design of the "legends" inscribed on the "leadpapered packets," and processes the information as a list of epithets, each naming the substantive in a particular way. The mental act of composing a list produces a regular rhythm, the first syllable of each epithet bearing an accent that actualizes the beat of the underlying rhythm: "chóice blend, fínest quality, fámily tea." While these accents communicate the *force* with which the written signs impress themselves on the mind, they also serve to differentiate the meaning of the adjective from the noun they qualify. The idea of purchasing tea reminds Bloom of Tom Kernan, the tea merchant from *Dubliners*, but the main thrust of the narrative concerns the transition from reality to fantasy, from everyday Dublin to the East Indies. One epithet in particular, "choice blend," recurs in the next paragraph, and motivates the dislocation of Bloom's mind into the world of fantasy: "The far east. Lovely spot it must be: the garden of the world, big lazy leaves float about on, cactuses, flowery meads, snaky lianas they call them. Wonder is it like that" (*U*, 5:29–31). As the fantasy of travelling to the Far East progresses, the rhythm of his thoughts condenses around the figure of another list, which replaces the language of advertising with the presumed language of the Cinghalese (or Sri Lankans): "cactuses, flowery meads, snaky lianas *they call them*." Here, the duration of Bloom's thoughts expand and contract around these images of pleasure, with the slow temporality of the Far East expanding like "big lazy leaves"; yet, the stretching span of time filled with the condensed pleasures of cactuses and "flowery meads." We can see from the construction of these two lists—one real, the other imaginary—that Bloom's mind possesses the tendency to catalogue desired objects into lists, such that the images float free of any grammatical association, becoming the raw material for his daydreams.

By separating the *image* of the commodity from its substantial basis, Joyce foregrounds the manner in which the productive realm is translated into the nominal world of language. As we have seen, the rhythmic form of the list mediates between the movement of the body and the stream of consciousness, for each act of naming implies a corresponding alteration to the visual field. Once the commodity has been named, however, the kinesthetic relationship between the moving body and the visual field recedes into the fringe of consciousness, for the concrete existence of the object is replaced by free-floating images of desire. Indeed, the separation of the *image* from its material substrate is made thematic by the "weightlessness" of the dead sea, which Bloom associates with the act of reading books:

> Where was the chap I saw in that picture somewhere? Ah, in the dead sea, floating on his back, reading a book with a parasol open. Couldn't sink if you tried: so thick with salt. (*U*, 5:37–9)

Attempting to explain the natural basis for the phenomenon of weight-lessness, Bloom seeks to reintegrate his desire for commodities within the real world of production. Nevertheless, his attempt to describe the law of displacement (used for measuring the volume of physical bodies) leads to the substitution of the concrete object for an *equivalent* volume of water:

> Because the weight of the water, no, the weight of the body in the water is equal to the weight of the what? Or is it the volume is equal to the weight? It's a law something like that. Vance in High school cracking his fingerjoints, teaching. (*U*, 5:39–42)

As the weight of water is used as a mathematical standard to measure the mass and density of other physical objects, it can be seen as a means of reducing the diversity of elemental substances to an homogenous quantity. Considering that Joyce uses images of fluidity to describe the circulation of money in the marketplace (air, water, beer, blood, and so on), the substitution of the weight of the body for its volume in water can be interpreted as a metaphor for the process of exchange. Indeed, "universality" is the first quality of water listed in the "Ithaca" episode, and its "democratic equality" indicates that it can be used as a standard of measure for all things.

By attempting to provide a mathematical explanation for the phenomenon of weightlessness, Bloom ascends into the ideal world of numbers; yet, his memorization of the mathematical formula reveals the extent to which his calculations remain inseparable from the performance of rhythms:

> The college curriculum. Cracking curriculum. What is weight really when you say the weight? Thirtytwo feet per second per second. Law of falling bodies: per second per second. They all fall to the ground. The earth. It's the force of gravity of the earth is the weight. (*U*, 5:43–6)

By alternating between the adjectives "college" and "cracking" in his naming of the "college," Bloom not only forms equivalent rhetorical periods in his mental stream, but also dramatizes the rhythmic techniques used to memorize the mathematical formula. As the acceleration due to gravity is calculated anew each second, Bloom constructs a periodic rhythm that enables the passage of time to be measured as such: "per second per second." By reciting the form of the mathematical formula learned under the tutelage of Vance at Erasmus Smith High School, Bloom has stumbled across a piece of wisdom that implies a rhythmic relationship between the intuition of space and time. Indeed, when Bloom repeats the phrase "per second per second," he uses the intuition of rhythm to construct equivalent temporal periods, and thereby discovers a *psychological* basis for the measurement of time. Having established a regular rhythm in his stream of consciousness, the refrain of "per second, per second" provides a temporal means of coordinating his thoughts with the movement of the body. Beating time with his copy of *The Freeman's Journal*, which the narrator compares to the "baton" of a musical conductor, Bloom continues his walk along the street:

> As he walked he took the folded *Freeman* from his sidepocket, unfolded it, rolled it lengthwise in a baton and tapped it at each sauntering step against his trouserleg. Careless air: just drop in to see. Per second per second. Per second for every second it means. (*U*, 5:48–53)

Rather than translating the physical movement of bodies into the abstract world of thought, the recitation of the formulae leads to the embodied performance of the rhythm and the reinscription of the ideal onto the world of social practice.

By foregrounding the relationship between the embodied performance of rhythms and the perception of images, Joyce therefore points to the *kinetic* involvement of the body in the *real* world of production and consumption that underlies the superficial appearance of commodities in the marketplace. In "Aeolus," Joyce constructs an analogy between the circulation of signs and machines, for the rhythmic chant of "The hoarse Dublin United Tramway Company's timekeeper" links the list of stations to the geographical configuration of the city as a whole:

> —Rathgar and Terenure!
> —Come on, Sandymount Green! ...
> —Start, Palmerston park (*U*, 7:8–13)

From this brief excerpt of the timekeeper's call, which is earlier paraphrased by the descriptive language of the narrator ("Blackrock,

Kingstown and Dalkey, *Rathgar and Terenure*, Palmerston park";
U, 7:3: my emphasis, WM), the reader begins to link the rhythm of
the timetable to the motion of the horse-drawn trams around the city.
Indeed, the pattern of call and response that governs the enunciation
of the place names is soon synchronized with the parallel movement
of the different trams, for as Joyce puts it, "Right and left parallel
clinging ringing a doubledecker and a singledeck moved from their
railheads, swerved to the downline, glided parallel" (*U*, 7:10–12).
In the section titled, "THE GENTLEMAN OF THE PRESS," furthermore, Joyce associates the composition of type for the newspaper
with the distribution of porter, for the conversation of the pressman
is punctuated by the movement of barrels from sea to shore (and vice
versa):

> Grossbooted draymen rolled barrels dullthudding out of Prince's
> stores and bumped them up on the brewery float. On the brewery float
> bumped dullthudding barrels rolled by grossbooted draymen out of
> Prince's stores. (*U*, 7:21–4)

Via these three snapshots of the city, Joyce links the spatial configuration of the city to its transportation network, and reveals that the
distribution of the printed word is dependent upon the movement of
machines (steam-powered presses, trains, and so on) that dislocate
the sensation of rhythm from the organic movements of the body.

The Stream of Life in "Lestrygonians"

As we have seen, modernist authors often use images of the sea to
describe the movement of machines and bodies in the modern metropolis; and this meditation on the "fluidity" or "flux" of modern life
can be extended to the "stream of consciousness," for it ought to be
analyzed as a *reflection* of the body's involvement in the movement
of the city. Considering that Pater uses the "stream of life" metaphor
to identify the temporal structure of the human personality with the
perpetual motion of bodies, it should come as no surprise to discover
that William James cites the very same source when inventing his conception of the "stream of consciousness." In a famous chapter of his
The Principles of Psychology (1890) titled "The Stream of Thought,"
James outlines the basic "characters" that distinguish real processes of
thought, including the notion that thoughts are always embedded in a
personal consciousness and that "within each personal consciousness

thought is always changing" (1890, 225). According to James, we can never perceive the same object twice, for the reason that every sensation involves a modification to the physiological structure of the brain. Even if a sensation could be analyzed as a simple idea, James argues that it could never be experienced twice in exactly the same way, for the person experiencing the sensation has changed:

> Even then we should have to confess that, however we might in ordinary conversation speak of getting the same sensation again, we never in strict accuracy could do so; and *that whatever was true of the river of life, of the river of elemental feeling, it would certainly be true to say, like Heraclitus, that we never descend twice into the same stream.* (1890, 233: my italics, WM)

Here we can see that the principle of change is traced to the physiology of the brain and the temporal structure of the modern subject, for the life history of the individual is altered with the passing of each moment. Despite the fact that there are gaps and qualitative alterations across the expanse of time, the subject nevertheless experiences his life history as a continuous unity:

> Consciousness, then, does not appear to itself chopped up in bits. Such words as 'chain' or 'train' do not describe it fitly as it presents itself in the first instance. A 'river' or a 'stream' are the metaphors by which it is most naturally described. *In talking of it hereafter, let us call it the stream of thought, of consciousness, of subjective life.* (James 1890, 239)

By reconstructing the genealogy that links both James and Pater to the metaphysics of Heraclitus, it can be seen that the stream metaphor involves a fundamental contradiction, for although it is used to demonstrate the principle of change in the structure of the human subject—the self-differentiation of the modern subject—it is also used to explain the ignorance of the subject towards the gaps and alterations that structure the so-called "stream of consciousness." Only a psychological explanation of the origin of the intuition of rhythm can resolve this paradox, for it provides a means of relating the succession of discrete moments (beats) to the continuous sensation of movement.

In a lecture titled "The Perception of Time," James discusses the metaphysical conception of the present as a "point" on the line of time (the Aristotelian notion of time as a mathematical dimension of space), and argues that it must be superseded by the concept of the "specious present," which takes into account the penetration of the past and the future into the actual experience of time. In this regard, it is significant that the inventor of the so-called specious present (Mr E. R. Clay) alludes to the temporal structure of music, because it demonstrates the extent to which the concrete duration of the present is shaped by the perception of rhythmic forms:

> The present to which the datum refers is really a part of the past—a recent past—delusively given as being a time that intervenes between the past and the future. Let it be named the specious present, and let the past, that is given as being the past, be known as the obvious past. *All the notes of a bar of a song seem to the listener to be contained in the present.* (quoted in James 1890, 609: my italics, WM)

The example of a bar of music illustrates the extent to which the perception of the present is informed by the retention of the previous beat and the anticipation of the next. Taking into account the fact that the sensation of rhythm has both a discrete (beats) and a continuous aspect (flow), James argues that the sensation of rhythm provides a sense of "order" in the stream of consciousness, for

> In the experience of watching empty time flow ... we tell it off in pulses. We say "now! now! now!" or we count "more! more! more!" as we feel it bud. This composition out of units of duration is called the law of time's *discrete flow*. The discreteness is, however, merely due to the fact that our successive acts of *recognition* or *apperception* of *what* it is are discrete. The sensation is as continuous as any sensation can be. All continuous sensations are *named* in beats. (1890, 622)

Here we can see that the process of counting involves an act of *naming* in which the abstract beats of the primary rhythm become the basis for the linguistic mediation on the rhythmic intuition. While the words "now" or "more" do not differentiate between one beat and the next, the alternation between "one" and "two" imposes order on the train of impressions, and creates the rudimentary space for the formation of a linguistic "cadence."

Although there is no textual evidence to suggest that Joyce actually read James's lectures on psychology, his familiarity with Pater's aestheticism reveals that his fiction was informed by a wider discourse surrounding the metaphysics of flux that attempted to trace the principle of change to the temporal structure of modern subjectivity. From the stage-notes to *Exiles*, we know that Joyce had encountered the philosophy of Bergson, a fact confirmed by the presence of Solomon's *Bergson* (1911) in his Trieste library. Indeed, Solomon's study reveals the extent to which the psychological discourse of the early twentieth century had been informed by the Heraclitan metaphysics of flux and the Jamesian notion of the "stream of consciousness." In a chapter simply titled "Change," Solomon begins with the assertion that "The world, whether as a whole or in its parts, is in constant change" (1911, 9). At a psychological level, he states that "conscious beings feel the contents of their consciousness to be ever changing" (1911, 9). As Bergson wishes to distinguish the continuous experience of *duration* or movement from the abstract measurement of time, Heraclitus's metaphysics of flux provides Solomon with a convenient way of introducing the French philosopher to his English audience:

> Heraclitus expressed in vivid metaphors and dark riddling language that at once stimulated and mystified his successors the central idea of the present chapter that the world was a universal flux, that existence was a perpetual change, to which our language with its words of definite meaning could never do justice. We name a thing, and straightway the name becomes inapplicable, for the thing has become different; "we cannot step twice into the same river." (1911, 27)

Alluding once again to the Heraclitan fragment from Plato's *Cratylus,* Solomon suggests that the act of naming involves an alteration not only to the form of the name, but also to the substance of the named object. Distinguishing Bergson's thought from the philosophy of Platonism, which tries to fix the meaning of words to a corresponding Idea, Solomon writes that "Bergson is the modern Heraclitus, insisting that existence is a perpetual change, but vindicating by exhibiting their origin the necessity and relative value of words, ideas, and intelligence" (1911, 28). Despite the differences among Pater, James, and Bergson, Solomon's study of *Bergson* reveals that the philosophical discourse of the early twentieth century drew from the Heraclitan metaphysics of flux, a conception of change that was associated with the stream of consciousness and the instability of language in the modern age.

In "Lestrygonians," Joyce uses the image of the river Liffey to embody the movement of the city as reflected in Bloom's stream of consciousness. At the beginning of the episode, Bloom pauses on O'Connell Bridge to observe a barge exporting Irish stout to England. As we have already seen, the growth of the brewing industry constituted a major exception to the general stagnation of the Irish economy in the late nineteenth and early twentieth centuries. Bloom associates the distribution of beer barrels on trains with the circulation of money

in the modern metropolis. Recalling the image of the grandfather rat
from "Hades," he compares the vats of porter to the coffins buried
at Glasnevin cemetery: "Vats of porter, wonderful, Rats get in too.
Drink themselves as big as a collie floating. Dead drunk on porter.
Drink till they puke again like christians. Imagine drinking that!
Rats: vats" (*U*, 8:47–9). Considering that Paddy Dignam's heart attack
was brought on by excessive drinking, the comparison between the
drunken Dubliner and the bloated rat is not misplaced. Indeed, if "an
Irishman's coffin is a house," then the image of a "rat" in a "vat" of
porter epitomizes the realization of the happy life. By placing these
vats on the surface of the river Liffey, Joyce makes explicit the thematic association among the consumption of porter, the stream of
consciousness, and the circulation of money, such that the image of
the "rat" in the "vat" becomes a general metaphor for the immersion
of the modern subject in the *phantasmagoria*. Yet, as this metaphor
reveals, excessive consumption is double-edged, for the unrestrained
consumption of images can lead to narcissism, depression, and death.
Following the flight of some gulls above the river Liffey, Bloom looks
down on the surface of the passing stream, and considers the possibility of suicide ("Throw myself down?"; *U*, 8:52). Recalling the story
of Reuben J. Dodd's son being rescued from the river Liffey, Bloom
associates the alienation of the modern subject with the economy of
credit and debt, for the Jewish money lender is mocked for putting
a monetary value on the life of his son (as Simon Dedalus puts it in
"Hades," "one and eightpence too much"; *U*, 6:291).

Following the train of images passing through Bloom's mind, it can
be seen that the so-called stream of life mediates between the circulation of images (or words) in the *phantasmagoria* and the impressions
entering Bloom's stream of consciousness. Throwing down a piece
of crumpled paper to the gulls, who do not mistake the apprehension
of images for the real consumption of food ("Not such damn fools";
U, 8:59), Bloom combines the formula for the acceleration due to gravity
with a religious advertisement for the return of Elijah: "Elijah thirtytwo
feet per sec is com" (*U*, 8:57–8). Realizing that spiritual fulfillment
is a substitute for material gratification, Bloom composes a rhyming
couplet that is inspired by the existential situation of the gulls:

The hungry famished gull
Flaps over the water's dull.

That is how poets write, the similar sounds. But then Shakespeare has
no rhymes: blank verse. The flow of the language it is. The thoughts.
Solemn.

Hamlet, I am thy father's spirit
Doomed for a certain time to walk the earth. (U, 8:62–8)

By juxtaposing his own rhyming verse to the quotation from *Hamlet*, which is composed in "blank verse," Bloom becomes self-consciously aware of the use of rhyme and rhythm to create poetry. Alluding to the so-called flow of the language, Bloom implicitly refers to the etymological connection between "rhythm" and the Greek verb for flowing (*rhein*), a predicate that is extended to describe the stream of speech. Yet, Bloom's poem also provides a way of condensing his experience of the passing moment into a concrete image. By translating the trajectory of the gull's flight into a line of poetry, Bloom creates a rhythmic correspondence between the flight of the gull and the plane of the river, the flapping of the bird's wings becoming a periodic measure for the continuous sound of the voice. In this way, we can see that the formation of the poetic image represents the spontaneous emergence of a rhythmic form in the stream of consciousness.

In contrast to the aesthetic form of Bloom's poem, which features rhythmic and harmonic correspondences, an advertisement for Kino's Trousers on the river Liffey emphasizes the *punctuated* manner in which the stream of impressions come to appearance.[8] Using the poetic technique of lineation to compare the advertisement to the structure of a poem, each line is perceived as a distinct impression by the mind:

Kino's
11/-
Trousers. (U, 8:90–3)

Rather than forming a metrical scheme, Bloom perceives each image as a single pulse of sensation; yet, he is able to retain the unity of the overall image as it appears over time. Lacking any grammatical structure, this advertisement exemplifies the fragmentary form of the "interior monologue" and its fidelity to the actual order of the impressions received by the mind. When Bloom comes to reflect on the medium which supports this image, however, it becomes clear that the image is transitory, for it is momentarily suspended in the stream of life:

Good idea that. Wonder if he pays rent to the corporation. How can you own water really. It's always flowing in a stream, *never the same*, which in the stream of life we trace. Because life is a stream. All kind of places are good for ads. (U, 8:93–6: my italics, WM)

As Fritz Senn (1987) has noted, this passage contains an allusion to Heraclitus's saying that "No one has ever passed twice over the same stream." Although it is unlikely that Bloom has ever read Heraclitus, Pater, or James, Joyce uses an image from Fitzball's *Maritana* to posit a subliminal connection between Bloom's stream of consciousness and the metaphysics of flux, for the phrase "which in the stream of life we trace" is taken from an aria titled "In Happy Moments by Day." As a part-time canvasser for *The Freeman's Journal*, Bloom is acutely aware of the ways in which public space can be used for private profit; yet, the fluidity of water challenges his preconceived notion that property must be located in a fixed geographical space. While the river Liffey represents the collective life of the city, the fluidity of the stream also embodies the circulation of money and the exchange of commodities in the marketplace. By superimposing the text upon the surface of the stream, Joyce highlights that the physical space of the city can provide the material substrate of the public sphere, making it difficult to distinguish between the act of reading a book and reading the signs of the city.

By embodying the image of the "stream of life" in a musical refrain, Joyce is perhaps suggesting that rhythms and melodies of popular songs provide the temporal medium in which the modern subject becomes immersed in the life of the city. In Fitzball's *Maritana*, "In Happy Moments by Day" is sung by Don Jose, a minister to the King who has fallen in love with the Queen. While the aria purports to recall the memory of a vision that cannot be altered, Bloom changes the wording of the refrain, for the wording of the second verse is as follows:

> Tho' anxious eyes upon us gaze,
> And hearts with fondness beat;
> Whose smile upon each feature plays,
> With truthfulness replete.
> Some thoughts none other can replace
> Remembrance will recall,
> Which in the *flight of years* we trace,
> Is dearer than them all. (cited in Gifford and Seidman 1988, 100: my italics, WM)

Although Fitzball's libretto is composed as a "fourteener," containing alternating lines of eight and six syllables respectively, the arranger William Wallace composes the song according to a rhythm in which the duration of each line is equalized. With the fourth syllable of each trimeter balancing the fourth, fifth, and sixth syllables of the preceding tetrameter, a rhythmic correspondence is created in the musical score that does not exist in the ballad form. In the critical edition of *Ulysses*, Gabler includes Joyce's alternative spelling of "thaaan" to indicate the duration of the musical phrase, for Bloom muses on the "heatwave" that has lingered in Dublin: "Won't last. Always passing, the stream of life, which in the stream of life we trace is dearer *thaaan* them all" (*U*, 5:563–4: my emphasis, WM). Indeed, this altered spelling reveals that the syllable is sustained over three tied notes, indicating the virtual presence of the musical performance in Bloom's stream of consciousness. From this typographical clue, we can see that Joyce intended for the line to be experienced as a musical phrase, causing the *duration of the musical phrase* to become the "chronotope" of Bloom's stream of consciousness. When the phrase recurs in "Lestrygonians," it is significant that Bloom alludes to the Heraclitan metaphysics of flux, for in addition to showing that the same object cannot be perceived in the same way twice ("never the same"), it also reveals that the mind alters the content of the memory in the act of reproducing the image.

Considering that Bloom's mind is immersed in the "stream of life," it should come as no surprise that the wording of Fitzball's aria is altered. From a textual point of view, however, the misquotation points out the contradiction implied in the notion of a *unique memory*—the idea that the act of recollection does not alter the content of the recollected image.[9] In Fitzball's libretto, Don Jose alludes to the irreplaceability of the original image, for he sings: "Some thoughts none other can replace | Remembrance will recall." While the song refers to the psychological act of reflection, a singular act in which the image as a whole is presented to the mind, Bloom's memory of the refrain unfolds as a continuous process, for his memory of the words is guided by an intuition of the rhythm and the melody of the tune. When we consider the wording of the alteration—from "the flight of years" to "the stream of life"—it can be seen that the *difference* between recollection and retention is retained at the level of meaning, for while the original expression emphasizes the temporal distance between the present and the past, and the separation of the mind from the remembered image ("in the flight of years"), the latter emphasizes the involvement of the mind in the act of memorization, and the lack of any separation between the present and the past ("in the stream of life"). In Bergsonian terms, the pure memory of the present is motivated by the actions of the past, such that no act of recollection is required to activate the scheme of bodily movement. As Solomon puts it in his commentary:

> The immersion in the water, when once we are able to swim sets going the motions needed to support and advance us in it. So the speaking and hearing the first line of the *Aeneid* sets going the motions that we call uttering the second line, as it is enough to say "Sing a song of six-pence" for a baby to continue with "a pocketful of rye." (1911, 53)

To the extent that the passive perception of any rhythmic form involves the activity of the listener (who anticipates the fulfillment of the next beat), the modern subject cannot avoid reproducing the images of commodities in the stream of consciousness. Indeed, inso-far that the *image* of the commodity can be embodied in a rhythmic form, the consciousness of the modern subject becomes *synchronized* to the circulation of money, for the rhythms of advertising jingles are triggered by the automatic memories of the body. In "Lotus Eaters," for example, Bloom reads an advertisement in the *Freeman's Journal* for "Plumtree's Potted Meat":

> *What is home without*
> *Plumtree's Potted Meat?*
> *Incomplete.*
> *With it an abode of bliss.* (*U*, 5:144–7)

While this jingle does not lead to any further reflection at the time of its reception, the image recurs in "Lestrygonians" when Bloom visits Davy Byrne's for lunch. Associating "potted meats" with a pun about the descendents of Noah ("Ham and his descendants mustered and bred there"), the momentary reappearance of the image leads to a reproduction of the underlying rhythm: "Potted meats. What is home without PlumTree's potted meats? Incomplete" (*U*, 5:742). As the recurrence of this jingle is embedded in the motor patterns of the body, the memory returns automatically to the surface of Bloom's mental stream, leading him to conclude, "What a stupid ad!" (*U*, 5:743). Becoming self-consciously aware of the power of the jingle over his mind, Bloom stops the rhythm at the dramatic point of the poem, for the line "incomplete" not only lacks a syllable for the realization of the third beat, but also signifies the absence of the commodity and the hunger of the consumer. Despite the apparent incompleteness of the poem, it is precisely the absence of this third beat that marks the effectiveness of the jingle, for in the act of anticipating the next measure, the mind is motivated to pass from desire to satisfaction.

As Bloom does not recall the fourth and final line of the jingle, however, he cannot complete the simulated circuit of consumption, and
remains suspended in a state of desire.[10]

Before Bloom can complete his performance of the jingle, the dramatic tension contained in the poem is diverted by a meditation on
the theme of cannibalism and ritual sacrifice:

> Under the obituary notices they stuck it. All up a plumtree. Dignam's
> potted meat. Cannibals with lemon and rice. White missionary too
> salty. Like pickled pork. Expect chief consumes the part of honour.
> Ought to be tough from exercise. His wives in a row to watch the
> effect. *There was a right royal nigger. Who ate or something the some-
> things of the reverend Mr MacTrigger.* With it an abode of bliss. (*U*,
> 8:744–9)

As it can be seen from this train of thought, a divergence has occurred
between the semantic significance of the phrase "potted meat" and
its metrical position in the jingle, for the final line appears only after
Bloom has made an association between consumptive satisfaction and
spiritual fulfillment ("with it an abode of bliss"). Indeed, in order to
complete the rhythm of the jingle, Bloom has inadvertently performed
the rhythm of a limerick, thereby becoming explicitly aware of the difference between the underlying rhythm and its realization in the syllables of verse (*Who ate or something the somethings of the reverend
Mr MacTrigger*). While it is fairly typical for Bloom to elide particularly words when reproducing formulaic phrases, the inclusion of the
indeterminate word "something" serves to highlight the duration of
the poem and the tendency of the mind to fill it with words. As this
scene progresses, the reproduction of this rhythm expresses Bloom's
motivation to eat a gorgonzola sandwich, for as he cuts it into strips, he
remembers the middle of the limerick ("*His four hundred wives. Had
the time of their lives*"). Anticipating the actual consumption of the
sandwich, Bloom associates the growing blob of cheese with the final
line of the poem, which emphasizes the increasing size of the cannibal's
penis: "*It grew bigger and bigger and bigger*" (*U*, 8:783). By creating a
parallel between the action of eating the sandwich and performing the
limerick, Joyce not only highlights the association between the theme
of cannibalism and the metamorphosis of commodities, but also provides a temporal schema for the coordination of the action. Just as the
tension of the limerick increases toward the end of the fourth line, so
does Bloom's anticipation grow as he remembers the poem. With the
delivery of the punch line, the relief of the rhythmic tension parallels
the satisfaction caused by the consumption of the sandwich.

Although Bloom cannot remember the exact wording of the limerick, he nevertheless senses a gap in his memory that needs to be filled, and the meaning of the final line reveals that the words "*or something the somethings*" refer to the penis of the consumed Reverend. According to William James, the affective involvement of the mind in shaping the temporal relationship between thoughts gives rise to certain "feelings of tendency" that orient the mind toward the anticipation of future events. Citing the example of a forgotten name, James claims that "it is a gap that is *intensively* active," for the attempt to reproduce the name is "beckoning us in a certain direction" (1989, 252). Although the mind may not be able to remember the exact sound of the name, it will nevertheless retain a sense of the rhythm, for it is inseparable from the feeling of tendency that motivates the stream of speech:

> The rhythm of the word may be there without sound to clothe it; or the evanescent sense of something which is the initial vowel or consonant may mock us fitfully, without growing more distinct. Everyone must know the tantalizing effect of the blank rhythm, of some forgotten verse, restlessly dancing in one's mind, striving to be filled out with words. (James 1890, 252)

Rather than separating the dimension of rhythm as one of the aesthetic qualities of language, James here claims that the tendencies of the mind express themselves in a rhythmic form, prior to symbolic mediation of language. Similarly, with the repetition of the phrase "or something the somethings," Joyce highlights the priority of rhythmic experience over the symbolic meaning of words, for the haunting presence of the underlying rhythm is maintained in the absence of any specific idea. Despite the apparent triviality of such incidents in *Ulysses*, the recurrence of rhythmic *motifs* in Bloom's stream of consciousness reveals the extent to which the temporal experience of the modern subject is already *ordered* by the motor patterns of the body, rhythmical movements that can be controlled through the subconscious performance of advertising jingles that circulate in the mass media.

Conclusion

With the invention of the "interior monologue" technique in *Ulysses*, Joyce directly stages the *psychological* experiences of his central characters; yet, the physical, physiological, and mechanical rhythms of "Sirens," "Proteus," and "Lestrygonians" demonstrate that the thoughts, feelings, and sensations passing through the stream of consciousness are motivated by the movements of the body and the city, whether it be the organic structure of the ear, the rhythm of walking, or the circulation of commodities. In "Sirens," Joyce foregrounds the relationship between the sounding of musical tones and the sympathetic vibration of tones in the inner ear, a creative process of transformation that modifies the sound of words as they are repeated. By alluding to the compound rhythms that differentiate the "tone-color" of vowels and consonants, Joyce overcomes the formal distance between music and language, creating an intoned, melodic language that evokes memories and emotions in Bloom's interior monologue. While the musical language of "Sirens" tends toward a feeling of *stasis*, typified by the mathematical ratios that govern the "harmony" of musical tones, the molecular transformations of the body in "Scylla and Charybdis" highlight the ontology of flux that characterizes the subjective response to the apprehension of modernity. In "Proteus," the source of endless change is attributed to the movement of the ocean; yet, the shifting colors of the sea and sand are ordered by the periodic movements of the body, for the rhythm of walking not only inspires the performance of poetry, but also provides a temporal schema for ordering the relationship between the movements of the body and the orientation of the visual field. In "Lotus Eaters" and "Lestrygonians," finally, Joyce relates the ontology of flux to the circulation of money and commodities in the marketplace, a set of economic relations that transforms the concrete object into an image in the mind of the consumer. When the desire for a specific commodity is embodied in an advertising jingle, the modern subject loses the capacity to resist the power of rhythm, for the performance of the metrical pattern is automatically remembered by the body.

Chapter 6

Conclusion

Recording Anna Livia Plurabelle

Throughout the course of this study, our understanding of the relationship between the rhythmic science of the modernist period and Joyce's stylistic practice has been for the most part limited to charting the influence of historical sources on his major works. As the physiological and psychological approach to the study of rhythm makes clear, however, literary authors are not always fully aware of the principles that govern the composition of their verses (or prose periods), for the intuition of rhythm occurs at the level of bodily sensations and movements. Indeed, prior to the composition of any literary work, the writer of poetry or prose possesses a certain *rhythmic competence* that is determined by an entire history of biological and physiological processes, a competence that is subsequently adapted to the composition of verses, dialogues, or cadences. In *Portrait*, for example, Joyce uses his knowledge of nineteenth-century psychology and prosody to describe the habitual practices that inform Stephen's development as a lyrical artist, including: (1) physical activities such as running or walking; (2) perceptual activities such as looking or listening; (3) musical activities such as singing and dancing; and (4) intellectual activities such as writing and reading. Taken together, these diverse activities form a set of rhythmic competences that move across generic boundaries, in the sense that a style of dance might inform a period of prose, or a poetic meter a perceptual pattern. While it is possible to give a fairly accurate description of Joyce's own rhythmic competence through an analysis of his literary works (a task that I have undertaken in this book), we can nevertheless gain an invaluable insight into his *unique* rhythmic practice through an analysis of a 1929 recording of Joyce performing the final section of the "Anna Livia Plurabelle" chapter of *Finnegans Wake*. In my view, this episode can be interpreted as the culmination of his rhythmic practice, as it incorporates the meters of English verse, the periods of prose, the beats of dialogue, and the habitual movements of the body.

In previous chapters, we have focused on specific genres of literature and analyzed the particular aspect of rhythm that was most prominently expressed in each of Joyce's major works. As Joyce began his career as a literary critic and poet, we focused on his rhythmic education at Belvedere and University College, suggesting that his understanding of rhythm *qua* meter was informed by both the quantitative meters of classical verse (most prominently Latin) and emerging science on the physiology and psychology of rhythm. To the extent, however, that Joyce composed the lyrics of *Chamber Music* with the intention of having them set to music, we also saw that his rhythmic practice was informed by the embodied practices of singing, dancing, and playing the piano, a set of motor activities that informed his preference for the style of the Elizabethan ballad (as typified by Ben Jonson). In the short stories of *Dubliners*—in particular, the dramatic dialogues of "Grace" and "Ivy Day"—we have seen that the beats of dialogue constitute a norm that socializes speakers: when the rhythm of the dialogue breaks down, the pathology of individual characters is revealed to the reader. As already mentioned, Joyce's *Portrait* describes the rhythmic education of the lyrical artist, linking the production and perception of motor and sensory rhythms to the intellectual activities of reading and writing. As the lyrical prose of this novel is designed to communicate the rhythmic sensations of the artist, the discourse of the narrator is frequently fused with the consciousness of the hero, eliding the distance between past and present and opening the space of the interior monologue. Finally, we have seen that the "waves of attention" passing though the interior monologues of *Ulysses* are informed by the bodily orientation of Joyce's characters, as the rhythm of walking alters the perspective of the visual field and orders the train of impressions that are continually striking the mind. As the vibration of musical tones in the atmosphere is reproduced by the nerve endings of the ear, the internalization of physical rhythms exemplifies the creative process of transformation that characterizes the poetic language of the narrator in "Sirens" and Stephen's interior monologue in "Proteus." While there is some resemblance between the style of the interior monologue and the narrative voice in the *Wake*—particularly in relation to the continuous flow of Molly's monologue in "Penelope"—it is also clear that the language of Joyce's last book resembles the poetic language of his youthful poems, returning full circle to the origin of the rhythmic phenomenon.

Joyce began writing "Anna Livia Plurabelle" in February of 1924, a text that would pass through many revisions before its New York publication in 1928. Apparently inspired by the vision of two women washing clothes on the banks of the Eure, Joyce decided to personify the river Liffey as the heroine of the *Wake*, amplifying the chattering dialogue of the two women (symbolized as a tree and stone on opposing banks of the river) to generate a mighty torrent of poetic prose (*JJ*, 563–4). As the episode came to epitomize the lyrical dimension of the *Wake*, the rhythmical style of Joyce's prose was used to legitimate the ongoing production of this difficult book (dubbed *Work in Progress* by Ford Maddox Ford), including a public performance of the French translation at Monnier's bookshop on March 26, 1931 (*JJ*, 637). Although Joyce himself did not perform at the séance, the author had recorded the English version of "Anna Livia Plurabelle" for C. K. Ogden at the Orthological Institute in August 1929, and a copy of the phonograph was played back to the French audience two years later (*JJ*, 617). Running for a total of 8 minutes and 39 seconds, this recording of the final section from *ALP* remains an invaluable source for contemporary scholars, because the specific choice of accentuation and phrasing employed by the author gives us an insight into his prosodic approach, as well as the multiple meanings contained in specific words.[1] The choice of this particular passage can be traced to Joyce's own opinion of his work. In response to some negative criticism from his patron, Harriet Shaw Weaver, Joyce wrote in January 1927: "Either the end of Part I Δ is something or I am an imbecile in my judgement of language" (*JJ*, 589). Indeed, Joyce consistently defended the difficult process of reading the *Wake* by alluding to the lyrical style of *ALP*, distinguishing the order of his own style from the chaos of *dada* to a friend: "It is an attempt to subordinate words to the rhythm of water" (*JJ*, 564).

In my opinion, "Anna Livia Plurabelle" represents the culmination of Joyce's stylistic development as an experimental modernist writer, as this chapter incorporates the metrical, dialogical, physiological, and psychological rhythms that distinguish his earlier works. By contrast, the style of *ALP* cannot be described by isolating any particular aspect of rhythm, for it employs all aspects *at the same time*: We can therefore accurately describe this episode as being "polyrhythmic." Indeed, beginning with the dramatic context of the episode, it can be seen that the physiological rhythms of the washerwomen is represented by the repetition of the word "flap," which creates the sensation of a primary rhythm (the bare perception of temporal intervals) through the sound of the wet clothes striking the stone. By altering the tone color of the word "flap" (flip/flep), Joyce creates a melodic pattern that is structured by the rising intonation of the question and the falling intonation of the answer. The parallelism between the tree and the stone on opposing banks of the river is therefore stylistically reflected by the symmetry of the rhetorical periods. Indeed, at the level of dialogue, the refrain "tell me all" or "tell me more" is repetitively echoed by the washerwomen on both sides of the river Liffey, establishing a pulse of dialogue that is maintained even when the conversation passes into narrative description. When the "discourse" (to use Benveniste's term) between the washerwomen passes into the "story" of HCE's fall and ALP's biography, the transition is marked by the use of poetic language, for the narrator employs the alliterative meters of Old English to create an epic style reminiscent of *Beowulf*: "every telling has a *t*aling and that's the *h*e and the s*h*e of it" (*FW*, 213:12: my emphasis, WM). Indeed, to the extent that ALP represents the evolution of the English language prior to the Norman invasions, her discourse can be described as a complex hybrid of Celtic, Germanic, and Roman words, a poetic language that captures the interaction between multiple languages and dialects. As the pulse of the dialogue is synchronized to the four beats of this alliterative rhythm, Joyce is able to pass seamlessly among dialogue, poetry, and prose. When at its most inspired, the voice of the washerwomen comes to embody the evolution of the English language, their individual voices blend with the sound of the rivers that run in a circular direction through the *Wake* as a whole.

A brief analysis of Joyce's oral performance as preserved in the recording of *ALP* will reveal that the author followed a number of metrical rules that enabled the "polyrhythmic" dimensions of the text to be heard. As already mentioned, the repetition of the word "flap" alludes to the bare perception of temporal intervals that is embodied by the movement of the washerwomen, creating a sense of the "primary rhythm" that underlies the oral performance as a whole (22–6: my numeration, WM). In the opening lines of the recording (1–2), however, Joyce uses the regular alteration between stressed and unstressed syllables to create a trochaic hexameter that mimics the style of the Homeric poems and establishes a "secondary rhythm" in the sense of the term used by Lanier. Due to the thematic association between the opening lines, Joyce pronounces the couplet as a complete phrase, creating a "tertiary rhythm" that emphasizes the act of telling the story and the cognitive processes of listening and understanding. As Joyce frequently enjambs lines to create associations between lines, I have used pointed brackets to indicate the beginning and end of phrases:

1.   < Wéll, you knòw or dón't you kènnet or háven't I tòld you
2.   évery télling has a tàling and thát's the hé and the shé of it. >

3. < Lóok, lòok, the dúsk is gròwing!
4. My bránches lòfty are táking ròot. >
5. And mý cóld chér's gone áshley.
6. Fíelùhr? Fílòu!
7. What áge is àt? It saón is làte
8. <'Tis éndless nòw senne éye or érewone
9. lást saw Wáterhóuse's clògh. >
10. < They tóok it asùnder, I húrd thum sìgh
11. Whén wìll they reassémble ìt? >
12. Ó, my báck, my báck, my bách!
13. I'd wánt to gó to Áches-les-Pàins.
14. < Píngpòng!
15. Thére's the Bèlle for Séxalòitez!
16. And Concépta de Sénd-us-práy! Pâng! >
17. Wríng out the clòthes! Wríng in the dèw!
18. < Gédavári, vért the shówers!
19. And gránt thaya gráce! Amàn.>
20. < Wíll we spréad them hére nòw?
21. Áy, we wíll.>
22. Flíp!
23. Spréad on yóur bànk and Í'll spread míne on mìne.
24. Flép!
25. It's whát I'm dòing.
26. Spréad!
27. It's chúrning chìll. Der wént is rìsing.
28. Í'll láy a féw stónes on the hóstel shèets.
29. < A mán and his brìde embráced betwèen them.
30. Élse I'd have sprínkled and fólded them ònly.>
31. < And Í'll tìe my bútcher's àpron here.
32. It's súety yèt. The stróllers will pàss it by.> (*FW*, 213:11–27)

After highlighting the act of telling the story, Joyce settles into a regular four-beat pattern that persists for the majority of the oral performance (3–17). As a general rule, the four-beat pattern is embodied by the dialogue of the washerwomen; yet, the play of call and response creates a "fourth-order" rhythm that allows the thematic relations between lines to be heard (8–9, 10–11, 14–16, 29–30, 30–31). In attempting to represent the metrical rules guiding Joyce's oral performance, I have used acute and grave accents to indicate the position of the primary and secondary accents, symbols that also reflect the rising and falling intonation of Joyce's voice. In rare instances, Joyce will pronounce a monosyllable as a complete period (16, "pang"), and I have used a circumflex to represent the rise and fall of the voice over the duration of the word. Although Joyce's text is arranged as a block of prose, the length of phrases corresponds closely to the punctuation, allowing the reader to divide longer utterance into poetic "lines" that reflect the intended meaning of each utterance. Taken together, these *metrical rules* may provide future readers with a means of interpreting and performing other sections of the *Wake*, for the position of commas and full stops tends to indicate the length of phrases and the division between thematic ideas.

In typically cryptic fashion, Joyce establishes a symbolic correspondence between the quantitative meters of classical verse, the beats of dialogue, and the ticking pulse of the Waterhouse clock, a well-known Dublin landmark that was placed above the window of a jewelry shop in Dame Street. In a passage from the recording that makes explicit the presence of the "discourse" between the two washerwomen, Joyce invokes the refrain at the opening of the episode, and transforms the call and response of the women's voice into a reflection on the process in which the rhythm of the narrative is generated:

Do you téll me that nów?	I dó in tróth.
Orára por Órbe	and póor Las Ánimas!
Ússa, Úlla,	we're Úmbas áll!
Mezha, dídn't you héar it	a déluge of tímes,
úfer and úfer,	respúnd to spónd?
Yóu déed,	yóu déed!
Í néed,	Í néed!
Ít's that írrawaddyng	I've stóke in my áars.
It áll but húsheth	the léthest zswóund. (*FW*, 214:5–10)

For the sake of analyzing Joyce's performance of this passage, I have divided the text into a number of poetic lines that represent the rise and fall of a poetic phrase or cadence. As can be seen from the placement of the accents, Joyce employs a four-beat pattern throughout this passage, a metrical rhythm that elides the generic difference among conversation, quotation, and narrative. Perhaps the most important prosodic feature of this passage, however, is Joyce's distinctive pronunciation of the phrases "I deed" and "I need," for the solemn rhythm of these lines is designed to dramatize the performance of a spondaic meter. Of course, the phrase "respund to spond" refers directly to the pattern of call and response that regulates the tempo of the conversation between the washerwomen (and presumably synchronizes the sound of their voices with the action of their hands); yet, the word "spond" also contains an allusion to a "spondee," a classical foot that consists of two long syllables. While it would be possible to perform the sequence as an iambic tetrameter ("You déed, you déed, I néed, I néed"), placing a stress only on the meaningful element of the verb, Joyce deliberately slows the tempo of his oral performance to extend the duration of each syllable, thereby creating a symmetrical sequence of four classical spondees. As made explicit by Quackenbos in *Practical Rhetoric* (1896), the Greek word *spondai* means a solemn treaty, a meaning that is reflected in Joyce's text by the reference to a legal "deed" and the obligations ("need") that it imposes on both parties. Presumably, the telling of the tale transforms the action (did/deed) into a legal precedent (need) that places obligations on all who subsequently transmit it. In this case, it is the obligation to tell the "troth."

In seeking to explain Joyce's choice of meter, it is significant previous scholars have identified no fewer than 13 allusions to Jespersen's *The Growth and Structure of the English Language* (1912) littered throughout the episode (Rosiers and Van Mierlo 2002, 63–4), for this text also contains a section on the alliterative meters of Old English poetry. From a brief glance at these references, it is clear that Joyce was reading the chapter on "The Scandinavians," for a single line from the *Wake* ("and his fringe combed over his eygs and droming on loft till the sight of the sterns"; *FW*, 199:6) condenses at least three references from Jespersen's work: *egg* is a Scandinavian word that has replaced the Old English *ey*; the native word *dream* (joy) has acquired the signification of the Danish word *drom* (to dream); the Old English word *star* has crowded out the Scandinavian *sterne*, a term that nevertheless survives as the name of a famous literary author (Lawrence Sterne). Considering that this line describes the gloomy figure of HCE after his internment for committing a crime in Phoenix Park, it is clear that Joyce's paternal hero is associated with the Scandinavian language and the Norman invasions of the eighth century. By contrast, "Anna Livia Plurabelle" is associated with the Germanic origin of Old English, for the phrase "with her femtyfyx kinds of fondling endings" (200:5) refers to the following passage from Jespersen's text: "In Dutch every child is a *kindje*; and every girl a meisje; every tree may be called a *boompje*; every cup of coffee or tea a *kopje*" (1912, 10). Considering that Jespersen lists Dutch and German as part of the Germanic family of languages of which English is a descendent, the eradication of these "foundling endings" from modern English can be attributed to the influence of Scandinavian languages such as Danish or Swedish. As ALP is associated with the generation and birth of

Earwicker's children, who are the product of a rape modeled on the archetype of Leda and Swan, it is fair to say that the erotic encounter between HCE and ALP symbolizes the conflict between the German and Scandinavian elements of middle English. The etymological evidence would therefore seem to suggest that Joyce was searching for a stylistic element to associate ALP with the state of the English language prior to the Norman invasion.

Taking into account the hybrid origins of Old English, including Celtic, Romanic, and German influences, it should come as no surprise to discover that Joyce chose to identify the character of Anna Livia with the poetic language of the period, a language that points to a time *prior* to the Scandinavian invasions. In the chapter titled "Old English," Jespersen describes the poetry of the period after the arrival of the Germanic tribes (Angles, Saxons, and Jutes), suggesting that the movement of the verse was slowed by the tendency of the Old English poets to multiply synonyms: "the movement is slow and leisurely; the measure of the verse does not invite us to move on rapidly, but to linger deliberately on each line and pause before we go on to the next" (1912, 51). Considering that Joyce tends to pause between cadences in his recording of the *Wake*, this description would seem to indicate that he wished to simulate the oral performance of the Old English poets. Listing all the synonyms used by the poet of *Beowulf* to describe the concepts of "hero," "battle," "sea," and "ship," Jespersen reveals that the diction of such texts must be considered to be a special poetic language that incorporates dialectical variations from all the locations in which such poetry was composed and performed. Significantly, Jespersen cites a long passage from *Beowulf* (340ff) where the hero announces his name for the first time, explaining that:

> Besides rules of quantity and stress, which were more regular than at might first appear, but were not so strict as those of classical poetry, the chief words of each line were tied together by alliteration, that is, they began with the same sound, or, in the case of *sp, sc, st*, with the same sound group. (1912, 56)

From reading such a passage, Joyce would have gained a practical understanding of the role which alliteration plays in positioning the accents of Old English poetry, explaining the presence of lines such as "delvan first and dulvin after" (*FW*, 197:20) or "drudgerous lands and devious delts" (*FW*, 197:22). It is also important to note that Jespersen cites a passage from Wultan where the alliteration is complicated by assonance or rhyme ("in mordre and on mane | in susle and on sare"), for it reveals another poetic technique used by Joyce to accentuate the dialect of the washerwomen, as in the line: "Flowey and Mount on the wishes of time make wishes and fears for a happy isthmass" (FW, 197:14–15).

It would be an oversimplification, however, to suggest that ALP is simply synonymous with the language of Old English, for the episode as a whole describes the founding of Dublin at the mouth of the river Liffey, a meeting of the river and the sea that is symbolized for the rape of ALP by HCE (who represents the Norman Invasions in Ireland). At the beginning of the episode, Joyce's paternal hero is cast in the role of Berard's Odysseus, "the gran Phenician rover" (FW, 197:31), but the helmsman of this ship should also be interpreted as a pillaging viking: "That marchant man he suivied their scutties right over the wash, his cameleer's burnous breezing upon him, till with runagate bowmpriss he roade and borst her bar" (FW, 197:33–5). Via an allusion to the relationship of adoration between the Queen of Sheba and King Solomon, Joyce makes more explicit the erotic significance of the salmon swimming from the mouth of the sea up the river Liffey: "When they saw him shoot up her sheba sheath, like any gay lord salomon, her bulls they were ruhring, surfed with spree" (FW, 198:3–5). From such accounts, it is clear that the story of the original sin between HCE and ALP represents not only the founding of Dublin, but also the hybridity of the English language, which maintains an historical record of the conflict and tension between a number of racial groups. As Jespersen points out, the language of the British Isles before the arrival of the German tribes was Celtic, indicating that the history of the English language preserves a colonial conflict that anticipates the arrival of the Vikings in Dublin. Although very few Celtic words were incorporated into English, the Christianization of the British Isles in the early eight century led to the inclusion of many Greek and Roman words that were associated with the institutionalized religion of the Catholic Church. In a description of ALP beautifying herself to tempt her lover, Joyce draws on the German word "fluss" (river) that is derived from the Latin verb "to flow," comparing the tresses of Anna Livia's hair to the currents of a river: "First she let her hair fal and down it flussed to her feet its teviots winding coils" (FW, 206:29). Elsewhere, Joyce alludes to the Greek verb *rhein* ("to flow") to describe the river of her speech-song, using words such as as "rima" (rhyme) and "rede" (German: discourse) stemming from this source (FW, 200:33–201:1). These classical sources indicate that ALP's poetic diction stems from a hybrid origin, as indicated by the term "creakorheuman" (Graeco-Roman; FW, 214:22) that humorously describes the "stream" (*rheuma*) of the washerwoman's speech as a burst of hot air. As the Greek word "rhythm" stems from the same source, ALP is clearly identified with the stream of poetic speech that epitomizes the act of storytelling and the passing of time.

Considering that Joyce uses alliteration and assonance to mark the position of the stresses in *ALP*, there are grounds to assert that the episode can be interpreted as a polyrhythmic poem that uses spelling and punctuation to guide the oral performance. While the diction of the *Wake* contains allusions to many different languages, the rhythm and syntax are peculiar to the English language, and the alternate spellings employed by Joyce often point to the idiosyncrasies of the Dublin dialect. Thus, when the washerwomen say "I hurd them sigh" or "I sar it again," Joyce is able to fuse local color with universal significance, for the tendency of Dubliners to roll the "r" also facilitates an allusion to two rivers: the Hurd and the Isar. Of course, when the text of the *Wake* is read aloud, the graphic dimension of the text disappears, causing the listener to miss the etymological associations created by Joyce's various puns. To the extent, however, that the stresses of the English language tend to be placed on the meaningful syllables of words, which are in turn determined by the way they are used, there will often be a way for the performer to reconcile this latent conflict between sound and meaning. As Jespersen explains in *Growth and Structure* (1912), the Germanic languages (including English) are distinguished from other Indo-European languages by two factors: the substitution of particular consonants (most notably *f* for *p*) and the tendency of English speakers to place the stress on the first syllable of the word. In contrast to Greek or Latin, where the significant element of the word is the inflexion (hence the classification of accents as ultimate, penultimate, and pre-penultimate), the words of the English language lack meaningful suffixes, and so the stress is largely placed upon the first syllable (which also usually carries the etymological root). In the description of ALP beautifying herself to seduce HCE, for example, the use of alliteration and assonance not only guides the reproduction of the rhythm, but also serves to highlight the meaningful elements of the words:

> And after that she wove a garland for her hair. She pleated it. She plaited it. Of meadowgrass and riverflags, the bulrush and the waterweed, and of fallen griefs of weeping willow. Then she made her bracelets and her ankles and her armlets and a jetty amulet for necklace of clicking cobbles and pattering pebbles and rumbledown rubble, richmond and rehr, of Irish rhunerhinerstones and shellmarble bangles (*FW*, 206:1–7)

In this passage, Joyce uses alliteration to create etymological associates between words, the "rhine" of the flowing voice becoming the "runes" of the written text.

Although Joyce was probably familiar with the accentual meters of Old English prior to reading *Growth and Structure*—Thomas Arnold delivered lectures on *Beowulf* when the Irish author was studying English at University College (*JJ*, 58)—Jespersen's account of synonymy in Old English may have provided Joyce with a useful means of transforming his "portmanteau" words into poetic passages. As pointed out by Lewis Carroll, the term can be used as a metaphor to describe words with two meanings, and for the most part, Joyce uses the technique of punning to achieve this effect. In the line, "Emme for your reussicher Honndu jarkon" (*FW*, 198:18), for example, Joyce superimposes the names of five rivers (Emme, Reuss, Cher, Hondu, and Yarkon) on an English phrase that might be rendered as "Um for your Russian Hindu Jargon." Yet, there are also many lines in *ALP* that use the technique of repetition to create a phonetic association between words, as in the opening speech of the episode:

> Or whatever it was they *threed* to make out he *thried* to two in the Fiendish park. He's an *awful old* reppe. *Look at the shirt of him! Look at the dirt of it!* He has all my water black on me. And it *steeping* and *stuping* since this time last wik. How many goes is it I *wonder* I *washed* it? I know by heart the places he likes to saale, *duddurty* devil! *Scorching my hand* and *starving my famine* to make his private linen public. *Wallop* it *well* with your battle and clean it. My *wrists* are *wrusty* rubbing the mouldaw stains. (*FW*, 196:9–18: my italics, WM)

As can be seen (similar words have been marked in italics), Joyce inserts a number of superfluous expressions that simply repeat the sound of earlier words, thereby establishing and maintaining a regular rhythm (and stream of sound). The repetition of similar words requires the addition of connectives such as "and," causing repeated phrases to evolve into long poetic passages, such as the description of ALP flowing through Dublin toward the sea: "Linking one and knocking the next, tapting a flank and tipting a jutty and palling in and pietaring out and clyding by on her easterway" (*FW*, 202:10–12). At a higher level, the repetition of syntactical formations creates structural rhythms that can be used to articulate symbolic relations, such as the differentiation of Ireland's four provinces by means of their accent: "And his derry's own drawl and his corksown blather and his doubling stutter and his gullaway swank" (*FW*, 197:4–6). At a more basic level, Joyce simply repeats words to create a stuttering effect, such as the echo between "Fieluhr" (German: what time is it?) and "Filou" (French: scoundrel), a call and response that not only restage the confusion of trench warfare in the Great War, but also epitomize the chatter between the two washerwomen (*FW*, 213:14). Toward the end of the passage, Joyce plays on the different variations of his own name, pronouncing the names "Shaun" and "John" in exactly the same manner, "Tell me of John or Shaun" (*FW*, 216:1). Such examples only demonstrate that the puns in the *Wake* always contain the possibility of being repeated as rhythmic motifs, a process that might be described as the unfolding of a "portmanteau."

As genetic scholars have noted (Landuyt 2007), the *ALP* episode emerged when the author was composing the Shem and Shaun chapter of the *Wake*, a section that deals with Joyce's autobiography and its transformation into the material of his literature. In the final paragraph of *ALP*, Joyce establishes a correspondence between the two washerwomen and Shem and Shaun, for Joyce writes "Telmetale of stem or stone" (*FW*, 216:3), a refrain that recalls the imperative to narrate the story of "Anna Livia Plurabelle." By eliding the difference between the mother (ALP) and her two sons, Joyce makes it clear that the story of HCE's fall is orally transmitted from generation to generation, explaining the association between Anna Livia and the alliterative meters of epic verse. In the section immediately preceding the "tale" of the episode recorded by Joyce, the washerwomen list all of ALP's children, who are named as "her furzeborn sons and dribbleberry daughters, a thousand and one of them, and wickerpotluck for all of them" (*FW*, 210:04). Imitating the catalogue of ships in the *Iliad*, the chattering discourse of the women is associated with the transmission of oral poetry, the gifts distributed to the children function as epithets to explain the meaning of each name. Thus, the life of James Clarence Mangan is condensed into a single phrase, "a collera morbous for Mann in the Cloak" (*FW*, 211:1), for the Irish poet died of Cholera (caused by "cloaca" or sewerage in the water) and went by the name of "Man in the Cloak" after publishing a short story of the same title. As the relationship between name and epithet reveals, the puns contained in words can be extended in narratives that explain their significance, demonstrating that the spatial dimension of the text (depth of meaning) is exchangeable for its temporal performance (rhythmic correspondences). It is also significant that the women list Shaun and Shem in the list, "a sunless map of the month, including the sword and stamps, for Shemus O'Shaun the post" (*FW*, 211:30–1), for the dual *personae* of Joyce himself become identified with the torrent of poetic speech flowing through the river

Liffey. In the final paragraph of *ALP*, the phrase "Can't hear with the waters of" becomes a melodic motif repeated by many voices, for "the chittering waters of" (*FW*, 215:31) and the "flittering bats" (*FW*, 215:31–32) become "All Livia's daughtersons" (*FW*, 215:35–6), before arriving at the "rivering waters of" (*FW*, 216:4) and the "hitherandthithering waters of" (*FW*, 216:4). Despite the shifting vocabulary, all of these phrases are propelled forward by a dactylic rhythm that captures the movement and sound of flowing water, including a melodic descent from the high-pitched I to the open A and closed O. Indeed, as the episode comes to a close, the meaning of the words fades behind the repeated rhythm and the intonation of the words, leaving us with the murmuring sound of a river that flows through the mouths of Joyce's characters.

To conclude, therefore, the poetic language of "Anna Livia Plurabelle" represents the culmination of Joyce's rhythmic practice, for it incorporates the metrical rhythms of *Chamber Music*, the dialogical rhythms of *Dubliners*, the psychological "tension" of *Portrait*, and the physiological movements of *Ulysses*. By identifying the stream of speech with the flowing movement of the river Liffey, Joyce fuses the classical figure of "Proteus" with a river that runs through the center of Dublin, creating a poetic symbol of both local and universal significance. Throughout the course of this study, we have seen that Joyce was both influenced by the rhythmic science of the late nineteenth century and anticipated developments in the twentieth century, for not only was he schooled in a wide variety of literary texts, but his stylistic practice represents a breakthrough that remains unparalleled to this day. Although the word plays and puns of the *Wake* remain obscure to most readers, the rhythmic and melodic aspects of his language remain accessible at the level of sound. To the extent that the *stresses* of English draw the listener's attention to the most meaningful words of a phrase or sentence, dramatic performance can make the meaning of the text translucent, if not transparent. In some instances, even, the peculiarities of the local Dublin accent reveal the deeper source of classical allusions. From this brief interpretation of the "Anna Livia Plurabelle" section of the *Wake*, therefore, we have tried to show how the *grain* of Joyce's unique voice can reveal the mysteries of this occult work. In relation to his wider *oeuvre*, however, the recording of ALP reveals to the reader a set of rhythmic competences that preserve Joyce's stylistic evolution over the course of a half century, a continuous experimentation with literary form that registers not only the influence of rhythmic science on his stylistic practice, but also the participation of his mind and body in the life of the modern, industrial city.

Notes

1 Introduction

1. We know for certain that Joyce possessed a copy of Maher's *Psychology* (1895) in his Trieste library (see Ellmann 1977), but John Rickard (1999) has argued that the Irish author read this work during his time at University College. Considering that Joyce read other "Manuals of Catholic Philosophy" from the "Stoneyhurst Series"—most notably, Rickaby's *General Metaphysics* (1890)—I find this argument to be persuasive.
2. In *The Human Motor* (1992), Anson Rabinbach has shown that Helmholtz's lectures on thermodynamics transformed our understanding of the human body in the mid-nineteenth century, for the body now becomes conceptualized as a machine for translating potential energy (food and nutrition) into actual energy (work and labour), a process which, if pursued continuously without rest, leads to the onset of fatigue.
3. In the first draft of *A Portrait of the Artist*, written in 1904, Joyce equates the concept of rhythm with the form of an Aristotelian substance, for the aim of the literary portrait is "to liberate from the personalized lumps of matter that which is their individuating rhythm, the first or formal relation of their parts" (*PSW*, 211). Considering that the artist is a living organism, the individuating rhythm would be equivalent to the Aristotelian "soul" or "entelechy" that ensures the harmonious growth and development of the animal. For an in-depth discussion of this passage, see Chapter 4.
4. It should be noted that Joyce reverses the order in which these operations are utilized, for he uses the term "selection" to describe the reception of impressions, and "reproduction" to describe the composition of aesthetic wholes.
5. While there are a number of sources that Joyce might have consulted, it is significant that the Shakespeare Head Press published an edition of *Shakespeare's Songs* in 1907, a collection that begins with "Ariel's Song" and "Full Fathom Five" from *The Tempest*. In "Proteus," the floating body of Alexander Kane reminds Stephen of "Full Fathom Five Thy Father Lies": "Five fathoms out there. Full fathom five thy father lies. At one, he said. Found drowned. High water at Dublin bar" (*U*, 3:470–1). In the later text, the allusion to Shakespeare becomes overloaded with mythic significance, for in addition to the classical reference to Proteus, "old Father Ocean," the same figures indicate the fall of Dedalus, the idealistic aesthete from *A Portrait of the Artist as a Young Man*.

2   "If Thou but Scan it Well"

1. According to Aubert (1992), Joyce cites the definition of movement from the Barthélémy-Saint-Hilaire translation of Aristotle's *Physique*: "Le movement peut être défini très convenablement: l'acte ou entéléchie du possible en tant que possible" (cited in Aubert 1992, 136).
2. Schork includes "Joyce's Latin Curriculum" as an appendix to his study of *Latin and Roman Culture in Joyce* (1997, 245–7), a list which is derived from the examination syllabi at Belvedere College. Significantly, he notes that Horace's *Odes* III were set for examination in Summer 1899, which means that Joyce would have translated *O Fons Bandusiae* in his final year.
3. From a brief survey of the songs contained in *A Book of British Song*, it can be seen that in 1904, the revival of British folk music was already well under way, for it includes songs from Walter Scott's *Songs from Northern England* (1833), Baring Gould's *Songs from the West* (1889), and Lucy Broadwood's *English County Songs* (1893). Although the revival of British folk music can be traced back to Allan Ramsay's *Tea-Table Miscellany: A Collection of Choice Songs Scots and English* (1740), which began to be published serially in 1724, the formation of the Folk Song Society in 1898 represents the beginning of a new aesthetic movement which began to intrude into the public sphere through the publication of popular anthologies. While Sharp's edition contains overtly patriotic anthems such as "Long Live the King" and "Rule Britannia," its political affiliation is not limited to the English tradition, as it also includes the revolutionary Irish ballad, "The Shan Van Vocht," as well as the "The Wearing of the Green," a song which protests against the British for outlawing the wearing of the shamrock on St. Patrick's Day. Although these examples are the exceptions rather than the rule, it does demonstrate that the folk Revival was a genuinely Pan-British phenomenon, and explains why Joyce may have felt sympathy for the movement. From the Irish perspective, Bunting had collected three volumes of Irish melodies, published in 1796, 1809, and 1840, which contained only the Gaelic titles, but these only became popularized when the poet Thomas Moore wrote English lyrics to fit the original melodies. The 1905 edition of Moore's *Irish Melodies and Song* needs to be understood in the context of the wider revival of British folk music, a text whose rhythms are woven throughout the fabric of *Finnegans Wake*. For further details, see Howes (1969).
4. "There's many a wind and way | And never a May but May; | We are in love's hand to-day; where shall we go? (Swinburne 1866).

3   "The Most Commonplace Conversation"

1. While Butcher does not explicitly translate end as *telos* in this passage, his choice of terminology is clarified in a footnote: "The true *ousia* or

physis of a thing is found in the attainment of its *telos*—that which the thing has become when the process of development is completed from the matter (*hyle*) or mere potential existence (*dynamis*) to form (*eidos*) or actuality (*entelecheia*)" (1895, 145).

2. In an article titled "Physiological Psychology in Germany" (1876), James Sully describes the basic premise shared by practitioners of this new science: "Their common presupposition is that every mental process, from the simple sensation which follows as the direct result of external stimulation up to the most subtle and complex operation of thought, has, as its obverse, a physical process, that conscious activity goes on at every point hand in hand with nervous activity" (21).

3. For a summary of how Joyce integrated these epiphanies into his novels, see the table in p. 273 of *Poems and Shorter Writings*.

4. Scott Klein (1999) was the first critic to suggest that Kernan's fall was not an accident, but rather a calculated punishment for his failure to repay his debts, a line of interpretation that has been pursued by Norris (2003, Ch. 14).

5. The scansion marks in the cited passage are my own. Each period of dialogue is divided by a bar line in a manner akin to a musical score, and rhetorical accents are placed at the beginning of each period. This method of scansion does not attempt to categorize feet, but simply seeks to determine how the rounds of speech are distributed between characters, and the extent to which turns of speech are synchronized to the underlying beats of the dialogue. For a more detailed analysis of rhythm in the context of dialogue, see Erickson and Schultz (1982) and Auer and Muller (1999).

6. Referring to "Ivy Day" and "Grace," Kershner notes that "both stories turn about silence, ellipses, the unspoken and the unspeakable; and in both, periphrasis, circumlocution, and verbal annoyance of a variety of sorts are highlighted (1989, 130).

7. A summary of Parnell's early parliamentary career can be found in chapter 1 of Lyons, F. S., *The Fall of Parnell, 1890–1891* (1960). A more extended discussion of the Home Rule movement can be found in O' Day, A., *Irish Home Rule* (1998). Parnell's cooperation with Davitt's Land League is described in Corfe, T., *The Phoenix Park Murders; Conflict, Compromise and Tragedy in Ireland, 1879–1882* (1968).

8. Under the leadership of William Gladstone, the liberal party was victorious in the elections of 1880, and significantly Joyce's father, John Stanislaus, played a prominent role in seeing a Nationalist and Liberal candidate elected in the seat of Dublin (Jackson and Costello 1997, 83–93).

9. By staging a dialogue between different genres of speech (dialogue/rhetoric/poetry), Norris (2003) argues that Joyce's short story engages in political practice, and is not simply a dialogue about politics. More specifically, she argues that the macropolitical views of Joyce's characters are dictated by their own private, micropolitical interests.

10. For a discussion of Connolly's opposition to the visit of King Edward, see Morgan (1988, 34–5).
11. The essay was published in the Italian journal *Il Piccola della Sera* (August 11, 1912) under the title of "L'Ombra di Parnell." For an English translation, see *CW*, Ch. 45.

4 "The Curve of an Emotion"

1. Gregory Castle (2003) has argued Joyce's *Portrait* invokes the conventions of a traditional *bildungsroman* (novel of culture or education) as typified by Goethe's *Willhelm Meister*, yet engages in a modernist critique of the genre that is motivated by the alienation of the artist from the institutions of society. More recently, Barbara Laman (2004) has suggested that Joyce's novel possesses more affinity to the genre of the *künstlerroman* as typified by the work of Schlegel and Novalis, for the reason that Stephen's education remains incomplete, and the novel is concerned with the artist's process of self-creation.
2. In the "Circe" episode of *Ulysses*, Joyce makes explicit the identification between the structural rhythm and the "entelechy" of an Aristotelian organism, for Stephen claims "that gesture, not music, nor odours, would be a universal language, the gift of tongues rendering visible not the lay sense but the first entelechy, the structural rhythm" (*U*, 15:105–7).
3. For Bakhtin, the quotation of a song in the novel creates a dialogue between poetry and prose that is mediated by the ironic distance of the author, because "The novelistic image of another's style (with the direct metaphors that it incorporates) must be taken in intonational quotation marks within the system of direct authorial speech (postulated by us here), that is, taken as if the image were parodic and ironic" (1981, 44).
4. Despite the distance that separates the serious performance of poetry from its ironic quotation in the novel, Bakhtin recognizes that the emotions contained in the poem can only be expressed in their given form, causing the distance between author and hero to be closed: "The hero is located in a zone of potential conversation with the author, in a zone of *dialogical contact*" (1981, 45).
5. Joyce possessed an account of the sensorimotor system in Solomon's commentary on the philosophy of *Bergson*: "The nervous system in man in part consists of afferent (ingoing) nerves and 'centres' in the brain to which the afferent nerves convey physical agitations caused by external bodies on the surface of our bodies; in part it consists of efferent (outgoing) nerves conveying agitations from the brain-'centres' towards the surface of the body, whereby limbs are set in motion and effect changes in the external world. The vital point is that agitation in brain-centres due to afferent nerves is passed on to efferent nerves and results in what we may call the return of the original agitation or movement to the external world" (1911, 44–5).

5 "Acatalectic Tetrameter of Iambs Marching"

1. In the field of English literature, the critical use of this term can be traced to the publication of Humphrey's *Stream of Consciousness in the Modern Novel* (1954) and Friedman's *Stream of Consciousness: A Study in Literary Method* (1955). Within the field of Joyce studies, more specifically, Steinberg (1973) has attempted to measure the degree to which the author's use of the interior monologue technique can be said to "simulate" the stream of consciousness, for as he puts it, "the stream of consciousness writer . . . tries to simulate reality, to give the impression to the reader that he is receiving the raw data of consciousness as they arrive in the mind of the character" (2).

2. In an essay titled "Ulysses, Order and Myth" (1923), T. S. Eliot famously argued that the Homeric parallel provided Joyce with "a way of controlling, of ordering, of giving a shape and a significance to the immense panorama of futility and anarchy which is contemporary history" (Eliot 1965, 681). In my view, the project of *ordering* the experience of modernity is already achieved via the rhythmic form of the interior monologue, for each sequence of impressions is integrated within an organic whole by the "waves of attention" (Bolton 1894) that structure the psychological experience of time.

3. Berkeley can be categorized as a "skeptic" because he refutes Locke's notion of the material substratum, attributing this delusion to the false belief in "general" or "abstract" ideas.

4. Ignoring the obvious allusions to Lessing, Joseph Duncan (1957) relates the meaning of the phrase "ineluctable modality of the audible" to the categories of scholastic logic, referring to judgments of possibility, actuality, or probability. Applying these categories to the changeable nature of the sensible world, he writes: "the ineluctable modality of the visible and the audible refers chiefly to the changing appearances and irregular sequences of the sublunary world, the product of potentiality and uncertainty, as these are perceived through seeing and hearing and are remembered" (290).

5. The incident is recounted in Tipton's account of Berkeley's philosophy: "Dr Johnson, who expressed his conviction about the corporeality of a stone by kicking it to show that it had a real and independent existence, exclaiming, as he did so, 'I refute it thus' " (1974, 16).

6. "Supply and demand are never completely adapted to each other; but each of them from time to time in excess, leads presently to an excess of the other. Farmers who have one season produced wheat very abundantly, are disgusted with the consequent low price; and next season, sowing a much smaller quantity, bring to market a deficient crop; whence follows a converse effect. Consumption undergoes parallel undulations that need not be specified. The balancing of supplies between different districts, too, entails analogous oscillations. A place at which some necessity of life is scarce, becomes a place to which currents of it are set

up from other places where it is relatively abundant; and these currents from all sides lead to a wave of accumulation where they meet—a glut: whence follows a recoil—a partial return of the currents. But the undulatory character of these actions is perhaps best seen in the rises and falls of prices" (Spencer 1880, 279).

7. "Frseeeeeeeeeeeeeeeeeeeefrong that train again weeping tone once in the dear deaead days beyondre call close to my eyes breath my lips forward kiss sad look eyes open piano ere oer the world the mists began I hate that istsbeg comes loves sweet soooooooooooong" (*U*, 18:874–7). For a further discussion of the relationship between Molly's monologue and modern technology, see Ziarek (2004).

8. Garry Leonard (1996, 23) has shown that advertising images possess the same structural form as images in Stephen's aesthetics, for the three qualities of *integritas, consonantias,* and *claritas* are translated by Bloom into the formal aspects of a poster. Significantly, the image must not exceed the span of the visual field and must be "congruous with the velocity of modern life" (*U*, 17:1773).

9. In his commentary on *Bergson* (1911), Solomon makes a distinction between memories *of* the past—in which the self is actually immersed—and the memories that are embedded in the thought process of the present, for he says that "when we do not so put ourselves in the past—a vital action which would alone be called "*pure* memory" by Bergson—images from it recur, but they recur so as to affect our present perception and to colour its object, not as images of the past" (51).

10. Mark Osteen (1989) has argued that the jingle for Pumtree's potted meet is a refrain associated with the character of Blazes Boylan, for not only does the phrase "potted meat" have phallic connotations, but Bloom's estrangement from Molly makes his abode incomplete.

6 Conclusion

1. Joyce also recorded a fragment from the "Aeolus" episode for Sylvia Beach in 1924 (Beach 1960, 25), which is remarkable for the author's impersonation of Professor MacHugh impersonating the historical figure of John F. Taylor, an Irish barrister who delivered a famous speech circulated in a pamphlet titled *The Language of the Outlaw* (Ellmann 1977, 34). While this recording illustrates Joyce's position within the tradition of Irish oratory, it does not reveal anything about his own rhythmic practice, as the style of Stephen's interior monologue is subordinated to Taylor's rhetorical periods.

References

Alighieri, Dante. 1992. *Vita Nuova*. Translated by Mark Musa. Oxford: Oxford University Press.

Allen, Grant. 1877. *Physiological Aesthetics*. London: Henry King & Co.

——— 1895. *The Woman who Did*. London: John Lane.

Aristotle. 1908. *The Works of Aristotle*. Translated into English under the editorship of W. D. Ross. Oxford: Clarendon Press.

Aristoxenus. 1989. *Elementa Rhythmica: The Fragment of Book II and the Additional Evidence for Aristoxenean Rhythmic Theory*. Texts edited with introduction, translation, and commentary by Lionel Pearson. Oxford: Oxford University Press.

Attridge, Derek. 1982. *The Rhythms of English Poetry*. London: Longman.

——— 2004. *A Peculiar Language: Literature as Difference from the Renaissance to James Joyce*. London: Routledge.

Aubert, Jacques. 1992. *The Aesthetics of James Joyce*. Baltimore and London: John Hopkins University Press.

Auer, Couper-Kuhlen and Muller. 1999. *Language in Time*. New York: Oxford University Press.

Bain, Alexander. 1867. *English Composition and Rhetoric: A Manual*. Revised Edition. New York: Appleton and Co.

——— 1872. *Mental and Moral Science*. London: Longmans & Green.

Bakhtin, Mikhail. 1975. *Voprosy Literatury i estetiki*. Moscow: Khudozhestvennaia literatura.

——— 1981. *The Dialogic Imagination*. Edited by Holquist. Translated by Emerson and Holquist. Austin: University of Texas Press.

Bauerle, Ruth. Ed. 1982. *The James Joyce Songbook*. New York: Garland.

Beach, Sylvia. 1960. *Shakespeare and Company*. London: Faber.

Benveniste, Émile [1951]. "The Notion of Rhythm in Its Linguistic Expression." In *Problems in General Linguistics*. Translated by Meek. Florida: University of Miami Press, 1971, pp. 281–8.

Bergson, Henri. 1908. *L'Evolution Créatrice*. Felix Alcan: Paris.

——— 1944 [1911]. *Creative Evolution*. Translated by Arthur Mitchell (authorized). New York: Random House.

Berkeley, George. 1910a. "A Treatise Concerning the Principles of Human Knowledge." In *Berkeley: A New Theory of Vision and Other Writings*. London: Dent & Sons, pp. 87–196.

——— 1910b. "Essay towards a New Theory of Vision." In *Berkeley: A New Theory of Vision and Other Writings*. London: Dent & Sons, pp. 1–86.

Boehme, Jacob. 1926. *The Signatures of All Things*. New York: EP Dutton St. & Co.

Bolton, Thaddeus. 1894. "Rhythm." *The American Journal of Psychology* 6, no. 2 (Jan), 145–238.

Brewer, R. F. 1893. *Orthometry: A Treatise on the Art of Versification and the Technicalities of Poetry.* London: C. W. Deacon & Co.

Bullen, Arthur Henry. ed. 1907. *Shakespeare's Songs.* Stratford-on-Avon: Shakespeare Head Press.

Bürger, Peter. 1984. *Theory of the Avant-garde.* Translated by Michael Shaw. Minneapolis: University of Minnesota Press.

Butcher, Samuel. 1895. *Aristotle's Theory of Poetry and Fine Art: With a Critical Text and Translation of the Poetics.* London: MacMillan & Co.

Brivic, Sheldon. 1990. "The Veil of Signs: Perception as Language in Joyce's *Ulysses.*" *ELH* 53, no. 3 (Autumn), 737–55.

Castle, Gregory. 2003. "Coming of Age in the Age of Empire: Joyce's Modernist *Bildungsroman.*" *James Joyce Quarterly* 40, no. 4, 665–90.

Connolly, Thomas E. 1966. "Kinesis and Stasis: Structural Rhythm in Joyce's *Portrait.*" *University Review* 3, 21–30.

Cope, Jackson. 1962. "The Rhythmic Gesture: Image and Aesthetic in Joyce's Ulysses." *ELH* 29, no. 1 (March), 67–89.

Corfe, Tom. 1968. *The Phoenix Park Murders; Conflict, Compromise and Tragedy in Ireland, 1879–1882.* London: Hodder & Stoughton.

Curran, C. P. 1968. *James Joyce Remembered.* New York: Oxford University Press.

Darwin, Charles. 1871. *The Descent of Man.* New York: D. Appleton & Co.

Dodge, Janet. 1902. *Twelve Elizabethan Songs.* London: A. H. Bullen.

Driesch, Hans. 1908. *The Science and Philosophy of the Organism.* Aberdeen: Printed for the University.

Duncan, Joseph. 1957. "The Modality of the Audible in Joyce's *Ulysses.*" *PMLA* 72, no. 1 (March), 286–95.

Eliot, Thomas S. [1923] 1965. "Ulysses, Order, and Myth." In Ellman and Fiedelson, eds, *The Modern Tradition: Backgrounds of Modern Literature.* New York: Oxford University Press, pp. 679–81.

Ellmann, Richard. Ed. 1957–1966. Vols 2 and 3 of *Letters of James Joyce.* 3 vols. London: Faber.

———— 1964. "The Growth of Imagination." In Joyce, James, *A Portrait of the Artist as a Young Man.* The definitive text corrected from Dublin Holograph by Chester G. Anderson and edited by Richard Ellmann. New York: Viking Press, pp. 388–98.

———— 1977. *The Consciousness of Joyce.* London: Faber.

———— 1982. *James Joyce: New and Revised Edition.* Oxford: Oxford University Press.

Erickson, Frederick and Schultz. 1982. *The Counselor as Gate-Keeper: Social Interaction in Interviews.* New York: Academic Press.

Farr, Florence. 1909. *The Music of Speech.* London: Elkin Matthews.

Fairhall, James. 1988. "Colgan-Connolly: Another Look at the Politics of 'Ivy Day in the Committee Room'." *James Joyce Quarterly* 25, no. 3 (Spring), 289–304.

Feshbach, Sidney. 1967. "A Slow and Dark Birth: A Study of the Organization of *A Portrait of the Artist as a Young Man.*" *James Joyce Quarterly* 4, no. 4 (Summer), 289–300.

Fogarty, A. 2006. "Parnellism and the Politics of Memory: Revisiting 'Ivy Day in the Committee Room.'" In Gibson and Platt, eds, *Joyce, Ireland, Britain*. Gainesville. University Press of Florida.

Foucault, Michel. 1972. *The Archaeology of Knowledge*. Translated by Sheridan Smith. New York: Pantheon Books.

—— 1977. *Discipline and Punish: The Birth of the Prison*. Translated by Sheridan. London: Penguin.

Friedman, Melvin. 1955. *Stream of Consciousness: A Study in Literary Method*. New Haven: Yale University Press.

Fuller, David. 1977. "Ben Jonson's Plays and Their Contemporary Music." *Music & Letters* 58, no. 1, 60–75.

Genette, Gérard. 1972. "Discourse du Recit." In *Figures III*. Paris: Editions du Seuil.

—— 1980. *Narrative Discourse*. Translated by Jane Lewin. Oxford: Blackwell, 1980.

Gifford, Don and Robert Seidman. 1988. *Ulysses Annotated: Notes for James Joyces Ulysses*. 2nd edn. Berkeley: University of California Press.

Gilbert, Stuart. ed. 1957–1966. Vol. 1 of *Letters of James Joyce*. 3 vols. London: Faber & Faber.

Gillespie, Michael Patrick. 1983. *Inverted Volumes Improperly Arranged: James Joyce and His Trieste Library*. Ann Arbor: UMI Research Press.

Golston, Michael. 2008. *Rhythm and Race in Modernist Poetry and Science*. New York: Columbia University Press.

Gordon, John. 2004. *Joyce and Reality: The Empirical Strikes Back*. Syracuse: Syracuse University Press.

Guest, Edwin. 1882. *A History of English Rhythms*. Revised Edition. Edited by Walter Skeat. London: George Bell & Sons.

Gumperz, John. 1982. *Discourse Strategies*. Cambridge: Cambridge University Press.

Hart, Clive. 1990. "The Rhythm of Ulysses." In Martin, Augustine, ed., *James Joyce: The Artist and the Labyrinth*. London: Ryan, pp. 153–67.

Hatzfeld, Adolphe and Médéric Dufour. 1899. *La Poetique d'Aristote*. Lille: Le Bigot Frères.

Helmholtz, Hermann Von. 1895. *On the Sensations of Tone as a Physiological Basis for the Theory of Music*. 3rd edn. Translated by Alexander Ellis. London: Longmans, Green & Co.

Herder, G. H. 1966. "Essay on the Origin of Language." In *On the Origin of Language*. Translated by Moran and Gode. London: University of Chicago Press.

Howes, Frank. 1969. *Folk Music of Britain—and beyond*. New Fetter Lane: Metheun & Co.

Humphrey, Robert. 1954. *Stream of Consciousness in the Modern Novel*. Berkeley: University of California Press, 1954.

Humphreys, Milton. 1892. "On the Equivalence of Rhythmical Bars and Metrical Feet." *Transactions of the American Philological Association (1869–1896)* 23, 157–77.

Jackson, John and Peter Costello. 1997. *John Stanislaus Joyce: The Voluminous Life and Genius of James Joyce's Father.* London: Fourth Estate.

James, William. 1890. *The Principles of Psychology.* New York: Henry Holt & Co.

Jespersen, Otto. 1912. *The Growth and Structure of the English Language.* Leipzig: Teubner.

Jonson, Ben. 1890. *Masques and Entertainments.* Edited by Henry Morley. London: Routledge.

Joyce, James. 1939. *Finnegans Wake.* London: Faber & Faber.

——— 1959. *The Critical Writings of James Joyce.* Edited by Ellsworth Mason and Richard Ellmann. New York: Viking Press.

——— 1963. *Stephen Hero.* edited by Theodore Spencer. 2nd edition. Norfolk: New Directions.

——— 1964. *A Portrait of the Artist as a Young Man.* The definitive text corrected from Dublin Holograph by Chester G. Anderson and edited by Richard Ellmann. New York: Viking Press.

——— 1966. *Letters of James Joyce.* Vol. I, edited by Stuart Gilbert. New York: Viking Press, 1957; reissued with corrections 1966. Vols II and III, edited by Richard Ellmann. New York: Viking Press, 1966.

——— 1969. *"Dubliners": Text, Criticism, and Notes.* Edited by Robert D. Scholes and A. Walton Litz. New York: Viking Press, 1969.

——— 1984. *Ulysses.* Edited by Hans Walter Gabler, et al. New York and London: Garland, 1984. References to Foreword, Critical Apparatus, Textual Notes, Historical Collation, or Afterword.

——— 1991. *Poems and Shorter Writings: Including Epiphanies, Giacomo Joyce and "A Portrait of the Artist."* Edited by Richard Ellmann, A. Walton Litz, and John Whittier-Ferguson. London: Faber & Faber.

Joyce, Stanislaus. 2003. *My Brother's Keeper: James Joyce's Early Years.* Cambridge, MA: Da Capo Press.

Kennedy, Benjamin Hill. 1866. *The Public School Latin Primer.* London: Longmans, Green & Co.

Kershner, R. B. 1989. *Joyce, Bakhtin and Popular Literature: Chronicles of Disorder.* Chapell Hill: University of North Carolina Press.

Klein, Scott. 1999. "Strongarming Grace." *James Joyce Quarterly* 37, no. 1–2 (Fall 1999/Winter 2000), 113–26.

Landuyt, Ingeborg. 2007. "Making Herself Tidal: Chapter 1.8." In Luca Crispi and Sam Slote, eds. 2007. *How Joyce Wrote Finnegans Wake: A Chapter-by-Chapter Genetic Guide.* Madison: University of Wisconsin Press.

Laman, Barbara. 2004. *James Joyce and German Theory: The Romantic School and all that.* Madison: Fairleigh Dickinson University Press.

Lanham, Jon. 1977. "The Genre of *A Portrait of the Artist as a Young Man* and 'the rhythm of its structure'." *Genre* 10, 77–102.

Lanier, Sidney. 1880. *The Science of English Verse.* New York: Charles Scribner & Sons.

Lee, Joseph. 1989. *The Modernisation of Irish Society*. Dublin: Gill & Macmillan.

Leonard, Garry. 1996. "The History of Now: Commodity Culture in Joyce." Ch. 1 of Wollaeger, Luftig, and Spoo. *Joyce and the Subject of History*. Ann Arbor: University of Michigan Press.

Lessing, Gotthold Ephraim. 1874. *Laocöon*. Translated by Robert Phillimore. London: Macmillan & Co.

Livorni, Ernesto. 1991. "Ineluctable Modality of the Visible": Diaphane in the 'Proteus' Episode'." *JJQ* 36, no. 2 (Winter), 125–69.

Lyons, F. S. 1960. *The Fall of Parnell, 1890–1891*. London : Routledge & Kegan Paul.

MacDougal, Robert. 1902. "The Relation of Auditory Rhythm to Nervous Discharge." *Psychological Review* 9, 460–80.

Maher, Michael. 1895. *Psychology*. Stoneyhurst Philosophical Series. London: Longman & Green.

Martin, Timothy.1991. *Joyce and Wagner: A Study of Influence*. Cambridge and New York: Cambridge University Press.

Marx, Karl. 1904. *A Contribution to the Critique of Political Economy*. Translated from the Second German edition by N. I. Stone. Chicago: Charles Kerr & Company.

Monro, Dennis. 1892. *The Modes of Ancient Greek Music*. Oxford: Clarendon Press.

Moore, Thomas. 1905. *Irish Melodies and Song*. London: Routledge.

Morgan, Austen. 1988. *James Connolly: A Political Biography*. Manchester: Manchester University Press.

Müller, Johannes. 1838. *Elements of Physiology*. London: Taylor and Walton.

Müller, Max. 1889. *Three Lectures on the Science of Language and Its Place in General Education*. Chicago: Open Court Publishing Co.

Murphy, Neil. 2004. "James Joyce's Dubliners and Modernist Doubt: The Making of a Tradition." In Frawley, ed., *A New and Complex Sensation: Essays on Joyce's Dubliners*. Dublin: Lilliput Press.

Nelson, James. 1985. "James Joyce's First Publisher: Elkin Mathews and the Advent of *Chamber Music*." *James Joyce Quarterly* 23, no. 1 (Fall), 9–29.

Noon, William. 1957. *Joyce and Aquinas*. New Haven and London: Yale University Press.

Norris, Margot. 2003. *Suspicious Readings of Joyce's Dubliners*. Philadelphia: University of Pennsylvania.

O' Day, A. 1998. *Irish Home Rule*. Manchester: Manchester University Press.

Omond, T. S. 1903. *A Study of Metre*. London: Grant Richards.

Osteen, Mark. 1995. *The Economy of Ulysses*. Syracuse, NY; Syracuse University Press.

Parsons, James. 1891. *English Versification for the Use of Students*. Boston: Leach, Shewell and Sanborn.

Pater, Walter. 1899. *The Renaissance: Studies in Art and Poetry*. London: MacMillan & Co.

Plato. 1953. *The Dialogues of Plato*. Translated by Benjamin Jowett. 4th edn. 4 Volumes. Oxford: Oxford University Press.

Plock, Vike Martin. 2009. "Good Vibrations: 'Sirens,' Soundscapes, and Physiology." *James Joyce Quarterly* 46, nos. 3–4 (Spring–Summer), 481–96.

———. Ed. 1914. *Des Imagistes: An Anthology*. New York: Albert and Charles Boni.

Quackenbos, John Duncan. 1896. *Practical Rhetoric*. New York: American Book Co.

Ramsay, Alan. 1740. *Tea-Table Miscellany: A Collection of Choice Songs Scots and English*. 4 Volumes. London: Millar & Hodges.

Rabinbach, Anson. 1992. *The Human Motor: Energy, Fatigue and the Origins of Modernity*. Los Angeles: University of California Press.

Reddick, Bryan. 1969. "The Importance of Tone in the Structural Rhythm of Joyce's *Portrait*." *James Joyce Quarterly* 6, 201–18.

Rickaby, John. 1890. *General Metaphysics*. Stoneyhurst Philosophical Series. London: Longman & Green.

Rickard, John. 1999. *Joyce's Book of Memory*. Durham, Duke University Press.

Rieber, R. W. Ed. 1980. *Wilhelm Wundt and the Making of a Scientific Psychology*. New York: Plenum

Rosiers, Erika and Wim Van Mierlo. 2002. "Neutral Auxiliaries & Universal Idioms: Otto Jespersen in *Work in Progress*." In Van Hulle, Dirk, ed., *Joyce and the Study of Languages*. Peter Lang: Bruxelles, pp. 55–70.

Ruckmich, Christian. 1913. "A Bibliography of Rhythm." *The American Journal of Psychology* 24, no. 4 (October), 508–19.

Ruskin, John. 1888. *Modern Painters*. 4 Volumes. New York: John Wiley & Sons.

Russell, George William. 1920. *The Candle of Vision*. London: MacMillan & Co.

Russel, Myra. 1981. "The Elizabethan Connection: The Missing Score of James Joyce's *Chamber Music*." *James Joyce Quarterly* 18, no. 2 (Winter), 133–45.

Sacks, Harvey. 1995. *Lectures on Conversation*. Edited by Gail Jefferson. Oxford, UK; Cambridge, MA, USA: Blackwell, 1995.

Sacks, Schegloff and Jefferson. 1974. "A Simplest Systematics for the Organization of Turn-Taking for Conversation." *Language* 50, no. 4, Part 1 (Dec), 696–735.

Saintsbury, George. 1906–1910. *A History of English Prosody from the Twelfth Century to the Present Day*. 3 vols. London: Macmillan & Co.

Scholes, Robert and Richard Kain. 1965. *The Workshop of Daedalus; James Joyce and the Raw Materials for A Portrait of the Artist as a Young Man*. Evanston, IL: Northwestern University Press.

———— 1973. "In Search of James Joyce." *James Joyce Quarterly* 11, no. 1 (Fall), 5-16.

Schork, Joseph. 1997. *Latin and Roman Culture in Joyce.* Gainesville: University Press of Florida.

Senn, Fritz. 1987. "In Classical Idiom: Anthologia Intertextualis." *James Joyce Quarterly* 25, no. 1 (Fall), 31-48.

Sharp, Cecil, ed. 1904. *A Book of British Song.* London: John Murray.

Shelley, P. B. 1965. *The Complete Works of Percy Bysshe Shelley.* Edited by Ingman and Peck. 10 vols. New York: Gordian.

Solomon, Joseph. 1911. *Bergson.* London: Constable and Company.

Spencer, Herbert. 1873. *Principles of Psychology.* New York: Appleton.

———— 1874. *The Study of Sociology.* New York: D. Appleton & Co.

———— 1880. *First Principles.* 4th edn. London: William & Norgate.

———— 1892. *The Philosophy of Style: Together with an Essay on Style.* Boston: Allen & Bacon.

Stedman, Edmund Clarence. 1892. *The Nature and Elements of Poetry.* Boston and New York: Houghton, Mifflin & Co.

Steinberg, Erwin. 1973. *The Stream of Consciousness and Beyond in* Ulysses. Pittsburgh: University of Pittsburgh Press.

Stetson, R. H. 1905. "Theory of Rhythm and Discrete Succession." *Psychological Review* 12, 250-70; 293-330.

Sully, James. 1876. "Physiological Psychology in Germany." *Mind* 1, no. 1 (Jan), 20-43.

Sullivan, Kevin. 1958. *Joyce among the Jesuits.* New York: Columbia University Press.

Swinburne, Charles Algernon. 1866. *Poems and Ballads.* London: John Camden.

Symons, Arthur. 1899. *The Symbolist Movement in Literature.* London: William Heinemann.

Tipton, I. C. 1974. *Berkeley: The Philosophy of Immaterialism.* London: Metheun & Co.

Tropp, Sandra. 2008. " 'The Esthetic Instinct in Action': Charles Darwin and Mental Science in *A Portrait of the Artist as a Young Man.*" *James Joyce Quarterly* 45, no. 2 (Winter), 221-44.

Tyndall, John. 1875. *Sound.* 3rd edn. London: Longmans & Green.

Wagner, Richard. 1895. "The Artwork of the Future." Vol. I of *Richard Wagner's Prose Works.* Translated by William Ashton Ellis, 2nd edn. London: Keegan Paul.

1895 "Opera and Drama." Vol. II of Richard Wagner's Prose Works. Translated by William Ashton Ellis, 2nd edn. London: Kegan Paul.

West, David. 2002. *Horace Odes III: Dulce Periculum. [Text, Translation and Commentary.]* Oxford: Oxford University Press.

Westphal, Rudolph. 1883. *Aristoxenus von Tarent: Melik und Rhythmik des classischen Hellenenthums.* Leipzig.

Wundt, Wilhelm. 1874. *Grundzüge der Physiologischen Psychologie.* Leipzig: Verlag.

————1897. *Outlines of Psychology*. Translated by Charles Hubbard. London: William & Norgate.

Yeats, William Butler. 1961. *Essays and Introductions*. London: MacMillan.

Ziarek, Ewa. 2004. "The Female Body, Technology and Memory in Penelope." In Attridge, Derek, ed., *James Joyce's Ulysses: A Case Book*. Oxford: Oxford University Press, pp. 103–28.

Index